INTERNATIONAL STRATIFICATION
AND
UNDERDEVELOPED COUNTRIES

INTERNATIONAL STRATIFICATION
AND
UNDERDEVELOPED COUNTRIES

by

GUSTAVO LAGOS

Chapel Hill
THE UNIVERSITY OF NORTH CAROLINA PRESS

PRINTED BY THE SEEMAN PRINTERY, DURHAM, N. C.

PREFACE

Looking at this book in perspective, it is apparent that it should be regarded more as a point of departure than as a point of arrival. To my knowledge, this is the first time that a Latin American scholar has attempted to apply modern knowledge of political science and sociology, available especially in the United States, to build up a theoretical approach to international relations focused on the underdeveloped countries. Myrdal has pointed out that the analysis of the problem of underdevelopment offers a challenge for social scientists of the underdeveloped nations. I am not certain that I am qualified to respond to this challenge that implies many risks, but the question may be asked: who is qualified? The fact is that international relations as a scientific field of inquiry is also in a state of underdevelopment, even in the United States in which the number and the quality of these studies has reached a point that would be difficult to equal in the combined efforts of all the other scholars in the Western world. The interest of sociologists in the study of the discipline is just beginning. For instance, the first attempt of Talcott Parsons to apply his theory to international relations is but one year old. In spite of the fact that some pioneering articles can be found in the *American Journal of Sociology* and in other publications, the great majority of sociologists are mainly concerned with the study of the national aspects of human society. Happily some journals, such as *The Journal of Conflict Resolution* and *World Politics,* have begun to put together the resources of different social sciences for the study of international relations. Paradoxically enough, when the world has been unified by mass communication media and applied science, when we begin to live in an era of global history, when foreign policy is the concern of every cultivated man throughout the world, the discipline of international relations finds itself lacking in scientific tools to deal with the problem of relations among nations.

There is not only a division of the world between developed and underdeveloped countries but also a division of the scientific world between developed and underdeveloped sciences. As the underdeveloped countries see in the developed societies the image of their own futures, so the underdeveloped sciences attempt to follow in some way or another the patterns of developed sciences in the attempt to discover in their methods the scientific tools to develop themselves. In the illuminating pages of his *Social Theory and Social Structure,* Merton has warned social scientists against the risks of such comparisons. The differences in the scope of achievement between the two worlds of science are so great that the question can easily arise: "Is a science of society *really* possible?" If that question can arise with respect to sociology—a science that is at an intermediate stage of development in the underdeveloped world of social sciences—it could be even more easily asked in connection with international relations.

But as Merton has pointed out, it would be more realistic and, perhaps, psychologically more rewarding to note the difference in age and hard-won experience of the developed sciences. "To perceive difference here would be to achieve proportion. It would be to avoid the error of assuming that all cultural products existing at the same moment of history must have the same degree of intellectual maturity." Only the reciprocal interaction of theoretical and empirical research, the cumulative knowledge built up by all the scholars working in social sciences, can contribute to reduce the gap between the two worlds of science. This book is an attempt in that direction. Its origin goes back to 1956. At that time, as the administrative head of a new international regional organization—the Latin American Faculty of Social Sciences (FLACSO) —I found myself in an unusual framework to observe the general trend of the development of social sciences in the world, particularly the efforts taking place in Latin America in comparison with those of Western Europe and the United States. The aim of the institution was to provide scholars of the region with opportunities for training at the post-graduate level in the field of social sciences.

The problem faced by FLACSO can be summarized as follows: how could the retarded stage of development of the social sciences in Latin America be improved in connection with the more advanced situation of these sciences in Western Europe and in the United States? How could the relative achievements of these sciences in the developed West be assimilated in a fruitful way by Latin Americans, meeting at the same times the needs of national societies that were trying to develop themselves? In various seminars held in Santiago, Chile, and in Brazil, with participation of European, American, and Latin American scholars, we began to study the methodology of teaching and research in the social sciences, the possible contribution of sociology, economics, and political science to the interdisciplinary study of the development processes, and the elements of resistance to social change in Latin American societies. It became evident, after this cross-fertilization of minds and areas of scholarship, that the main focus of attention of the social sciences in Latin America should be on the problem of national development and that, following the universalistic pattern of UNESCO, we should bring together the efforts of all scholars concerned with the study of this problem without regard to nationality. Our device was to learn from the entire world in our task of formulating the scientific foundations of what the Mexican professor, Pablo González Casanova, so rightly called in one international meeting "the social sciences of development."

Peter Heintz of the University of Cologne and Lucien Brams of the Centre National de la Recherche Scientifique of Paris, both sociologists who had been members of the staff of FLACSO since the creation of the institution, encouraged me to study the processes of international relations from the viewpoint of sociological theory, taking advantage of what knowledge I had acquired of international life as participant observer in international meetings of diverse nature and through negotiations with governments and international agencies. Without this initial encouragement and guidance, I would not have undertaken so difficult a task. The theoretical framework of this book was exposed in a partial and embryonic form in 1960 in a new course at the University of Chile entitled with some audacity "Sociology of International Relations."

An invitation of the Center for International Studies of the University of Paris to participate in an international symposium on "The Newly Independent Countries in International Relations" contributed considerably to enlarging my vision of the field, permitting me to obtain important source materials and to compare the problems of international relations of Latin American countries with those of Asia and Africa. At the same time, I realized how difficult it was for French and British scholars to avoid a certain trend to study the foreign-policy problems of Asian and African nations from the viewpoint of their own countries, the former colonial powers of those newly independent nations. For reasons linked to the sociology of knowledge, this trend can lead to distortion of judgments without relationship to the quality of the scholarship involved. A century ago, Spencer noted this problem in the chapter "The Bias of Patriotism" in *The Study of Sociology*. This fact convinced me even more that an approach to the study of international relations of underdeveloped countries made from the perspective of these nations—and not from the standpoint of the great powers—could contribute to the enrichment of the incipient theory of international relations. Obviously, it is necessary to avoid the opposite distortion in this new perspective.

A grant from the Ford Foundation allowed me to proceed in the research in 1961, working in the stimulating intellectual environment of the Department of Political Science and the Institute of Latin American Studies of the University of North Carolina. Two lectures sponsored by the International Studies Committee of the University contributed to clarifying the theoretical approach of the book through a fruitful discussion with scholars in the various social sciences. It was also rewarding to continue this experience during the spring semester of 1962 as Visiting Professor in the Department of Political Science. The final chapter of the book was written as a result of discussions with graduate students of political science and economics who participated in the seminar on "Theories of International Politics." Without this framework for developing my thinking, the content of that chapter would undoubtedly have been different.

Having explained the origins of the book, it seems appropriate to describe the general outline of its theoretical approach. The main purpose is to provide a conceptual scheme that may serve for the analysis of international relations of underdeveloped countries. Because of my acquaintance with the problems of Latin American countries, I have illustrated, in many cases, the general theoretical approach with the empirical reality of those nations. Nevertheless, the theory is not limited to the case of Latin America but aims also to embrace the foreign-policy problems of Asian and African underdeveloped nations. Although some elements of the Parsonian theory of action have been used, the study is guided by the scientific orientation that Merton calls "the theories of the middle range," that is, theories that have a delimited range of social phenomena and are not "all inclusive speculations comprising a master conceptual scheme." The main components of the theory, explained in Chapter I, describe the structure of relations among nations as a stratified system in terms of economic, power, and prestige variables, and they define in this system the situation of underdeveloped countries. Some concepts of the sociological theory of social stratification, principally the concept of status, have been applied to the nation as a human group. Several other theoretical insights also have been used, but I am aware that not all have been employed with the same intensity. From the use of the social stratification approach there has emerged the concept of *atimia*—a Greek word meaning a loss or degradation of status—which the underdeveloped countries have experienced as a consequence of their comparison with the developed nations within the stratified international system. This concept could be easily related to the idea of relative deprivation used by Merton in his reference group theory. It seemed preferable to use the word *atimia* because of its heuristic value. The expression "*atimic* process" was coined to describe the evolution of the international system that has ended in a loss or lowering of status of the underdeveloped nations.

In this context, the underdeveloped countries arrive at a general definition of their international situation, characterized by their low *real status*, which is in open contradiction to the *formal status* that they are presumed to enjoy according to equalitarian ideology. In agreement with this ideology, the underdeveloped nations have equal rights, equal capacity to exercise their rights, and equal duties along with the nations of higher economic status or power. But next to this ideological world, the nations find that the hard facts of their real status are characterized by the relationship of super-ordination and subordination within the international system. The principal hypothesis is that, within this general definition of the situation, diverse international actions take place and their total orientation is the elevation of the real status of the underdeveloped nations. This approach permits the study of international relations of these countries as systems of action oriented to enhance the real status of the nation in a stratified world, dominated by the values of wealth, power, and prestige.

In the second part of the book the analysis is focused on the identification of types of international actions of the underdeveloped countries in the three basic stratification variables. The typologies presented in Chapters II, III, and IV are not the only ones that could have been identified. For instance, in the analysis of international behavior of an underdeveloped nation in the pattern of power presented in Chapter III, no attempt has been made to examine the role of guerrilla warfare in connection with military power of underdeveloped nations nor to analyze the role of political union as an effort to enhance the power status of these nations. The frustrated cases of the United Arab Republic and the Mali Federation in Africa probably would have provided empirical references for such study. The typologies, then, should be regarded only as examples not as an exhaustive consideration of this broad field.

Chapters V and VI are dedicated to the building of a model of rational international behavior of an underdeveloped nation that attempts to react against the *atimic* process within the stratified system. As all models in the social sciences, this model is an abstraction of reality based on various postulates and prerequisites; its methodological foundations have been identified in Chapter V, and Chapter VI presents the model itself. The data classified in the typologies have been used, as far as possible, as empirical references in the process of model building. The model has been constructed as an action system of rational international behavior, and it is in this connection that some elements of the Parsonian theory have been applied. It is evident that not all of the rich potentialities of the Parsonian theory for the study of international behavior have been used. Finally, in the last section of Chapter VI a short outline for the comparison of the model with reality is presented.

The influence of Rostow's book, *The Stages of Economic Growth,* needs hardly to be emphasized because it would be apparent to any reader. The debt to the group of social scientists of Massachusetts Institute of Technology who wrote the penetrating work, *The Emerging Nations,* must also be acknowledged. To Frederic N. Cleaveland and Federico G. Gil, who provided the opportunity to initiate and complete the research in the stimulating environment of the Department of Political Science and the Institute of Latin American Studies of the University of North Carolina, and to all of my colleagues of the department who often guided me through the rich American bibliography in this field, I also want to express a deep debt.

This study was completed in June, 1962, and since that time new international situations of deep implication have taken form on the world scene. Some notable examples are: the U.S.-Soviet crisis concerning the nuclear buildup in Cuba; the French refusal to admit England to the European Common Market; and the armed conflict between India and Communist China. These issues have affected the pattern of relationships within the bipolar system, the future of the North Atlantic Community and of the Western bloc, and the political situation in Asia. No attempt has been made to modify the text to cover these recent events. It seems that the theoretical framework presented in the book permits the analysis of these phenomena and even confirms some of the interpretations presented in the study.

Mrs. Molly Schmidlin made the translation of the Spanish text, with the exception of Chapter VI which was translated by Gary L. Hyde, a graduate student in my seminar at the University of North Carolina. Mr. Hyde also read the final draft of the manuscript and made numerous valuable suggestions. It is a pleasure for me to thank both of them publicly. I am also grateful to the Ford Foundation for a grant that made possible the financing of the translation. Mrs. Patricia Rodgers and Mrs. Mary Shannonhouse typed the manuscript and I wish to thank them for their patient work.

There are two other persons who need little acknowledgement, because both of them already know all of my gratitude. One is Mrs. Gwen Duffey, without whose invaluable assistance this book probably never would have reached an acceptable editorial presentation. The other is my wife, without whose moral support during the long process of research and writing, I surely would not have had the energy to overcome the difficulties of this task.

June 5, 1962
Mount Bolus, Chapel Hill
North Carolina

CONTENTS

PART THREE

A MODEL OF RATIONAL INTERNATIONAL BEHAVIOR OF AN UNDERDEVELOPED NATION

TABLES

PART ONE

INTERNATIONAL INEQUALITY AND THE STATUS OF
THE NATION

CHAPTER I

INTERNATIONAL STRATIFICATION
AND ATIMIA

1. *Inequalities among social classes and among nations*

A major trend has recently appeared that characterized the world situation in the second half of the twentieth century.*

The problem of human inequality, of social stratification—to use a concept of sociological theory—continues to be an essential question, but its terms of reference have been widened and transformed. In the past, the problem of inequality among social classes within a nation occupied the attention of the academic world and the world of politics, but now, political leaders and an increasing number of authors have pointed out that the problem of inequality among nations is a matter of major concern and analysis.[1]

Nations and classes have become major symbols of identification,[2] and nations seem to have superseded classes in symbolic attraction. The workers of industrialized countries have not recognized the bond of their common interests in an international movement but have acknowledged primarily the bond of the nation to which they belong. To be sure, a radical movement that obliterates local, regional, and even many national antagonisms is developing today, but it is not the labor movement of the industrialized countries as Marx envisaged it. It is, rather, an international protest movement against those countries in the Western civilization in which industrialization has bestowed major benefits on the working masses.[3] Bernard Barber in his study of social stratification, has pointed out that the conflicts of the classes operate as a dividing

* This chapter is a revised version of an article published in *Soziologie der Entwicklungsländer* (Kiepenheuer und Witsch, Köln, 1962), edited by Peter Heintz.

force within the nation; on the contrary, "nationalism has been an important source of solidarity among classes of the modern world. Inspired by nationalism, the lower and upper classes of a modern industrial society may set aside their differences of class interest and cooperate to keep the society and the stratification system intact against some external enemy."[4]

If, inspired by the equalitarian ideology, a utopian social revolution would aim to suppress the economic aspects of class inequality and to distribute the wealth of an underdeveloped nation on an equal basis, the standard of living would still be extremely low. In Table I, it can be seen that the underdeveloped nations, which comprise a population of 1,368,740,000 (45.7 per cent of the world total), produce only $305,568 million of the real GNP (17.5 per cent of the world total). The average real GNP per

TABLE I
WORLD GROSS NATIONAL PRODUCT AND POPULATION, 1961

	GNP ($ U.S. million)	% of World Total	Population (thousand)	% of World Total	GNP Real Terms ($ U.S. million)	% of World Total	GNP Per Head	Real GNP Per Head
							(U.S. dollars)	
Developed Countries:								
Western Europe	284,774	20.6	260,999	8.7	384,898	22.0	1,091	1,472
Oceania	17,781	1.3	16,095	0.5	24,360	1.4	1,105	1,513
United States	515,000	37.3	184,566	6.2	515,000	29.4	2,790	2,790
Canada	37,506	2.7	18,313	0.6	37,506	2.1	2,048	2,048
Japan	36,326	2.6	94,791	3.2	58,122	3.3	383	613
South Africa	6,495	0.5	15,215	0.5	9,093	0.5	427	598
	897,882	*65.0*	*589,974*	*19.7*	*1,028,979*	*58.7*		
Communist Bloc:								
U.S.S.R.	175,960	12.7	214,968	7.2	212,032	12.1	818	986
Eastern Europe	54,745	4.0	99,556	3.3	82,117	4.7	550	825
China	57,844	4.2	693,957	23.2	115,688	6.6	83	167
North Korea	989	0.1	9,418	0.3	1,978	0.1	105	211
North Viet Nam	1,749	0.1	16,661	0.6	3,323	0.2	105	199
	291,287	*21.1*	*1,034,560*	*34.6*	*415,138*	*23.7*		
Underdeveloped Countries:								
Africa	20,565	1.5	205,814	6.9	33,657	1.9	100	164
America	65,292	4.7	210,145	7.0	89,344	5.1	311	425
Asia	65,309	4.7	779,800	26.1	119,765	6.8	84	154
Europe	20,943	1.5	66,845	2.2	33,509	1.9	313	501
Middle East	19,906	1.4	106,136	3.5	29,293	1.7	187	257
	192,015	*13.8*	*1,368,740*	*45.7*	*305,568*	*17.5*		
WORLD TOTAL	*1,381,184*	100	*2,993,279*	100	*1,749,685*	100		

TABLE II
World Income Distribution

Countries with GNP Per Head	"Money" GNP		"Real" GNP	
	% of World Population	% of GNP	% of World Population	% of Real GNP
$100 or less	50.1	8.5	0.4	0.1
($150 or less)	(57.1)	(10.2)	(26.6)	(6.3)
$101-$300	15.7	6.1	59.9	16.6
($151-$300)	(8.7)	(4.4)	(33.7)	(10.4)
$301-$600	10.7	10.1	8.7	6.4
$601-$1,200	16.7	35.3	15.1	21.9
Above $1,200	6.8	40.0	15.9	55.0

NOTES FOR TABLES I AND II: The gross national product figures were taken from *World Income*, 1957, by Mikoto Usui and E. E. Hagen, M.I.T., November, 1959, and from the U.N. *Yearbook of National Accounts Statistics 1959*, United Nations, New York, 1960.

The gross national product estimates have been calculated as follows:

Western Europe: Derived from the 1958 figures of the U.N. *Yearbook of National Accounts Statistics 1959* with the following growth rates:

Common Market (except Belgium)	5 per cent per annum
Belgium	3½ per cent per annum
Free Trade Area	3½ per cent per annum
Rest of Europe	3 per cent per annum

Oceania: Derived from Usui and Hagen, *op. cit.*, with a 3 per cent per annum growth rate. These figures seem to underestimate Oceania's income. They show the GNP per family for Oceania equal to 72 per cent of those of Sweden, Switzerland, and Luxemburg, 8.2 per cent of those of Belgium and the United Kingdom, 92 per cent of France, and less than that of Western Germany. With a real wage higher than that of Germany and the United Kingdom and a relatively more even distribution of income, as well as high farm incomes, the GNP per family in Australia and New Zealand should come out at only slightly less than that of Sweden or Switzerland. The nominal and real income of Oceania should, therefore, be raised by 33 to 35 per cent.

Canada: Estimate taken from D. E. Armstrong, *Canada's Prospects—A Reassessment*, Moorgate & Wall Street, London, 1960, giving a 1960 figure. A growth rate of 2 per cent is assumed for 1960-61.

United States: Direct estimate of $505 billion for 1960 and an assumed 2 per cent growth rate.

Japan: Usui and Hagen, *op. cit.*, and a growth rate of 7 per cent per annum from 1957 to 1961.

South Africa: Usui and Hagen, *op. cit.*, and a growth rate of 3 per cent per annum from 1957 to 1961.

China: Calculated on a direct estimate for 1961 gross national product of $83 per head.

U.S.S.R.: Calculated from a direct estimate for 1961 gross national product of $813 per head.

North Korea and North Viet Nam: Calculated from a direct estimate for 1961 gross national product of $105 in both cases.

Eastern Europe: Calculated on the following direct estimates for 1961 gross national product per head:

Albania	$240
Czechoslovakia	$650
Bulgaria ⎫	
Poland ⎬	$440
Rumania ⎭	
Hungary	$475
East Germany (including East Berlin)	$700

Real GNP per head (last column) indicates the purchasing power of the GNP compared to United States prices. It is a rough estimate of an order of magnitude. The purchasing power of various countries has been increased by rates varying from 20 per cent to 100 per cent. Western Europe, according to Milton Gilbert & Associates, *Comparative National Products and Price Levels, A Study of Western Europe and the United States*, Paris, O.E.E.C., 1958. U.S.S.R. plus 20 per cent, India plus 100 per cent. . . . For an alternative calculation of "Real" GNP estimated globally, see Everett E. Hagen, "Some Facts About Income Levels and Economic Growth," this *Review*, XLI (February, 1960).

SOURCE OF TABLES I AND II: P. N. Rosenstein Rodan, "International Aid for Underdeveloped Countries," *The Review of Economics and Statistics*, XLIII (May, 1961), p. 118.

capita in the underdeveloped countries fluctuates between $154 and $501. Table II shows world income distribution and demonstrates another aspect of the tremendous differences between developed and underdeveloped countries.

It is within the international framework that underdeveloped areas must find the instrumentation to solve the problem of their low standard of living. In essential terms, this instrumentation is financial, scientific, and technological assistance that the industrialized countries can provide the underdeveloped countries to promote their national development. The Stanford Research Institute has developed a table (Table III) showing the various fields of science and technology in which the underdeveloped countries can receive technical help from more advanced countries.

Thus, a relationship of subordination and dependence of the underdeveloped areas has been created with respect to those that are developed, a structure of superordination and subordination that is typical of a system of social stratification.[5] In this structure it is the nation, not the social class, that emerges as an adequate channel to promote the improvement of the living standards.[6] The experience of industrialized countries shows, furthermore, that contrary to one of the basic components of Marxist theory, the workers in the lowest social classes have successfully obtained an appreciable measure of the fruits of socio-economic development and have achieved an adequate standard of living. The situation of these classes in the countries of Western Europe and in the United States serves as a reference group for the same classes in the underdeveloped countries.[7]

The recent trend of the United States foreign policy, founded on the principle that international assistance must be based on the national programs of socio-economic development, tends to define even more clearly the role of the nation. In effect, the nation appears as the unity in which a solidarity of movement among the classes must be established as a prerequisite to the movement toward international solidarity.

These factors contribute to the idea that the basic problem of inequality is embedded primarily in terms of nations rather than in terms of classes. As Bendix has pointed out, the class differences in underdeveloped areas have remained subordinate to the more decisive conflict between these areas and the industrialized countries.[8]

2. *International stratification and the real status of a nation*

In this study, we shall assume that the nations of the world can be considered a great social system composed of different groups

TABLE III

EXAMPLES OF PROBLEMS ON WHICH SCIENTIFIC RESEARCH AND
DEVELOPMENT WOULD MATERIALLY ASSIST UNDERDEVELOPED
COUNTRIES

(This tabulation is by no means exhaustive)

Selected problems	Stage of scientific and technological development at which work is presently required			
	Basic science (1)	Invention of new or improved technology (2)	Adaptive invention (to fit known technology to other countries and cultures) (3)	Introduction and spread of known technology (4)
A. PHYSICAL				
1. Simple and cheap power sources for villages and towns:				
(a) Electric generator driven by animal power, by energy from agricultural crops or waste materials, or other locally familiar resources	—	—	X	X
(b) Gas from agricultural wastes, cow dung, etc.	—	—	X	X
(c) Wind-powered pump and electric generator	—	—	—	X
(d) Solar energy uses	X	X	X	X
(e) Efficient storage of energy (for intermittent operation of wind, solar, or other sources)	X	X	—	—
(f) Small nuclear power systems	X	X	—	—
2. Improved but simple and cheap housing materials and construction methods:				
(a) Hand-operated press and stabilizers for making durable building blocks from common soils	—	—	X	X
(b) Designs and insulation methods adapted to tropical climates and local materials	—	—	X	X
3. Abundant and cheap water for irrigation and industrial uses:				
(a) Control of runoff, river valley development, etc.	—	—	X	X
(b) Locating underground water	X	X	X	X
(c) Well-drilling techniques	—	—	X	X
(d) More efficient water-raising techniques (e.g. modern pump adapted to local power sources)	—	—	X	X
(e) Solar pump	X	X	X	X
(f) Cheap desalting of water	X	X	—	—
(g) Prevention of water storage losses (evaporation inhibitors)	X	X	X	X
(h) Re-use of waste water	—	—	X	X
4. Simple, cheap methods of refrigeration for foods and for cooling of houses:				
(a) Solar-powered refrigeration	—	X	X	—
B. BIOLOGICAL				
1. Environmental sanitation:				
(a) Simple, cheap, culturally acceptable outdoor latrines and indoor toilets requiring no running water	—	—	X	X
(b) Simpler and cheaper water purification methods	X	X	X	X
(c) Controls for flies and other pests	X	X	X	X

(TABLE III Cont.)

Selected problems	Stage of scientific and technological development at which work is presently required			
	Basic science (1)	Invention of new or improved technology (2)	Adaptive invention (to fit known technology to other countries and cultures) (3)	Introduction and spread of known technology (4)
2. Special disease problems (schistosomiasis, hepatitis, filariasis, brucellosis, trachoma, dysenteries, etc.)	X	X	X	X
3. Food preservation:				
(a) Storage methods adapted to tropical conditions	—	—	X	X
(b) Adaptations in conventional preservation methods (canning, drying, etc.)	—	—	X	X
(c) Unconventional methods (irradiation? others?)	X	X	—	—
4. Improvement in food crops and animals:				
(a) Selection and genetic improvement of promising local plants and animals	—	X	X	X
(b) Local adaptation and improvement of plants and animals imported from abroad	—	—	X	X
5. Control of population growth:				
(a) Good, cheap oral contraceptive or its equivalent	X	X	—	—
C. PSYCHOLOGICAL AND SOCIAL				
1. Improvement in techniques of planning development programs:				
(a) Better means of anticipating social impacts of introducing scientific and technological changes	X	X	X	X
(b) Better theory and methods for determining best allocation of limited funds among diverse projects	X	X	X	X
(c) Better organization, administration, and training methods for planning agencies	X	X	X	X
(d) Comparative studies and improved techniques to assist in anticipating future needs for trained manpower	X	X	X	X
2. Simple, cheap methods of mass education:				
(a) Special adaptations of conventional methods of teaching and teacher training	—	—	X	X
(b) Use of radio, T.V., films, etc., in new ways	—	X	X	X
(c) Unconventional methods such as teaching machines	X	X	X	—
(d) Inexpensive methods of meeting special educational problems, such as communicating birth control information to illiterate people	X	X	X	X
3. Methods of introducing agricultural and rural improvements communicating effectively with people and motivating them to adopt better practices:				
(a) Finding the most efficient agricultural extension and rural community development methods and spreading them	—	X	X	X

(TABLE III Cont.)

Selected problems	Stage of scientific and technol gical development at which work is presently required			
	Basic science (1)	Invention of new or im proved technology (2)	Adaptive invention (to fit known technology to other countries and cultures) (3)	Introduction and spread of known technology (4)
(b) Better understanding of special sociological problems in rural areas of particular cultures and adjustment of technical assistance methods accordingly	X	X	X	X
4. Methods of introducing modern industrial techniques and meeting problems of industrialization:				
(a) Improvement and spread of techniques of management training, worker training, industrial counseling, organization of industrial estates, etc.	X	X	X	X
(b) Ways of finding, stimulating, and developing business and industrial entrepreneurship in nonindustrial cultures	X	X	X	X
(c) Urbanization problems and possibilities of decentralizing industry	X	X	X	X
5. Governmental methods compatible with democratic ideals but more suitable to special circumstances of underdeveloped and newly independent countries than methods copied from highly developed countries	X	X	X	X
6. Better methods of identifying the most suitable persons for "overseasmanship" and methods of training and briefing them	X	X	X	X

SOURCE: *Possible Nonmilitary Scientific Developments and Their Potential Impact on Foreign Policy Problems of the United States.* A study prepared at the request of the Committee on Foreign Relations, United States Senate by Stanford Research Institute (Washington: G.P.O., 1959), pp. 90-92.

interacting[9] and that these national groups occupy various positions within the social system. These positions can be ranked in terms of economic stature, power, and prestige, and they constitute the status of the nation. Each nation occupies various positions in these three patterns; thus, we may speak of the status of a nation from the viewpoint of its economic stature, of its power, or of its prestige, and the relative positions of these three ratings may very well not coincide, as we shall see later. The real status of the nation is determined by the complex that results from the distinct positions of the previously mentioned ratings, that is to say, its status set.[10] Sociological theory has established that every system of social stratification is the product of the interaction of social differentiation and social evaluation.[11] Consequently, the system of international stratification would be the result of the differences between the various nations appraised in terms of the prevailing values.

These values are precisely those of economic stature, power, and prestige, and the great distances that now separate the underdeveloped areas from the more advanced nations have been created through the growing differentiation of economic stature and power so as to present repercussions in the pattern of prestige.

Differences have always existed among nations that have been characterized by predominance of one over another. Historians speak of a period of Spanish predominance, of a period of French predominance, and a period of English predominance in modern times.[12]

The principal characteristic of the period before the twentieth century was the absence of a necessary relationship between the economic stature of a nation and that nation's position in the pattern of international power. This explains how a nation as small as Sweden was able to acquire the rank of a great power in the seventeenth century and how, in the epoch of the greatest splendor of Spanish predominance, Emperor Charles V was forced to turn to the house of Fugger to finance his military undertakings. To give an example from the Western Hemisphere, it would suffice to point out the case cited by Spykman in his now classic opus, *America's Strategy in World Politics;* in the nineteenth century "the Chilean navy was strong enough at the time of the Pacific War to discourage the United States from backing up with force her demands for a revision of the peace terms."[13]

When coercive dimensions in the power of a nation begin to depend more and more on its economic stature and are allied with technological advancement, the process of differentiation between the nations that distinguishes the actual system of international stratification is initiated. This period begins with the English Industrial Revolution in the late eighteenth century and the early nineteenth century. From this point on, we are able to observe the economic growth of the nations as a succession of stages that lead to a high degree of economic development, which serves to a large degree as a prerequisite to its participation in international power politics.

The studies of Professor Rostow have distinguished five stages in this evolution: "The traditional society, the pre-conditions for take-off, the take-off, the drive to maturity, and the age of high mass consumption."[14]

It is beyond the scope of this study to enter into a detailed consideration of these stages. We only wish to bring out this central idea in Rostow's work, which serves to distinguish traditional society from the following stages and which also characterizes the so-called stage of maturity. "The central fact about the traditional society is that a ceiling exists on the level of attainable output per head. This ceiling results from the fact that the potentialities which flow from modern science and technology were either not available or not regularly and systematically applied."[15]

It is in the period of take-off that the stage of economic self-sustained development is initiated. "The forces making for economic progress . . . expand and come to dominate society. Growth becomes its normal condition . . . the slow-moving changes of the pre-conditions period, when forces of modernization contend against habits and institutions, the values and vested interests of the traditional society, make a decisive break-through; and compound interest gets built into the society's structure." During the take-off period the economy is "focused around a relatively narrow complex of industry and technology." After take-off, the economy extends "its range into more refined and technologically often more complex processes" until reaching the stage of maturity. It is only in this latter period when a society can effectively (normally, regularly, systematically) apply "the range of (then) modern technology to the bulk of its resources."[16]

The following chart is offered by Rostow to roughly date the technological maturity of several countries:

Great Britain	1850	Sweden	1930
United States	1900	Japan	1940
Germany	1910	Russia	1950
France	1910	Canada	1950

We can see that, with the exception of the unique case of Great Britain, the most advanced countries have reached maturity in the twentieth century. As societies achieved this period of economic growth, "two things happened: real income per head rose to the point where a large number of persons gained a command over consumption, which transcended basic food, shelter and clothing; and the structure of the working force changed in ways which increased not only the proportion of urban to total population, but also the proportion of the population working in offices, or in skilled factory jobs—aware of and anxious to acquire the consumption fruits of a mature economy."[17]

"In addition to these economic changes, the society ceases to accept the further extension of modern technology as an over-riding objective. It is in the post-maturity stage, that through the political process, Western societies have chosen to allocate increased resources to social welfare and security. The emergence of the welfare state is one manifestation of a society's moving beyond technical maturity."[18]

Consequently, scientific progress and its technological applications have played a fundamental role in the process of economic growth, permitting the countries that have reached technological maturity to reach maturity in their economic development at the same time and to create the conditions of their social development. Social development has expressed itself in a rise in the standard of living that can be measured approximately by the per capita income and by a much more precise method utilizing the studies on the definition and measurement of standards and levels of living that have been made by a series of expert committees convened by the United Nations and the specialized agencies.[19]

Both types of maturity, economic and technological, with their repercussions on the standard of living, have constituted the basic factor of international differentiation, since only a small group of nations have reached this stage, separating themselves from the nations that have continued in the phase of traditional society or in the preconditions of take-off.

But economic and technological maturity carry implicitly the second factor of international differentiation, differentiation in terms of coercive power. In effect, economic and technological advance permitted some nations to apply these capacities to the production of new methods of warfare, and the world entered the nuclear era with the production of the atomic bomb in 1945.

TABLE IV
GNP OF SOME MAJOR POWERS, 1955, EXPRESSED IN BILLIONS OF
1955 U.S. DOLLARS

Power	GNP
United States	390
U.S.S.R.	120-150
United Kingdom	60- 70
West Germany	50- 70
France	40- 60
Canada	30- 40
Italy	20- 40
Japan	20- 40

SOURCE: Charles J. Hitch and Roland N. McKean, *The Economics of Defense in the Nuclear Age* (Cambridge, Mass.: Harvard University Press, 1960), p. 88.

Within a decade and a half of this date, they were developing the hydrogen bomb, the rocket artillery capable of hurling objects beyond the immediate sphere of terrestrial gravity, the ICBM, the IRBM, the artificial satellites, and the atomic submarines. Thus, in the second half of the twentieth century, the process that united economic development and technological maturity was achieved and this, in turn, was joined to military power. The technological leadership of a nation had transformed itself into an indicator of economic potential and military power. We began to live in an era in which "a single technological mutation can far outweigh in military importance the substance resource advantages of a nation."[20]

Only two nations had both the economic and technological capacities necessary to create the maximum expression of power in its dimension of force: the Soviet Union and the United States. England and France had but a limited capacity to produce some of these means of warfare. In 1952, England entered the nuclear club with the atomic bomb and, in 1957, could manufacture the hydrogen bomb. France, in a dramatic attempt to elevate herself to the level of a nuclear power, was able to produce her first atomic bomb in 1960.

In Table IV, we can see that, eliminating the case of West Germany because of its special case in the post-war world, an exact correlation exists between the capacity to create the maximum expression of warlike power and the national economic stature as expressed in terms of gross national product.[21]

Once a nation has reached the stage of maturity in its economic and technological development, with the consequent effects already pointed out in the standard of living of its inhabitants, the gross national product can be considered as a useful indicator of its basic economic strength.

Following Hitch and McKean's *The Economics of Defense in the Nuclear Age,* we grant that the utility of GNP as an indicator of economic stature is more significant than a long list of specific resources, such as steel, electrical energy, etc.   In effect the underlying determinants of the gross national product are: (1) initial stock of basic resources and their use (manpower, stock of capital equipment, state of the arts and knowledge, degree of efficiency in the use of resources); (2) growth (a) increase in manpower, (b) growth of capital stock, (c) advances in the state of the arts —amount of resources devoted to research and education and incentives to explore new ideas, (d) efficiency in taking advantage of innovations—incentives to introduce innovations and mechanisms for reshuffling resources in response to innovations.[22]

Many scholars have pointed out the importance of the population factor as a source of national power.   Although historical testimony on the rise of the gross national product in the United States reveals that its increase "has far outstripped the growth in the quantities of capital and labor,"[23] the size of the population continues to be an important factor in the determination of the economic strength of a country.

Kingsley Davis, trying to measure the demographic foundations of national power, points out in a study published in 1954 that "for a top rank among the world's nations, a country must have a large population—at least 60 million."[24]   Although this statement could be right at that time, it clearly appears that developed nations with that population do not have at the present the necessary size to rank in the top level within the stratified international system.   The case of England is a significant illustration of this fact.

If a country is already developed, the population factor is one of the bases of national power.   If the country is underdeveloped a great and rapidly growing population can be a source of weakness instead of being a source of power.   That is why it is better to use the size of the gross national product as one of the indicators

TABLE V
DEFENSE BUDGETS, 1955

Power	Defense Expenditures		
	Domestic currency (billions of units)	As a per cent of GNP	As a range in U.S. dollars (rounded to nearest billion)
United States	40.5 (U.S. dollars)	10%	41
U.S.S.R.	153 (rubles)	13%	19- 31
United Kingdom	1.6 (pnds. sterling)	8%	5- 7
France	1102 (francs)	7%	2- 4
West Germany	7.4 (D.M.)	4%	2- 3
Canada	1.8 (Can. dollars)	7%	2- 3
Italy	551 (lire)	4%	1- 3
Japan	142 (yen)	2%	0- 1

SOURCE: Charles J. Hitch and Roland N. McKean, *The Economics of Defense in the Nuclear Age* (Cambridge, Mass.: Harvard University Press, 1960), p. 95. For a statistical analysis of the level and pattern of defense expenditure of the NATO countries over the past ten years, according to British and NATO sources, see the study made by the National Institute, "Defence Expenditure," *National Institute Economic Review*, 10 (July, 1960), 28-39. There are no significant differences between the data of this study and the figures shown in Table V.

of power and economic stature. In effect, the GNP reflects the population factor and its important, but relative, role in the creation of economic stature.

And also, the gross national product allows us to relate easily economic and military strength. The measure, in this case, is the percentage of the gross national product that a nation can dedicate to this end, which is translated into its defense budget.

In Table V we can observe the military budget of the major powers in billions of dollars and in the percentage of gross national product. We may establish, also, that there exists an exact correlation between the nations with the highest military budget and the nations that have achieved the use of nuclear arms.

The situation of France and England clearly illustrates one fact: a high degree of technological and economic development is not sufficient to raise a nation to the rank of world power. It is also essential that the economic stature of the nation be of sufficient magnitude to participate in the technological race for the perfection of modern arms and their production in sufficient quantity for military use. The English had to abandon the production of "Blue Streak" before it was completed because it had already been superseded by the technological advance of the Russian rockets, and the desperate, dramatic attempt of France to become a nuclear power has been evidence of the economic weakness of the nation. The appropriate legal steps were taken without the approval of the Congress, which considered the financial burden too great for the country. Indeed, the program only allocated 700 million francs for the development of the rockets, only one fourth of the amount that the English proportioned fruitlessly to project "Blue Streak."[25]

In Table V we can see that the military budgets of France and England differ considerably in magnitude from the Russian and American budgets. The French and English budgets have not been able to achieve, because of the size of the gross national product of these countries, the necessary magnitude to underwrite the scientific and technological investigations necessary to participate in the technological race for military use. Hitch and McKean have estimated that "using accepted definitions, military research and development in the late 1950's was costing about 6 billion dollars per annum in the United States. Expenditure really devoted to advancing science and technology in areas of special military interest is much less—perhaps 1 to 2 billion dollars."[26]

Now we have all of the elements to comprehend the great social system formed by nations as a stratified system of economic and power status.

The elements of economic status are the following: (a) the degree of economic (and technological) development measured by the placement of the nation on one of the five stages of economic growth pointed out by Rostow; (b) the economic strength measured by the quantity of gross national product; and (c) the degree of social development measured by the average standard of living. It is the combination of these three elements that determines the economic status of a nation. Let us examine some illustrations of this concept.

Canada and Sweden have similar positions in factors (a) and (c) because both countries have arrived at technological maturity; they have achieved the stage of "high mass consumption" and the standard of living of their inhabitants is high. Nevertheless, the international position of Canada, from the economic point of view, is superior to that of Sweden, because the gross national product is three times larger than Sweden's.

Italy and India have comparable gross national products, that of India being slightly larger; however, the economic status of Italy is above that of India because there exists a marked difference in factors (a) and (c). While Italy has already reached technological maturity, India is only beginning the take-off; while Italy has achieved acceptable social development, India has one of the lowest standards of living in the world.

With respect to the three elements of economic status, all the underdeveloped nations are in a similar position because: (1) in factor (a) they find themselves in the stages preceding take-off or attempted take-off; (2) in factor (b) they have a gross national product that is small even in the case of countries such as Indonesia and Pakistan, whose population, greater than 80 million, produces a gross national product smaller than that of Sweden—only Communist China, with its population in excess of 600 million, has been able to achieve a relatively high gross national product, which according to some estimates is 55 billion dollars and according to others 90 billion dollars; and (3) in factor (c) they have a low degree of social development and, thus, a low standard of living. (See Tables I and II.) In any of the three elements of economic status, the underdeveloped countries are classified in the lowest level.

Now let us look at the components of national status on the level of power. Other factors being equal, these components are the following: (a) technological maturity; (b) a gross national product of sufficient quantity that a percentage of it, which fluctuates between the 2 per cent and 15 per cent that is destined for the defense budget, reaches a minimum sum sufficient to permit its influencing the world balance of military power (this sum was, in 1955, one billion dollars and, according to the projections of Hitch and McKean for 1965 and 1975, will fluctuate between 2 and 5 billion dollars); and (c) a defense budget of sufficient quantity to permit participation in the technological race in military terms. As we have pointed out, this budget fluctuated in the decade of the 1950's between one and 2 billion dollars up to 6 billion dollars in the case of the United States.

Only a few countries of high economic status meet factor (b) and only two, Russia and the United States, can meet factor (c).

TABLE VI

COMPARISON BETWEEN SPENDING FOR NATIONAL U.S. SECURITY AND
SELECTED PROJECTIONS OF GNP OF SOME UNDERDEVELOPED REGIONS
($ Billion)

Spending for National U.S. Security (1960)	Selected Projection of Gross National Product[2] Estimated 1960 Total (orders of magnitude only)
45.1[1]	22 Near East (incl. Greece, Turkey, and Egypt)
	40 South Asia
	25 Free Far East (excluding Japan)
	30 Africa
	50 Latin America

1. *New York Times*, January 22, 1961.
2. *Goals for Americans*, The Report of the President's Commission on National Goals, The American Assembly, Columbia University, 1960, p. 369. All estimates in 1958 U.S. dollars.

TABLE VII

COMPARISON BETWEEN THE DEFENSE BUDGET OF A MIDDLE-RANGE
POWER (CANADA)[1] AND THE FOREIGN CAPITAL INFLOW REQUIRED
ANNUALLY FOR DEVELOPMENT PROGRAMS OF SOME
UNDERDEVELOPED NATIONS
($ Million)

Annual Defense Budget of a Middle-Range Power[2]	Foreign Capital Inflow Required Annually for Development Programs during 1961-66[3]
2.000-3.000 Canada	1.677.7 India
	172.3 Indonesia
	331.6 Pakistan
	1.522.7 20 Latin American Republics

1. For the definition of Canada as a middle-range power, see Hugh L. Keenleyside (and others), *The Growth of Canadian Policies in External Affairs* (Durham, N.C.: Duke University Press, 1960).
2. Charles J. Hitch and Roland N. McKean, *The Economics of Defense in the Nuclear Age* (Cambridge, Mass.: Harvard University Press, 1960), p. 95. The estimate is for 1955.
3. P. N. Rosenstein-Rodan, "International Aid for Underdeveloped Countries," *The Review of Economics and Statistics*, XLIII, No. 2 (May, 1961). The amount of aid required for technical assistance is not included in the concept "foreign capital inflow" used by Professor Rosenstein-Rodan; for the exact meaning of the concept, see his article, especially pp. 109-10. The foreign capital inflow per annum required for the development of the 20 Latin American Republics does not coincide with the official estimates made in the Alliance for Progress; this estimate is $2 billion.

This has determined that the stratification of power standards be even greater than the stratification of economic standards. The first factor automatically excludes all the underdeveloped countries from participation in the world balance of power in its military aspect, and the second only reinforces this exclusion.

In Tables VI and VII we present two aspects of international stratification in terms of economic stature and of power. In the first, we compare the military defense budget of the United States with the gross national product of the underdeveloped countries by regions. In the second are contrasted the annual exterior capital necessities of four underdeveloped groups—India, Indonesia, Pakistan, and Latin America—with the defense budget of a middle-range power such as Canada.

As can be seen, in the first case the military budget of the United States reaches a sum slightly inferior to that of the total gross national product of Latin America, the region with the highest level in this factor. In the second case, Canada's annual defense budget is greater than the annual exterior capital needs of the four groups mentioned.

Up to this time, we have analyzed the international stratification in terms of economic and power status. Now let us analyze the third factor of a nation's status, prestige.

In order to do this, we must refer, beforehand, to the objective and subjective aspects of stratification. On studying the components of status on the levels of power and economics, we determined the *objective* aspects of the stratification, that is to say, those elements that give greater economic stature to a nation, or greater power to a nation, in agreement with external indexes. But as we pointed out previously, status is always a product of a social evaluation of certain differences between individuals or groups; the status is created by the opinions that establish the relative positions of these differences.[27] This is the subjective aspect of the stratification. If the values, in agreement with which the social evaluation is produced, coincide with the factors that produce the differences, we have a coincidence of the *image of the nation* and *what the nation is in reality*. It is highly improbable that a total coincidence occurs between the image and the actuality, but since at the present time wealth and power are the prevailing values in the world, one will be able to expect at least a high correlation. This correlation will be greater when the amount of information acquired by the groups or individuals who evaluate the differences is greater.

Prestige is the image that one has of an individual or a group, when this image is associated with a positive evaluation of the qualities of the individual or group. Prestige exists when the image is imbued with social esteem, honor, or admiration. "Prestige is a sentiment in the minds of men that is expressed in interpersonal [or intergroup] interaction: deference behavior is demanded by one party and granted by the other. Obviously, it can occur when there are values shared by both parties that define the criteria of superiority."[28]

W. Lloyd Warner, who has done the most extensive studies of prestige of individuals and families in the United States, has suggested that the prestige hierarchy represents the synthesis of all the other stratification variables;[29] this includes possessions, interaction patterns, occupational activities, and value orientations.

We believe that these same criteria can be applied, in large part, to the system of international stratification. Prestige would be determined by two factors: (1) by the synthesis of the status of a nation on the levels of power and economy; and (2) by the grade of accord between the international conduct of the nation and the value orientations of the international system.

With reference to the first factor, our hypothesis is that the prestige of a nation will be greater as its economic and power status increases. The difficulty of access to such status, and the capacities necessary for a nation to develop in the economic, scientific, and technological patterns in order to achieve it, will constitute the sources of its prestige. In the international system real status is not ascribed, but rather acquired. In large measure it is the capacities associated with the acquisition of status as an economically developed nation, or a nation with great power, that confer prestige in the international system.

Let us see an example of this situation in the Western Hemisphere. Before the Cuban Revolution, Morgenthau accurately stated:

The superiority of the United States in the Western Hemisphere is so obvious and overwhelming that prestige alone is sufficient to assure the United States the position among the American republics commensurate with its power. The United States can even at times afford to forego insistence upon the prestige that is its due, because the self-restraint thus manifested will make its hegemony more tolerable to its neighbors to the south. Thus the United States has made it a point, since the inauguration of the Good Neighbor policy, to have Pan-American conferences meet in Latin-American countries rather than in the United States. Since in the Western Hemisphere the United States has the substance of unchallengeable power, it may well deem it the better part of wisdom not to insist upon all the manifestations of the prestige that goes with such overwhelming power, and to allow some other country in the Western Hemisphere to enjoy at least the appearances of power in the form of prestige.[30]

With reference to the second factor, our hypothesis is that the value orientations of an international system play an important role with respect to prestige. Power and economic strength are main values in the international system, but in addition there exist, at least in the free world, other value-orientations determined by democratic values, national independence, self-determination, and equal rights of all nations, etc. The degree of accord between the behavior of a nation and these value orientations will have an important influence in the determination of its prestige.

For example, the prestige of Costa Rica or Uruguay in the Inter-American System will be greater than, doubtless, that of the Dominican Republic, because Costa Rica and Uruguay have reached a high degree of democratic evolution conforming to the values of the Inter-American System, while the Dominican Republic has lived for many years under a system of dictatorship. In the same way, the contradiction between the democratic values held by the United States and its behavior with respect to some of the Latin American dictatorships in the past has contributed to the decrease of its prestige in Latin America.

In agreement with this hypothesis, the prestige of Nasser in Africa and in the Middle East can be interpreted in the emergence of the Arabian government as the leader in values of national independence and the self-determination of the people. These values are particularly important for that region as it is composed primarily of countries that have recently been granted independence and are trying to affirm their new position.

The case of France and the Algerian War provides another example. France, which contributed greatly to give the world the political concepts of liberty, equality, fraternity, and national sovereignty, has been involved in a struggle with Algeria, which was looking for the recognition of these ideas. This conflict has no doubt influenced France's loss of prestige on the international scene.

The underdeveloped nations can, therefore, achieve a certain status on the prestige level through the co-ordination of their conduct with value orientations, but in the long run "high social prestige, if it is to persist over time, must have an institutional basis."[31] On the international scene, these bases are the institutions that make it possible for a nation to achieve a high status on the levels of power and economics.

3. *Atimia and the ideology of equalitarianism: a distinction between the formal status and the real status*

International stratification, in terms of economic stature, power, and prestige, was produced at the same time that the ideology of equalitarianism was holding sway in the field of international relations.[32] The distinctive trait of this ideology is the affirmation that all states, from the moment they are constituted as such and from the moment they acquire independence, are free, sovereign, and equal. Sovereignty implies that each nation has the supreme authority to manage its external and internal affairs, with the exclusion of authority from any other nation, "in so far as it is not limited by treaty or . . . common . . . international law."[33] All nations have the obligation to respect that independence or sovereignty and, in consequence, cannot interfere in its internal or external politics; "equality . . . is nothing but a synonym for sovereignty, pointing to a particular aspect of sovereignty. If all nations have supreme authority within their territories, none can be subordinated to any other in the exercise of that authority."[34] Out of "the principle of equality a fundamental rule of international law is derived which is responsible for decentralization of the legislative and, in a certain measure, of the law-enforcing function: the rule of unanimity. It signifies that with reference to the legislative function all nations are equal, regardless of their size, population and power. . . ."[35] The vote of Panama counts as much as the vote of the United States.

The ideology of equalitarianism was one of the basic principles of Wilsonian thought. "An evident principle," he said, introducing his famous Fourteen Points in January, 1918, "runs through all the programme I have outlined. It is the principle of justice for all peoples and nationalities and their right to live on *equal terms* of liberty and safety with one another, *whether they be strong or weak*."[36] The ideology of equalitarianism has always been the basic principle of international law, and it inspired the system of the League of Nations. The Charter of the United Nations did not give full recognition to the principle, because the veto power of some great nations was established. This situation was explained as a consequence of the fact that the great powers had an additional function: the maintenance of peace and security. In the field of inter-American relations, the ideology of equalitarianism found full recognition in Article 6, the Charter of the Organization of American States: "States are juridically equal, enjoy equal rights and equal capacity to exercise these rights, and have equal duties. The rights of each state depend not upon its power to ensure the exercise thereof, but upon the mere fact of its existence as a person under international law."

This ideology is also in perfect agreement with the thinking of the classical economists for whom the differences of economic stature among nations seemed unimportant. As Professor Triffin pointed out, interpreting the classical economic thought, "They would also point out . . . that if each nation state acted rationally and embraced free trade, little or no damage could be done by the existence of separate political sovereignties and that the size of nations would then be irrelevant to their economic prosperity."[37]

The concept of formal status of a nation emerges from this ideology. All nations have the same formal status; their positions, their rights, their duties in the system of international relations are the same. The achievement of these rights and duties is not influenced by size, population, wealth, historical age, military power, or political power.

In opposition to the formal status of the nation, the real status is found. While the first is derived from the equalitarian ideology, we have seen that the second is derived from the position that the nation occupies in the system of international stratification in its three basic variables, economic stature, power, and prestige. While in agreement with the first concept—all nations are equal—the structure of the stratified system also determines relationships of superordination and subordination among nations.

Before the present system of international stratification was established, when all nations were underdeveloped, the differences between nations still existed, but they were less accentuated. In such a period, a political leader such as Jefferson could think of assigning equal roles to the Brazilian and United States navies in the defense of the Western Hemisphere; today the American military budget is three times greater than the gross national product of Brazil, according to the most optimistic estimates of the latter.

There existed in that period less distance between the formal status of the nation and its real status, but now, the fact that only a few nations have increased their real status to a considerable fashion has meant a degradation of real status for the rest.

Let us use a Greek word, *atimia,* which signifies the loss or deterioration of status, to designate this situation, and let us call the evolution or social change that ends in a state of *atimia* the *atimic* process. *Atimia* has manifested itself in various forms. Always its essential characteristic is the lowering of status, but this lowering can acquire total or partial characteristics.

Total *atimia* occurs when a nation has not been able to develop the necessary capacities to reach economic and technological maturity. This incapacity impedes its social development and maintains the economic stature—measured in terms of gross national product—on its lowest level. *Atimia* is manifested here in the three elements that constitute the economic status of the nation. As a consequence, the nation sees itself impeded in reaching a status on the power level, requiring, as a basic condition, technological maturity and a high gross national product.

All of the so-called underdeveloped countries that existed as independent nations, when international stratification developed, have suffered this process; as typical examples let us point out the Latin American nations and those of the Middle East. On the other hand, countries that have recently gained their independence in Asia and Africa have been born into an independent life in an already highly stratified international system. Although they have not experienced an *atimic* process, since they previously did not exist and in consequence could not suffer a lowering of a status that they did not have, they acquired formal status in a world in which there existed enormous differences between the formal status and the real status. Their positions in the international system doubtless would have been different had they acquired their independence when the rest of the world was underdeveloped, as happened with the United States and Latin America at the end of the eighteenth and beginning of the nineteenth centuries. To use a metaphoric comparison in describing the system of national stratification, we can say that the countries that suffered the *atimic* process became the lower class in consequence of their *atimia,* while the countries who recently gained their independence were born into the lower class.

Partial *atimia* is produced when the nation, in spite of having acquired technological and economic maturity and social development, has not had the necessary economic stature, measured in terms of gross national product, to participate in the technological race, which is interpreted as the creation of the maximum expressions of military power. As typical cases of partial *atimia,* we may point out France and England. Although the *atimia* is evidenced in this case in power status, its economic implication is also clear since the lack of sufficient economic stature limits the capacity of the nation.

The most notorious indicator of total *atimia* is the lack of social development that is expressed by low standards of living. The most notorious indicator of partial *atimia* is the incapacity for technological leadership.

Total or partial *atimia* is also manifested in the pattern of prestige of the nation, because prestige needs institutional bases. Total *atimia* implies the lack of institutional bases of prestige linked with economic and technological maturity and with social development, while in the case of partial *atimia* institutional bases that permit a technological leadership have been lacking.

In this study we shall limit ourselves to analyzing the international consequences of total *atimia,* which is the common characteristic of underdeveloped countries.

4. *Underdevelopment and atimia as a general definition of the situation of the underdeveloped countries*

The highly stratified international system that we have described has created interactions of a peculiar nature among the nations that have experienced the *atimic* process—or its consequences—and those that have achieved a high status in economy and power.

The first result of this interaction has been the comparison of inequalities—a comparison that is typical of every system of stratification, as T. H. Marshall has pointed out: "Comparisons sustain both the sense of superiority of the rich over 'the great unwashed' and the sense of resentment of the poor against the 'idle rich.' Such feelings may be shared by any number of persons from a single individual to a whole nation."[38]

The comparison of inequalities has been expressed in various dimensions. The governing elite of the underdeveloped countries have been able to appreciate from a close perspective the *atimic* situation in terms of military power, economic stature, and institutional development. The common man has perceived the most evident aspect of international inequality, the difference in standards of living.

As a typical example of the perception of inequality by the political head of a country, let us cite the words of President Kubitschek of Brazil as he explained the objective of Operation Pan-America: "Upon hearing a stronger voice for Latin America in the community of nations, the Pan-American Operation is not unaware that, in the hard realities of power politics, that voice will not be given a hearing unless it has its origin in countries of healthy economy and perfectly stabilized social institutions. . . . We cannot affirm our action unless we resolutely affirm our capacity for action. We cannot express our opinion with assurance on our neighbors' problems if we show ourselves incapable of solving our own problems. We wish to join the Free World but we do not wish to become its proletariat."[39]

The common man has perceived international inequalities through the modern means of mass communication that has spread the social goals of the advanced countries on a large scale in the underdeveloped countries and has made known the high standard of living that exists in them.

It is *atimia* in one of its dimensions—the lack of social development—that has reached him.

Poverty is not new. But now there is a new factor. This is the awareness of poverty, the realization that it is not the inevitable lot of man, and the determination to do something about it. This new awareness, often referred to as the revolution of rising expectations, has come about largely as an indirect consequence of modern science and technology. . . . The wealth-producing capacity of science and technology was demonstrated in the more developed countries, proving that dire poverty for the masses is not inevitable. . . . This vast movement can be characterized as a quest for change in man's affairs by large sectors of population who previously had lived within static social patterns. This accelerated transition and transformation causes many strains and pressures throughout the social organism. . . . The world is divided into two camps, the traditional and the modern, the rich and the poor, the hungry and the satiated, the illiterate and the educated, the free and the oppressed. Potentially the most tremendous social force in the world of the 1960's will be the people who know they no longer have to be hungry and poor, who want education and freedom, who want bicycles, refrigerators, movies and radios, who want to see the city, who want it now. This force, this revolution in expectations, may prove to be the principal modern impact of science on man—the impact on his way of thought and on his values.[40]

The expression "underdeveloped country" is recent. It was mainly the United Nations and its specialized agencies who coined it when the differences between these countries and the more advanced nations became apparent. The fact that, in 1947, when the creation of the Economic Commission for Latin America was discussed in the Economic and Social Council of the United Nations, they described all the conditions of underdevelopment, but still did not use the word, is significant. In 1952 the United Nations published "The Preliminary Report on the World Social Situation," in which the social conditions of the world are described in the following terms: "More than half the population of the world is still living at levels which deny them a reasonable freedom from preventing disease; a diet adequate to physical well-being; a dwelling that meets basic human needs; the education necessary for improvement and development; and conditions of work that are technically efficient, economically rewarding and socially satisfactory."[41] Although it is still difficult to establish the date on which the term "underdeveloped country" began to acquire universal usage, it may be stated that its use is little more than ten years old.

As Myrdal has pointed out it is interesting to note, concerning the use of this term, that it has a dynamic connotation.

The expression commonly used until quite recently was the static term "the backward countries." Both terms . . . are value-loaded, and it is conducive to clarity in our thinking that we are aware of this fact. The use of the concept "the underdeveloped countries" implies the value judgment that it is an accepted goal of public policy that the countries so designated should experience economic development. It is with this implication that people in the poorer countries use the term and press its usage upon people in the richer countries. When they, in their turn, accept this term and suppress the old one, "the backward countries," they also accept the implication. The change from the static to the dynamic concept thus implies in the richer countries a registration of a positive attitude [toward] . . . the poorer countries and, therefore, an acknowledgment—given naturally, only in a general and therefore necessarily vague form—that those countries are right in demanding higher standards of income, a bigger share in the good things of life, and greater equality of opportunity.[42]

The principal result of the comparison of international inequalities and of their expression has been the appearance of a group consciousness in the underdeveloped countries of their underdeveloped condition. The indications of such a consciousness are rich and varied. Let us point out several examples:

I. The term appears frequently in the official documents of the governing bodies of the underdeveloped nations. On opening the third meeting of the Committee of Twenty-one of the OAS, the President of Colombia, Alberto Lleras Camargo, stated: "It is probable that in human history there has been no other case of such rapidity in the extension and intensity of a public preoccupation as that which has occurred with the problem of development, so that, for the third time, the countries of Latin America have dedicated another meeting exclusively to this matter."[43]

During President Eisenhower's trip to Brazil, Argentina, Chile, and Uruguay in February and March of 1960, joint declarations were formulated by the President of the United States and the presidents of each of the countries visited in which development appears as the essential theme.[44]

II. The use of the term is not limited to governmental spheres alone but has also reached political parties, which means that it has penetrated the language of political communication on the national level.

III. The fight against underdevelopment has come to be the essential objective of diverse international organizations sponsored by contributions from the governments. As an illustrative example we may point out: (a) the organizations of the Inter-American System that compose the administrative bodies of Operation Pan-America and the Alliance for Progress; (b) the creation of the International Development Association whose goals are to promote the economic development, increase the productivity, and, in this way, to raise the standard of living in the less developed regions of the world;[45] (c) the Colombo Plan for Co-operative Economic Development in South and South-East Asia.

IV. The emergence in the heart of the United Nations of a group of fifty-seven underdeveloped countries of Asia, Africa, Latin America, and Eastern Europe with common hopes and interests concerning the problem of underdevelopment.[46]

V. The fact that the Soviet leaders, in their propaganda, make the U.S.S.R. appear not so much the leader of world communism but rather the sustainer of underdeveloped countries reveals that the concept is readily accepted by public opinion in these countries.[47]

VI. The debate of the Second Committee of the Fifteenth United Nations General Assembly, in which speaker after speaker pointed out that the rich nations were getting richer faster than the less developed nations, with the result that year by year the gap between the living standards of the two groups was growing wider.[48]

The contradiction between the formal status and the real status of the underdeveloped nations has tended to accentuate the group consciousness of the state of underdevelopment. In agreement with the ideology of equalitarianism, the nations know that they have "equal rights, equal capacity to exercise these rights, equal duties" along with the nations of high economic status or power. They know also that their rights "do not depend on their power." But next to this ideological world, they find also the realities of power, of economic stature, and of prestige, all built on a complex gradation of status that is characterized by relationships of superordination and subordination.

In this context, the underdeveloped nations arrive at a general definition of their international situations, characterized by their low status as a consequence of the *atimic* process. In this study, our principal hypothesis is that, within this general definition of the situation, diverse international actions take place and that their total orientation is the elevation of the real status of the nation.

As the real status is composed of economic, power, and prestige variables, our effort will be directed to the study of these variables. We shall try to construct a conceptual scheme that may serve for the analysis of the variables and of their interrelationships, a conceptual scheme that may permit the sociological investigation of the international actions of the underdeveloped countries by means of empirical investigation. Our task falls then within the scientific orientation that Merton calls "theories of the middle range," theories that have a delimited range of social phenomena and are not "all inclusive speculations comprising a master conceptual scheme."[49]

The orientation of these systems of action throws new light on the interpretation of the nationalist phenomenon. Nationalism, understood as the promotion of national interests in a world of sovereign states, acquires new perspectives from the point of view of the *atimic* process. The rise in real status appears to be for the underdeveloped nations the correct interpretation of the international dimensions of their national interest.

In his study *The Stages of Economic Growth,* Rostow pointed out that "as a matter of historical fact a reactive nationalism—reacting against intrusion from more advanced nations—has been a most important and powerful motive force in the transition from the traditional societies, at least as important as the profit motive."[50]

Nationalism of the underdeveloped countries is also a reactive nationalism—reacting against *atimia* or its consequences—attempting to enhance the status of the nation in a stratified world that is dominated by the values of wealth, power, and prestige.[51]

NOTES

1. Gunnar Myrdal, *Rich Lands and Poor* (New York: Harper & Brothers, 1957); Pierre Moussa, *Les Nations Proletaires* (Paris: Presses Universitaires de France, 1960); Karl Deutsch, *Nationalism and Social Communication* (New York: John Wiley & Sons, Inc., 1953); Reinhard Bendix, "Social Stratification and Political Power," in *Class, Status and Power,* eds., Reinhard Bendix and Seymour Martin Lipset (Glencoe, Ill.: The Free Press, 1953); Francois Perroux, *La Coexistence Pacifique* (3 vols.; Paris: Presses Universitaires de France, 1958);

Robert Theobold, *The Rich and the Poor: A Study of the Economics of Rising Expectations* (New York: Clarkson N. Potter, Inc., 1960); Georges Balandier (ed.), *Le "Tiers Monde": Sous-developpement et developpement* (Paris: Presses Universitaires de France, 1956). For a selected bibliography on this subject, see Max F. Millikan and Donald L. M. Blackmer (eds.), *The Emerging Nations* (Boston: Little, Brown and Company, 1961), pp. 161-68.

2. Harold D. Lasswell, "Nations and Classes: The Symbols of Identification," in *Reader in Public Opinion and Communication*, eds., Bernard Berelson and Morris Janowitz (Glencoe, Ill.: The Free Press, 1953), pp. 28-43.

3. Reinhard Bendix, "Social Stratification and Political Power," in Bendix and Lipset, *Class, Status and Power*, p. 598.

4. Bernard Barber, *Social Stratification* (New York: Harcourt Brace & Co., 1957), p. 259. In the same sense, Edward Hallet Carr, "Socialization of Nationalism," in *Conflict and Cooperation among Nations*, ed., Ivo D. Duchacek (New York: Holt, Rinehart and Winston, Inc., 1960), pp. 60 ff.; George Schwarzenberger, *Power Politics* (London: Stevens and Sons, Ltd., 1951), p. 62.

5. Talcott Parsons, "Social Classes and Class Conflict in the Light of Recent Sociological Theory," in *Essays in Sociological Theory* (Glenco, Ill.: The Free Press, 1954), pp. 323-35.

6. Karl Deutsch, "The Growth of Nations: Some Recurrent Patterns of Political and Social Integration," *World Politics*, V (1953), 168-95.

7. According to an article by Harry Schwartz which appeared in the *New York Times*, March 4, 1962, Moscow revised this aspect of Marxist economic theory:

"Teachers of economics in the Soviet Union have been instructed to stop telling their students that workers' wages in capitalist countries always go down. This assertion is to be replaced by a more sophisticated argument intended to show that workers' conditions get worse under capitalism even when wages go up.

"This change has been disclosed by the chief economic organ of the Communist party's Central Committee, *Ekonomicheskaya Gazeta* in an article reporting on major changes recently introduced in the curricula of economics courses in Soviet universities.

"The announcement of the change was presented as if it were an effort merely to correct an error by 'some teachers,' but an examination of the leading Soviet economics textbooks showed that the repudiated doctrine had been the official line."

"According to *Ekonomicheskaya Gazeta*, the change made is the following:

" 'In the subject of wages, a proposition has been included about the lag of wages behind the material and cultural needs of the worker and his family in the conditions of capitalism. The proposition has important significance since the analysis of the dynamics of wages there has sometimes been over-simplified exposition.

" 'Some teachers have said, for example, that the quantity of the means of existence and services purchasable with wages constantly declines. In doing this, they have not given attention to the fact that they were speaking about the decline in the quantity of the means of existence and services in comparison with that which is necessary for normal reproduction of the labor force.'

"*Facts Conflict with Theory*

"This circuitous wording has presumably been required because it apparently has proved impossible to reconcile the traditional Communist argument about the 'increasing misery of the working class under capitalism' with the facts known to ever larger numbers of Soviet citizens about the sharp improvements in living standards in the advanced industrial nations of Western Europe and the United States.

"The traditional Soviet teaching of this subject was presented in a textbook on political economy published by the Soviet Academy of Sciences in 1954. The section based its discussion on Marx's statement: 'the general level of the real wages of the working class as a whole declines under the influence of the capitalist labor market.'

"The new doctrine apparently abandons the old argument about the absolute decline of wages under capitalism and substitutes for it the argument that even when wages increase there is still a relative worsening of the condition of the working class.

"Soviet authors who have argued this point maintain that with general economic progress workers' requirements rise with the general increase in prosperity of a society. Thus it has been argued that a worker may be relatively worse off than his father or grandfather even though he has an automobile and a refrigerator, which neither his father nor his grandfather had.

"But apparently in both the old line and the new the case of workers who have all the conveniences of modern technology is dismissed because these are held to be members of a 'working-class aristocracy' *whose welfare is a bribe paid by the capitalists at the expense of the poorer workers and the colonial peoples."* (Italics supplied by author.)

8. Bendix, "Social Stratification and Political Power," in Bendix and Lipset, *Class, Status and Power*, p. 598. In a similar sense, Reinhold Niebuhr, "Power and Ideology in National and International Affairs," in *Theoretical Aspects of International Relations*, ed., William T. R. Fox (Notre Dame, Ind.: University of Notre Dame Press, 1959), p. 114.

9. For the study of the concept of international system, see Morton A. Kaplan, *System and Process in International Politics* (New York: John Wiley and Sons, Inc., 1957); Stanley Hoffmann (ed.), *Contemporary Theory in International Relations* (Englewood Cliffs, N.J.: Prentice-Hall, Inc., 1960); Klaus Knorr and Sidney Verba (eds.), *The International System: Theoretical Essays, World Politics*, Special Issue, XIV (1961); James N. Rosenau (ed.), *International Politics and Foreign Policy: A Reader in Research and Theory* (Glencoe, Ill.: The Free Press, 1961); see especially Talcott Parsons, *Order and Community in the International Social System*, pp. 120-29. For a treatment of interactions among nations as a great social system in a general textbook of sociology, see William F. Ogburn and Meyer F. Nimkoff, *Sociology*, (3rd ed.; Boston: Houghton Mifflin Company, 1958), p. 525 ff.

10. We are following here Robert K. Merton, for whom "the status set refers to the complex of distinct positions assigned to individuals both within and among social systems," *Social Theory and Social Structure* (rev. ed.; Glencoe, Ill.: The Free Press, 1957), p. 380.

11. Barber, *Social Stratification*, p. 2.

12. See *Peuples et civilisations*, published under the direction of Louis Halphen and Philippe Sagnac—Henri Hauser, *La prepondérance espagnole (1559-1660)* (3rd. ed.; Paris: Presses Universitaires de France, 1948), Vol. IX; Philippe Sagnac and A. de Saint-Leger, *La prepondérance francaise: Louis XIV (1661-1715)* (Paris: F. Alcan, 1935), Vol. X; Pierre Muret, with the collaboration of Philippe Sagnac, *La prepondérance anglaise (1715-1763)* (2nd. ed.; Paris: Presses Universitaires de France, 1942), Vol. XI.

13. Nicholas John Spykman, *America's Strategy in World Politics* (New York: Harcourt Brace and Co., 1942), p. 61.

14. W. W. Rostow, *The Stages of Economic Growth* (New York: Cambridge University Press, 1960), p. 4.

15. *Ibid.*

16. *Ibid.*, pp. 7, 36, 9, 59.

17. *Ibid.*, p. 10.

18. *Ibid.,* p. 11.

19. United Nations, "Report on International Definition and Measurement of Standards and Levels of Living" (New York, 1954).

20. Charles Hitch and Roland McKean, *The Economics of Defense in the Nuclear Age* (Cambridge, Mass.: Harvard University Press, 1960), p. 18.

21. *Ibid.,* p. 88.

22. *Ibid.,* pp. 34-35.

23. *Ibid.,* p. 36.

24. Kingsley Davis, "The Demographic Foundations of National Power," in *Freedom and Control in Modern Society,* eds., Monroe Berger, Thomas Abel, and Charles Page (Princeton, N.J.: D. Van Nostrand Company, Inc., 1954), p. 223.

25. On the failure of the "Blue Streak" see "The Moral of the Blue Streak," *The Economist,* 195 (April 23, 1960). The English spent 65 million pounds sterling on perfecting this rocket. On the French nuclear program and its financial repercussions, see Jules Moch, "La Force de Frappe," *Le Monde,* XII (1960), 6-7.

26. Hitch and McKean, *The Economics of Defense,* p. 246.

27. Ogburn and Nimkoff, *Sociology,* p. 157.

28. Joseph A. Kahl, *The American Class Structure* (New York: Rhinehart and Company, 1959), p. 19.

29. *Ibid.,* pp. 21-25.

30. Hans J. Morgenthau, *Politics among Nations* (3rd. ed.; New York: Alfred A. Knopf, 1960), p. 82.

31. Bendix and Lipset, *Class, Status and Power,* p. 11.

32. We employ the concept of ideology in the sense defined by Mannheim in *Ideology and Utopia* and which Haas has synthesized: "Ideology postulates belief in a set of symbols which, even though they may be 'false,' objectively, still characterize the total myth system of social groups and are essential to the spiritual cohesion of a ruling group which would lose its sense of control if it were conscious of the 'real' state of affairs." Ernst Haas, "The Balance of Power: Concept, Prescription or Propaganda," in *Theory and Practice of International Relations,* eds., David S. McLellan, William C. Olson, and Fred A. Sondermann (Englewood Cliffs, N.J.: Prentice-Hall, Inc., 1960), p. 224.

33. Morgenthau, *Politics among Nations,* p. 315. See also in the same sense, Richard C. Snyder and Edgar S. Furniss, *American Foreign Policy: Formulation, Principles, and Programs* (New York: Rinehart and Company, 1954), p. 761.

34. Morgenthau, *Politics among Nations,* p. 315.

35. *Ibid.,* p. 316.

36. Cited by Elie Kedourie, *Nationalism* (London: Hutchinson and Co., 1960), p. 130.

37. R. Triffin, "The Size of the Nation and Its Vulnerability to Economic Nationalism," in *The Economic Consequences of the Size of Nations,* ed., Austin Robinson (New York: St. Martin's Press, Inc., 1960), p. 248.

38. T. H. Marshall, "The Nature of Class Conflicts" in Bendix and Lipset, *Class, Status and Power,* p. 84.

39. *Revista Brasileira de Politica Internacional,* Ano II, No. 5 (Março, 1959), 139.

40. *Possible Nonmilitary Scientific Developments and Their Potential Impact on Foreign Policy Problems of the United States,* study prepared at the request of the Committee on Foreign Relations, United States Senate, by Stanford Research Institute (Washington, D.C.: G.P.O., 1959), pp. 42-43.

41. United Nations, "The Preliminary Report on the World Social Situation" (New York, 1952), p. 4.

42. Myrdal, *Rich Lands and Poor,* pp. 7-8.

43. *Panorama Económica,* 216 (October, 1960, Santiago, Chile).

44. "President Eisenhower's Visit to Brazil, Argentina, Chile and Uruguay," February-March, 1960, Department of State Publication 6974, Inter-American Series 59.

45. Article 1 of the Constitutional Covenant of the International Development Association.

46. Thomas Jovet, *Bloc Politics in the United Nations* (Cambridge, Mass.: Harvard University Press, 1960), pp. 44-45.

47. In the content analysis of the report presented by Khruskchev to the 21st Congress of the Communist party, it is revealed that the U.S.S.R. appears thirty-seven times as the sustainer of underdeveloped countries and not once as the guide of world communism. See Stuart R. Schram and Francoise Guillaume, "Communisme et nationalisme dans les pays sous-developpes," Fondation Nationale des Sciences Politiques, Centre d'Etudes des Relations Internationales, Paris, Mai, 1960.

48. Speech of the Minister of Education of the United Kingdom to the XI General Conference of UNESCO.

49. Merton, *Social Theory and Social Structure,* p. 5.

50. Rostow, *Stages of Economic Growth,* p. 26.

51. Compare the similarity of this definition that arises logically from our theory with the definition of Karl Deutsch: "Nationalism is the preference for the competitive interest of [the] nation and its members over those of all outsiders in a world of social mobility and economic competition, dominated by the values of wealth, power and prestige, so that the goals of personal security and group identification appear bound up with the group's attainment of these values," in "The Growth of Nations: Some Recurrent Patterns of Political and Social Integration," *World Politics,* V (1953), 169.

PART TWO

SOME TYPOLOGIES OF INTERNATIONAL ACTION OF
UNDERDEVELOPED COUNTRIES

CHAPTER II

INTERNATIONAL ACTION AND THE ECONOMIC STATUS OF A NATION

1. Economic development as a primary component of the real status of a nation

In the preceding chapter the study of the components of the real status of a nation demonstrated that status in military power depended on economic status. The analysis also showed that on the international scene the institutional basis of the real status in the pattern of prestige depended on the institutions that make it possible for a nation to achieve a high status in the patterns of economic stature and military power.

It is clear, therefore, that economic status is the basic element of real status. If we now analyze the components of the economic status of a nation, we can see that of the three basic elements there are two—the degree of social development and the amount of the gross national product—that depend on a third, the degree of economic development evaluated by the position that the nation occupies in some of the stages of economic growth described by Rostow.

Economic development appears as the primary component of real status, and therefore it is understood that total *atimia*—or its consequences—occurs when a nation is classified as low in this aspect. This same fact explains that economic development has become a focal point towards which public opinion is directed, together with the attention of political leaders and governments. In this way the idea of economic development becomes confused with development in all of its aspects. The development of a society as a whole and economic development are not synonymous.

The recent use of the expression "national development" in some significant official documents (Act for International Development of the U.S. and the Charter of Punta del Este establishing the Alliance for Progress) refers to the first meaning. We shall deal extensively with the deep implications of this distinction in Chapter VI. For the analysis in the present chapter we shall deal mainly with the economic aspects of the development process.

Our plan is to identify the types of international action of underdeveloped countries in the economic pattern of status, i.e., to observe the international behavior of nations in achieving their economic development and thus in securing a rise in their real status.

In the previous chapter we stated the hypothesis that the systems of action of the underdeveloped countries can be studied as a reaction to the *atimic* process or to its consequences.

Therefore, our analysis will first determine how *atimia* manifests itself from the economic point of view and then identify the kinds of international action adopted by countries as a reaction against it.

2. *Economic manifestations of atimia and international dependence of underdeveloped countries*

The superordination-subordination relations that characterize the system of international stratification are manifested, from the economic point of view, in a high degree of international dependence of the underdeveloped countries upon those which have achieved a high real status.

In the analysis of the relations of dependence, three basic aspects can be pointed out: (1) the satellite character of underdeveloped economies, (2) the need for foreign capital to finance development, and (3) the need for technical aid for development.

It is beyond the scope of this study to enter into an exhaustive consideration of each one of these three aspects; we shall refer only to those elements which are directly related to our purpose of establishing a typology of international action of underdeveloped countries in the economic field. As we shall see, although the field in which these actions occur is economic, no action can be adopted without a previous decision of a political nature.

Hoselitz, in his study *Sociological Aspects of Economic Growth* has pointed out

... the dichotomy between countries with a "dominant" and those with a "satellitic" pattern of economic growth. The ideal case of a dominant pattern would be exhibited by a country with a fully autarchic economy, with no need to resort to foreign borrowing for purposes of capital accumulation and without exports. At the other extreme we would have a society which draws all its capital for development from abroad and which develops only those branches of production whose output is entirely exported. If we further stipulated that all or the bulk of the capital imports come from one source and that all or the bulk of the exports go to one destination, we have the ideal-typical case of a country with a "satellitic" pattern of growth. It is obvious that neither of these two extremes is, or even can be, realized in practice.[1]

Underdeveloped countries approximate, to a greater or smaller degree, the satellite type of economic development.

As is known, the foreign trade of these countries depends on one or two primary products[2] which places underdeveloped countries, with respect to the terms of trade, in a position that has been described as "traditionally precarious and vulnerable"[3] by the experts of the United Nations. "For reasons well explored in economic analysis, primary commodities, especially industrial raw materials, are subject to particularly violent swings in price. Nor can the fall of primary commodity prices be compensated for by an increase in volume of exports. Often effects of changes in quantities are added to those of change in prices, with the result that values of total exports may vary from year to year as much as 30 per cent; change in the same direction may also go on for consecutive years, resulting in a total fall in value of more than 50 per cent within a few years."[4]

In the case of Latin America, this fact and the "heavy demand for imported capital goods, foodstuffs, fuels and raw materials for development purposes"[5] compose the two structural elements that are translated into "the chronic inadequacy of Latin America's capacity to import."[6]

Referring to the repercussions of this situation, ECLA, in its "Economic Survey of Latin America, 1958," states: "in any event, the disequilibrium in the balance of payments made it essential to resort once again to compensatory loans, which were obtained as a rule from the usual sources. United States banks, both official and private, were responsible for most financing of this type."[7]   These foregoing facts are too well known to dwell further upon them.   What we wish to point out is the relation between them and the *atimic* process.

From a triple point of view, the problem of raw materials affects the economic status of underdeveloped countries: (1) because price fluctuations of these commodities can destroy the beneficial effects of foreign financial aid, (2) because market instability is an impediment for economic development and, in consequence, a great obstacle for a rise in status, and (3) because trends in prices and quantums of these commodities on the world market accentuate the distance between underdeveloped countries and industrialized countries.   With relation to this last aspect, it has been asserted, "The terms of trade between primary and manufactured commodities entering into international trade moved against primary commodities for the sixty years between 1873 and 1937. During this period primary commodities lost nearly 40% of their value in terms of manufactures."[8]   In a recent study of the United Nations, it has been established that the "trends in price and quantum of primary commodities, when taken together, have meant that, by comparison with trade in manufactures, the total value of trade in primary commodities has shown relatively slow growth. The share of the primary producing countries in total world trade has accordingly declined since the early post-war years.   Whereas their share in world trade amounted to 38% in 1948, it fell to 36% in 1953 and declined still further to 31% in 1959."[9]

The second factor of dependence of underdeveloped countries is the need for foreign capital to finance economic development. The situation "is in the nature of a vicious circle.   Economic development cannot proceed because the rate of saving is inadequate; saving does not take place because there is insufficient development."[10]   In 1951 a group of United Nations experts pointed out the need and the urgency of providing the underdeveloped countries with the necessary capital to raise their level of living more rapidly, calling attention to the fact that the amount of this capital was much greater than was currently supposed.   In the decade of 1950, consciousness of this need was affirmed to such an extent that today it constitutes a universally accepted fact.

United Nations calculations estimated the amount of the aid at 4 billion dollars annually in 1958, composed of 2.4 billion dollars of government aid and 1.6 billion dollars from private capital. Including Soviet aid of 700 million dollars per year, the total figure amounts to 4.7 billion.[11]

But this sum is obviously insufficient to achieve a rapid increase in the standard of living of the underdeveloped areas of the world. It is evident that a precise estimate of the necessary aid is difficult to arrive at, as it depends on the objectives or goals of the economic development plans, on the capacity of the country receiving the aid to absorb foreign capital, on the cost and productivity of the various types of investment planned, on the rate of demographic growth of the recipient country, etc. Paul Hoffman has calculated, in general and approximately, that if the aim pursued is to double, in the 1960 decade, the annual per capita rate of economic growth compared with the existing 1950 rate in the one hundred countries and territories mentioned in his study, whose population is 1.25 billion people, "it will mean increasing the per capita economic growth rate of the less developed countries from an average of 1 per cent a year in the 1950's to an average of 2 per cent in the 1960's. To do this, it will be necessary for the less developed countries to sustain an annual rate of economic growth of 4 per cent. This will mean a total increase of about 40 per cent and a per capita increase of nearly 25 per cent in ten years. It will mean increasing per capita income from the estimated figure of around \$100 to \$125 in 1970. This means increasing per capita income in the 1960's by about 25 per cent per person or an average of about \$2.50 per person per year."[12]

Studies made in the United States and Europe, regarding the quantity of additional capital required to achieve the previously mentioned aim, agree in general on an approximate sum of 3 billion dollars per year, which added to the present 4 billion would give a total of 7 billion dollars annually.

P. N. Rosenstein-Rodan has made the most recent study of the amount of international aid required for underdeveloped countries. Table VIII, derived from this study, shows the estimated capital inflow required per annum by underdeveloped countries for the period 1961-76.

TABLE VIII
ESTIMATED CAPITAL INFLOW REQUIRED PER ANNUM BY UNDERDEVELOPED COUNTRIES, 1961-1976
(Million Dollars)

Region	Total Capital Inflow	Capital Aid	Private Investment
A. 1961-1966			
Africa	430	275	155
Latin America[1]	1,550	840	710
Asia	2,695	2,395	300
(Asia)	(2,520)	(2,240)	(280)
Middle East	640	475	165
Europe	385	305	80
TOTAL I	5,700	4,290	1,410
TOTAL II (Asian alternate)	(5,525)	(4,135)	(1,390)
TOTAL III (I minus Europe)	5,315	3,985	1,330
B. 1966-1971			
Africa	605	395	210
Latin America[1]	1,495	585	910
Asia	2,380	1,965	415
(Asia)	(2,910)	(2,430)	(480)
Middle East	750	525	225
Europe	455	305	150
TOTAL I	5,685	3,775	1,910
TOTAL II (Asian alternate)	(6,215)	(4,240)	(1,975)
TOTAL III (I minus Europe)	5,230	3,470	1,760
C. 1971-1976			
Africa	740	415	325
Latin America[1]	1,010	180	830
Asia	1,250	910	340
(Asia)	(2,270)	(1,710)	(560)
Middle East	400	180	220
Europe	360	185	175
TOTAL I	3,760	1,870	1,890
TOTAL II (Asian alternate)	(4,780)	(2,670)	(2,110)
TOTAL III (I minus Europe)	3,400	1,685	1,715

[1] Excluding Puerto Rico and the Virgin Islands.

NOTE: This table summarizes for each of the next three five-year periods the estimated total capital inflow required by regions of the world and the estimated division of these totals between capital aid and private investment. Some elements of what has come to be called "foreign aid" in the American aid program are omitted from these figures (e.g., technical assistance and the emergency fund) because they do not constitute capital inflow in the usual sense. Also excluded are those elements of defense support which do not contribute directly to capital formation; that portion of surplus agricultural products which cannot properly be regarded as providing capital; and expenditures for so-called social development, encompassing such items as education, health, and administration, which are not normally included in economists' statistical estimates of new productive capital.

The first column in this table estimates the capital inflow which would be required to produce the rates of growth assumed as reasonable. . . . In general, the method was to estimate total investment requirements by applying a capital-output ratio to the growth figures and then to subtract estimates of the level of domestic savings which each of the countries could be expected to achieve. India bulks so large in the figures for Asia that it has seemed useful to present an alternative estimate for that continent. The first estimate accepts the assumptions made in the draft outline of the Indian Third Five-Year Plan as to rates of growth and as to domestic average and marginal savings rates. The alternate estimate is based on somewhat less optimistic assumptions both as to the capital-output ratio and as to domestic savings. The division of capital inflow in the last two columns into capital aid and private investment is based on exceedingly rough estimates and serves only illustrative purposes. In comparing the three periods, it will be noted that the required capital inflow falls off in 1971-76 because domestic savings are assumed to take over a larger share of the substantially increased capital requirements. It will also be noted that the role of private investment is assumed to increase over the fifteen years.

SOURCE: Max F. Millikan and Donald L. M. Blackmer (eds.), *The Emerging Nations: Their Growth and United States Policy* (Boston: Little, Brown, 1961), pp. 156-57.

Whatever the validity of these calculations may be, the fact we wish to stress is that the very existence of such calculations demonstrates the pronounced situation of dependence of the underdeveloped countries upon those that are capable of providing economic assistance.   It is true that such an amount of capital represents only a small part of the total investment that the underdeveloped countries must make to realize their goal; the largest part of the investment will always have to be financed by domestic capital.   However, it is evident that economic development cannot be achieved without foreign aid.

This relation of dependence between the countries of the underdeveloped areas and those of the developed areas has been translated into an interaction of a special character.   Lines of interaction have been created in accordance with the expectations that have arisen which are related to the real status of nations from an economic point of view.   Hence, the underdeveloped countries look toward the countries of a higher economic status as the natural distributors of financial aid.   In their turn, these countries consider it socially permitted behavior for the aid to be solicited or even demanded.   The country of the highest economic status—the United States—considers it natural to request the co-operation of the countries of the Atlantic Community in assisting the underdeveloped world.   And, lastly, it is suggested that "both Europe and the United States should consider ways in which countries at an intermediate stage of economic growth can be brought into the process of developing the underdeveloped countries."[13]   A similar phenomenon is seen in the relations of the Soviet Union and the countries within its orbit, in the sense that the more developed countries of the Communist world, such as Czechoslovakia, for example, must contribute equally to the Soviet effort of economic aid.   So it is that the countries with the lowest economic status look towards the two nations of highest status—the United States and the Soviet Union—these, in turn, try to incorporate into their roles as givers of aid those countries of high economic status but of a lower power status.   Both try jointly to persuade the countries of middle-range economic status to participate to some measure in aiding the underdeveloped nations.   A concrete proposal for dividing equitably among the developed countries the burden of supplying capital aid

TABLE IX

A Proposal for Sharing the Burden of Capital Aid*

Country	Number of Families (thousands) (1)	A. "Money" GNP				B. "Real" GNP				
		GNP per Family (dollars) (2)	Tax per Family (dollars) (3)	Contribution (per cent)		Weight Used (6)	GNP per Family (dollars) (7)	Tax per Family (dollars) (8)	Contribution (per cent)	
				With Soviet Union (4)	Without Soviet Union (5)				With Soviet Union (9)	Without Soviet Union (10)
Belgium	2,303.2	5,392	495	1.0	1.1	1.23	6,632	729	1.2	1.4
Canada	4,578.2	7,954	1,002	4.1	4.3	1.00	7,954	1,002	3.4	3.7
Denmark	1,152.7	4,774	380	0.4	0.4	1.33	6,349	676	0.6	0.6
Finland	1,128.5	3,573	164	0.2	0.2	1.44	5,145	449	0.4	0.4
France	11,478.0	4,815	389	4.0	4.2	1.20	5,778	568	4.8	5.3
West Germany	14,072.0	4,452	326	4.1	4.3	1.43	6,366	679	7.0	7.7
Italy	12,385.7	2,491	0	0	0	1.44	3,587	164	1.5	1.6
Luxembourg	83.0	6,084	626	0.04	0.04	1.23	7,483	900	0.05	0.06
Netherlands	2,910.5	3,815	209	0.5	0.6	1.55	5,913	594	1.3	1.4
Norway	906.7	4,895	398	0.3	0.3	1.29	6,315	670	0.4	0.5
Oceania	4,023.7	4,419	317	1.1	1.2	1.33	5,877	585	1.7	1.9
Soviet Union	53,742.0	3,274	110	5.3	—	1.20	3,928	227	9.0	—
Sweden	1,889.7	6,228	653	1.1	1.2	1.30	8,096	1,033	1.4	1.6
Switzerland	1,343.6	6,222	652	0.8	0.8	1.25	7,778	944	0.9	1.0
United Kingdom	13,075.0	5,383	493	5.8	6.1	1.30	6,998	799	7.7	8.4
United States	46,141.5	11,161	1,728	71.3	75.2	1.00	11,161	1,728	58.6	64.4

* Based on the current U.S. progressive income tax schedule. Also assuming GNP per family as a measure of income with family consisting of four members.

NOTE: This table illustrates the application of a suggested principle for dividing equitably among the developed countries the burden of supplying capital aid to the underdeveloped countries. The principle proposed is that relative shares should be determined by applying to the per family GNP (in dollars) of the developed countries a rate of taxation which progresses with increasing income on the same basis as the present U.S. income tax. In Section A of the table this principle is applied to family incomes expressed in "nominal" or "money" figures, that is, in local currencies converted at the effective rates of exchange. Section B of the table applies the same principle to per family GNP computed in "real" terms, that is, by valuing all elements of GNP at U.S. prices.

SOURCE: Max F. Millikin and Donald L. M. Blackmer (eds.), *The Emerging Nations: Their Growth and United States Policy* (Boston: Little, Brown, 1961), pp. 158-59.

to the underdeveloped countries was made by a working group of social scientists of M.I.T. Table IX shows the application of this idea.

The same situation arises with respect to the need for technical assistance for development (see Table III), the third aspect of international dependence of the underdeveloped countries from the economic point of view. The British and the countries of Southeast Asia were the first to demonstrate this fact in a concrete plan of action in 1950 in the Colombo Conference, when they pointed out the need for "the provision of technical assistance and advice, without which the countries will be unable to increase their agricultural and industrial development."[14]

Essentially, the term "technical assistance" or "technical co-operation" means the introduction of programs for "the international interchange of technical knowledge and skills designed to contribute to the balanced and integrated development of the economic resources and productive capacities of economically underdeveloped areas. Such activities may include, but need not be limited to, economic, engineering, medical, educational, agricultural, fishery, mineral, and fiscal surveys, demonstration, training, and similar projects that serve the purpose of promoting the development of economic resources and productive capacities of underdeveloped areas."[15] Although the role of technical aid is not as spectacular as that of financial aid, its importance is perhaps as great or even greater.

It was stated in Chapter I that the distinguishing traits of the stages of economic development, which Rostow terms "take-off" and "technological maturity," are that society begins to apply systematically and regularly the potentialities of modern science and technology to the bulk of its resources and that, with the new knowledge, the level of income and welfare in which traditional society found itself is significantly raised. The nation thus achieves a degree of efficiency in the use of its resources unknown in the previous stages. The role of efficiency in economic development is made evident in the following: a better allocation of the resources among the possible alternative uses; methods of organization that utilize the scientific and technological knowledge of which society disposes; the creation of social incentives to production; a greater degree of efficacy in the use of innovations and mechanisms which, in turn, opens new avenues for the resources in answer to the innovations themselves; incentives created to explore new ideas; the increase of research and education in general; and, in short, a maximum use of human resources which, in turn, leads to a full use of the resources of capital and labor available to society.

What is the exact role that efficiency plays in increasing the gross national product with relation to the other factors influencing its growth? As Myrdal has pointed out this role was usually kept outside the analysis of classical economists. We mentioned in Chapter I, "Recent studies have begun to shed light on the answers to these questions. These studies indicate that the rise of GNP in the United States has far outstripped the growth in the quantities of capital and labor."[16]   More specifically, they suggest that half or more of the increase in national product must be attributed to rising productivity of the inputs.   One researcher concludes: "Of the historic increase in GNP, about half represented the effect of increased resources, and half, the effect of increased efficiency of resource use."[17]   According to another inquiry, an index of factor input (capital and labor combined) quadrupled between the decades of 1869-78 and that of 1944-53, while over the same period net national product grew to thirteen times its original size.[18] "Such results indicate that new ideas and their efficient and widespread application may be of overriding importance to growth."[19]

Other studies lead one to believe that this same phenomenon is particularly applicable to underdeveloped countries.   Research carried out in Mexico and Brazil with relation to agricultural development has indicated this.   "In Mexico, for example, the relatively large crop producing sector increased its output 60 per cent from 1925-29 to 1945-49, using however only 27 per cent more input; thus output per unit of aggregate input rose by 26 per cent.   Farm production in Brazil was 55 per cent larger in 1945-49 than in 1925-29.   The input index rose only 30 per cent; and, accordingly, output per unit of aggregate input increased 20 per cent."[20]

Given the role of efficiency in economic development, one might restate the role of technical aid by the following question: Is technical aid enough to bring about the change required to create the cultural patterns that are favorable to the development of "efficiency"?   The answer is negative.   Technical aid consists essentially of the contribution and transmission of scientific and technical knowledge and skills, but science and technology, of which the knowledge and skills transmitted form a part, arose in a given social and cultural context, that of the developed countries. It is one thing for foreign experts carrying out a program of technical assistance to succeed in transmitting certain scientific and technological knowledge and skills to small groups in a nation, but it is quite another thing for the total society, to which the small groups receiving the technical aid belong, to succeed in changing its beliefs, patterns of values, and behavior in such a way that the necessary mental attitudes and cultural patterns for the development of science and technology can be produced. The first process defines the role of technical aid; the second process depends upon a profound and complex social and cultural change in which the factors introduced by technical aid represent only one of many elements. Only when this social and cultural change has begun can society reach the "take-off stage" and later proceed to the technological maturity that allows this society to apply regularly and systematically the potentialities of modern science and technology to the development of its resources.

The problem, then, for underdeveloped countries is the achievement of this socio-cultural change necessary for their development without losing those values and worthy traditions that are compatible with the socio-cultural complex of a modern society.

The defense of those values of the underdeveloped in-group, with respect to the values of the developed out-group, can be observed in the case of India which pursues economic development rationally and systematically through its five-year plans[21] and at the same time endeavors to bring about the change in such a way that its cultural and religious values are not lost.

Paradoxically, the dependent situation of the underdeveloped countries with respect to the developed countries obliges the former to enlist technical aid in order to realize their development and to achieve a greater independence; but at the same time, because of the process of socio-cultural change we have noted, they run the risk of losing those precise values on which the feelings of in-group independence are built.

3. *Reactions to atimia, international action, and economic development*

We have seen up to this point that *atimia*, or its consequences, implies a high degree of economic dependence of the underdeveloped countries upon the developed world.

Within the plan of our analysis, we shall now identify the types of international action employed by the underdeveloped countries in their effort to emerge from the *atimic* state, to raise their real status as a consequence, and, as far as possible, to approach a formal status of independence and equality with respect to other nations.

A. *The policy of induced development*

In this reactive process, the need for a major decision becomes more and more evident, a decision that leads the underdeveloped nations to adopt a policy of economic development and to link that policy to its aspirations of strengthening its independence not only formally but also economically. It is true that complete economic independence cannot exist in a world characterized by interdependent relations; the desired goal is the eradication, insofar as it is possible, of the satellite character of national economies and the placing of interdependence on a level of equality not of domination. To illustrate this idea we need only compare the case of a small country that is highly developed, as is Switzerland, with a small country that is underdeveloped. We have stated some of the foreign-trade characteristics of the underdeveloped countries; the comparison of these with the Swiss economy shows great similarities and profound differences. As with underdeveloped economies, the Swiss economy is strongly oriented toward export. "Nothing could more strikingly illustrate the export orientation of the Swiss economy than the fact that four important branches of industry (watches, dyes, pharmaceutical preparations and perfumes, and embroideries) export 95 per cent of their output."[22]

The profound differences derive from the fact that the highly diversified industrial economy, whose quality is assured by a specialized labor force and by a high level of technological research and business capacity, allows Switzerland to have a great variety of export commodities and of markets for placement. Some 69 per cent of the export is placed in twelve large foreign markets, from neighboring Germany to distant nations such as India, China, and Australia; the remaining 31 per cent is marketed in seventy-five countries throughout the world. Hence, the high level of efficiency of its economy permits it a wide degree of flexibility and adaptability to the fluctuating conditions of the world economy in contrast to the degree of vulnerability of the underdeveloped economies.[23]

When the underdeveloped countries speak, therefore, of economic independence, they are referring not to the suppression of economic interdependence among nations—which is impossible—

but to the suppression or decrease of the effects of domination by means of compensatory economic mechanisms, such as the Swiss and other highly developed economies have been able to create.

On stating that the first visible reaction to international economic dependence is the decision in favor of economic development, it may be asked: What is the meaning of this decision and who must make the decision and translate it into action?

The decision in favor of economic development consists essentially of the will to achieve a rational utilization of determined means for reaching the goals and proposed objectives with a maximum yield. Whatever the scope of this decision may be and, in consequence, whether the goals be near or far in time, the final objective can be no other than that of attaining the stage of self-sustained economic growth and technological maturity. This stage brings with it, from an internal point of view, the raising of the standard of living and, from an international point of view, a greater independence in the relative sense defined above. A decision in favor of development, then, necessarily involves planning.

The nature of the decision in favor of economic development—or development planning—clearly indicates the agent who must make the decision and carry it out.

This agent can be no other than the state—in other words, the government—for the simple reason that "it is the principal organ of common action of the community"[24] and only the government is in a position to evaluate the given means, available at present or capable of being obtained, to reach the aim of economic development.

Having overcome the controversy that confused planning with socialism,[25] "it is interesting to observe the unanimity with which central economic planning is instituted as a policy in underdeveloped countries."[26]

In 1951 the United Nations experts in charge of establishing measures for economic development in the underdeveloped countries recommended to the governments of these nations, as a measure to create the preconditions and the institutional framework to promote economic development, the need to

. . . establish a central economic unit with the functions of surveying the economy, making development programmes, advising on the measures necessary for carrying out such programmes and reporting on them periodically. The development programmes should contain a capital budget showing the requirements of capital and how much of this is expected from domestic and from foreign sources.

In order to promote rapid economic development [continued the report of the experts] an under-developed country should take the following measures: (1) Survey the ways in which production, distribution and finance are organized in each of the major sectors of the economy and take measures to improve their efficiency; (2) Survey the prospects of creating new productive employment by industrialization, by bringing more land under cultivation, by developing mineral resources or by other means; and announce its programmes for expanding employment; (3) Survey the possibilities of increasing agricultural yields and announce the measures it proposes to adopt in order to effect rapid improvement of yields; (4) Prepare a programme covering a period of years, for the improvement of public facilities by capital investment; (5) Prepare a programme of education and research showing its goals and its proposed expenditures for such periods as five years; and showing separately what is proposed for agricultural extension services, for industrial training, and for the training of scientists and administrators; (6) Prepare programmes to stimulate domestic savings, including the extension of savings institutions and measures involving taxation; and (7) in order to ensure that capital moves into the most productive uses, establish a development bank and an agricultural credit system and, if necessary, take other measures for influencing the direction of investment, such as credit controls, foreign exchange controls, or licensing of buildings or capital extensions.[27]

As can be seen, none of these measures can be carried out without state support, without a stable plan drawn up by the government that sets the goals for development within a certain period and co-ordinates the roles of the public and private sectors to meet these goals.

Lately some agencies of the United Nations, especially the regional Economic Commissions have stressed the need for vigorous state action to promote economic development. In the case of Latin America, ECLA has defined the "principal aims of state intervention in economic development."[28]

The conciousness of underdevelopment and the acceptance of planning as an unavoidable need in the policy of development have led the governments of Asia, Africa, and Latin America to establish development plans of varying degrees, especially with regard to public investment. The principal characteristics of these plans may be observed in Table X.[29] Referring to this fact the "World Economic Survey for 1959," published by the United Nations pointed out:

While there have been significant differences among under-developed countries in their approach to planning, it has been a common practice to create special public bodies responsible for the formulation and implementation of investment programmes. The nature of these entities and the range of their responsibilities, however, have varied considerably among countries. In some, they have been of a very comprehensive character, taking the form of national planning commissions empowered to prepare and direct over-all plans of economic development. In others, they have been more limited in scope. Generally, they have consisted of development banks or corporations whose area of responsibility has been confined to specific sectors of the economy, such as industry or agriculture, and whose functions have been the provision and guarantee of finance and the planning or promotion of new projects. In some of these countries, a single entity has undertaken both the financial and the planning functions, while in others each function has rested with a separate body. Finally, in certain circumstances, entities of an even more specific character have been established to promote investment in particular industries, such as petroleum.

Inevitably, the effectiveness of such development institutions has varied considerably from country to country. While there are many which have been judged very successful from the national viewpoint, others appear to have accomplished relatively little. In some instances, this has reflected the limited resources available to the institution. In others, activity has been confined to the formulation of programmes, and governments have done little to translate these plans into effective action.[30]

For the reasons previously indicated, there is a profound difference between the type of development that the less developed countries are at present undergoing and the development of such countries as the United States or those of Western Europe at a similar stage of evolution. While in those countries economic development grew spontaneously with a minimum of state intervention, in the underdeveloped nations, as has been seen, vigorous state action is required.

Hoselitz, in the work previously cited, has constructed two ideal types of economic development to clarify the differences between the two kinds of social change. The two ideal types are spontaneous

TABLE X
Principal Features of Investment Plans, Selected Countries

Country	Plan or programme	Period	Scope or object	Principal planning or implementing authority
Asia and the Middle East				
Burma	Four-year implementation programme	1956/57-1959/60	Mainly public sector plan to restore pre-war level of production and to develop basic facilities	Ministries and special agencies
Federation of Malaya	Five-year capital expenditure plan	1956-1960	Public expenditure plan largely for agricultural development	Ministries
India	Second five-year plan	1956/57-1960/61	Comprehensive plan for a 25 per cent increase in national income during the plan period	Planning Commission and ministries
Indonesia	Five-year development plan	1956-1960	Comprehensive plan to raise national income by about 3 per cent per annum	State Planning Bureau and ministries
Iran	Second seven-year development plan	Period ending 22 September 1962	Public sector plan for agricultural development and basic facilities	Plan Organization
Iraq	Second five-year programme	1955-1959	Public sector plan for providing mainly irrigation and other basic facilities	Development Board
Pakistan	First five-year plan	1955/56-1959/60	Comprehensive plan to achieve 15 per cent increase in national income during the plan period	Planning Commission and ministries
Philippines	Three-year programme of economic and social development	1959/60-1961/62	Part of a long-range programme of development	Office of National Planning and ministries
UAR (Egypt)	Five-year industrialization plan	1957-1961	Development of industrial sector	Economic Organization and Ministry of Industry
Africa				
Belgian Congo	Ten-year development plan	1950-1959	Basic facilities and services through public investment	Secrétariat du Plan Décennal
Ghana	Second development plan	1959-1964	Mainly a public investment programme to supply basic economic and social services; also, special aid to agriculture and industry	Ministries and special agencies
Latin America				
Argentina	Petroleum development	1959-1961	Self-sufficiency in crude oil	Yacimientos Petrolíferos Fiscales
Bolivia	Agricultural development	From 1952	Agricultural sector	Agricultural Bank
Brazil	Transport and electric power development	1957-1961	Expansion of basic facilities	National Development Bank
	Petroleum development	From 1953	Import substitution	Petrobras

(TABLE X Cont.)

Country	Plan or programme	Period	Scope or object	Principal planning or implementing authority
Chile	Agricultural and transport development	1954-1961	Import substitution and relief of transport bottleneck	Development Corporation and Ministry of Agriculture
	"Chillan Plan"	From 1954	Regional and agricultural development	Ministry of Agriculture and official agencies
Mexico	Agricultural development programme	From 1943	Import substitution and development of agricultural sector	Ministries and special agencies
Peru	Food expansion programme	From 1951	Import substitution	Ministry of Agriculture and special agencies
Venezuela	Rice expansion programme	From 1949	Self-sufficiency	Development Corporation

NOTE: It must be mentioned that the data shown in the table are not now up-to-date. In the case of Latin America, for instance, the establishment of the Alliance for Progress has stressed the need to formulate national development plans. This situation has been fully acknowledged in the statement made by Felipe Herrera, President of the Inter-American Development Bank, at the inaugural session held on April 23, 1962, of the third meeting of the Board of Governors of the Bank: "It is interesting to note," said Mr. Herrera ". . . that, during the past year, Chile, Colombia, and Bolivia have submitted their development programs for review; that Ecuador, Venezuela, and Panama have drawn up programs covering from 4 to 5 years; that Guatemala and Honduras have prepared 4-year public investment plans; that Brazil has made considerable progress in the field of regional planning, and that Nicaragua, El Salvador, Paraguay, the Dominican Republic, Argentina, and Uruguay have established councils or agencies to program and coordinate their development policies."

SOURCE: United Nations, *World Economic Survey 1959*, pp. 81-82.

economic development[31] and induced economic development. Spontaneous economic development "is one in which all decisions affecting economic growth are made by individuals other than those holding political power. In other words, in the entirely liberal state. . . . At the other extreme is the social system in which economic decisions are entirely determined by a central-planning agency. . . . All economic growth in such a system would be strictly induced, that is, provided for and planned by a central authority. No contention is made that these ideal types of distributing decision-making functions among holders of political power and independent private individuals are realized anywhere in practice."[32]

The United States from 1830 to 1890, Canada until 1900, and France and Germany during the nineteenth century, to cite only a few examples, experienced an economic growth that approximated—to a greater or lesser degree—spontaneous economic development. On the other hand, the underdeveloped countries are found to be closer to the induced type of development, as we have indicated.

In economic development of the induced type, the basic decisions are decisions of a political nature.[33]   For this reason a planned economic development depends on the political will of the leading groups in the government.[34]

B. *The relationship between international action and the policy of induced development*

With the foregoing established, we may now analyze the types of international actions a government can adopt in carrying out a policy of induced development.

Since the international dependency of the underdeveloped countries is based on the satellite character of their economies, on the need for foreign capital, and on the need for technical aid, we shall examine the types of international actions of these nations in the attempt to deal with the components of their dependence.

We shall first deal with international actions related to the satellite character and secondly with those referring to the need for foreign capital and technical aid.

The need of meeting the problem of the satellite character of the underdeveloped economies creates three critical factors from the domestic point of view: that of industrialization, that of lessening the external vulnerability of these countries, and that of finding means to counteract the pernicious effects of price fluctuations in the raw materials market.

We have said that planning consists of the rational use of determined means to achieve the aims of economic development. In relation to these three great needs, a basic question arises regarding the means of determining whether the framework of the national economy is the most adequate framework for the promotion of economic development.   In other words, is the underdeveloped nation the best economic unit through which the goals of development can be achieved?   Will this economic unit be able to meet the three requirements indicated?   Or, on the contrary, does a supranational economic unit appear to be the adequate channel for achieving development?

Supranational integration in common markets has been considered an answer to the requirements of industrialization and the attenuation of external vulnerability.[35]   It is obvious that as un-

derdeveloped nations industrialize and lessen their external vulnerability, the diversification of production offers at least a partial
solution to the problem of fluctuations of the raw materials market,
because the importance of raw materials in the whole structure of
foreign trade decreases. However, since these are only long-term
effects, there is an urgent need for international actions to meet this
acute problem in the underdeveloped countries.

For this reason, although economic development offers a general answer to the problem of the satellite nature of the underdeveloped economies, we shall deal separately with the question of
"supranational integration" as distinguished from that of the
problem of raw materials.

(a) *The reaction to atimia and supranational economic integration*

In the study of "supranational integration" a dichotomy is
implied: "economic development in supranational integration"
vis-à-vis "economic development within the national framework."

The primary fact to consider in the analysis of this dichotomy
is the comparison of the advantages of the large nations with respect to the smaller ones. "Among the large nation's advantages
the following are the most common:

"(a) By virtue of its geographical size and economic and
political power it can exercise domination effects on international
markets;

"(b) The size of its domestic market enables it to sell the
bulk of its production at home and so to make the economy less
sensitive to economic fluctuations originating abroad;

"(c) For the same reason it can take full advantage of the
economies of scale deriving from mass production."[36]

Now, the great majority of the underdeveloped nations of
Africa, Asia, and Latin America have a population of less than 10
million inhabitants, twelve have a population between 10 and
20 million, eleven have a population fluctuating between 20 and
40 million, and only four—India, Indonesia, Pakistan, and Brazil
(excluding Communist China)—a population over 60 million.

Studies made by the International Economic Association con-
cluded that "most of the major industrial economies of scale could

be achieved by a relatively high-income nation of fifty million; that nations of ten to fifteen million were probably too small to get all the technical economies available."[37]

The above data shows that on the strength of these facts, the underdeveloped nations, with the exception of the four countries mentioned, should look for ways of broadening their markets if they desire to promote industrialization.[38]

Other elements related to the system of international stratification are added to these factors of purely economic nature. The existence of developed nations acts as a reference group for the underdeveloped nations. The interaction in a stratified system makes these nations appear as "models" whose very high status creates imitation and attraction. This force of attraction increases when the developed nations themselves appear to be seeking and achieving supranational integration as a means of reaching even higher levels of development while, at the same time, strengthening their power status. Thus, the European Common Market appears to the underdeveloped nations as a reference group par excellence, and it holds a double fascination because the participating countries are "developed" and they have been able to limit their sovereignties by a formula of supranational integration.

On the other hand, the creation of these new forms of economic co-operation provokes adjustments in trade and international economy that oblige nations of other areas to co-operate among themselves to counteract the unfavorable effects of the new forms of co-operation in their own economies. The effect of the European Common Market with respect to Latin America is a typical case in point.

The European Common Market, states ECLA, however undeniable the advantages for the six countries forming it and however beneficial its indirect repercussions for Latin America, does have some unfavorable effects, principally because of the preferential measures it establishes for the overseas territories. Whatever a concerted action of the Latin American countries may do to lessen these effects, it may be supposed that they can never be completely avoided. Moreover, the European Common Market will give considerable impulse to the technological revolution that is already taking place in agriculture and in the production of synthetic raw materials; and all of this will have adverse repercussions on the producing countries of Latin America. However, it is not sufficient to be limited by a purely negative reaction. The positive reaction of Latin America should be the regional market.[39]

The rationality of supranational economic integration for the policy of induced development and the role of the reference groups has had various effects on the underdeveloped nations. In his recent study, "Economic Regionalism Reconsidered," Lincoln Gordon has pointed out that in the underdeveloped areas the movement toward economic integration has been

... obscure in purpose and uncertain in content. . . . The most definite cases so far are the Latin American Free Trade Area Treaty of Montevideo (whose seven members are Argentina, Brazil, Chile, Mexico, Paraguay, Perú, and Uruguay) and the Central America Free Trade Area of Guatemala, Honduras, Nicaragua and El Salvador, paralleled by the broader but vaguer economic integration program of these four countries together with Costa Rica. In addition, there have been discussions of some seriousness concerning common market or free trade areas arrangements in North Africa, West Africa, South East Asia, and the Middle East, but only the last named shows much current promise of developing real substance.[40]

Consequently, until the present time, only a number of the Latin American countries have taken the first steps towards supranational integration. The nations of the Arab League are moving in this direction but they have not yet arrived at the same stage. "At a meeting of the Economic Council of the Arab League in March, the member-states approved in principle the formation of an Arab Common Market within ten years, and voted to refer to a special committee on economic unity the question of the steps to be taken toward implementation."[41]

Curiously, the Latin American countries and the members of the Arab League have a longer record of independence than the other underdeveloped nations. This fact gives a certain plausibility to the Myrdal hypothesis that the movement towards supranational integration requires previous national integration. Following this reasoning, these two groups of nations, because of their longer period of independence, have achieved a greater degree of national integration than the rest of the underdeveloped nations and this explains their greater receptivity to the idea of supranational integration.[42]

This hypothesis also permits the conjecture that, of the nations recently acquiring independence, those which have achieved a more advanced stage in their political and socio-economic structure during the colonial period and have formed a directing elite, because of the policy of the mother country, may possess the necessary prerequisites for national integration. Those nations in which the mother country did not practice this policy are consequently lacking in these requirements. The former English colonies serve, in general, as examples of the first, and the former Belgian Congo presents an extreme case of an underdeveloped nation lacking the indispensable elements to promote its national integration.

To reduce the analysis of supranational economic integration to only the factors of rationality in economic development planning and the attraction of the reference groups would undoubtedly be an over-simplification of the problem. It is outside the scope of this study to present a theory of supranational economic integration; we merely propose to show the point at which international actions of an integrative nature arise and not why these actions are produced. However, it seems necessary to point out two elements in addition to those already mentioned that result from the observation of the empirical cases of supranational integration previously cited; these elements are directly related to the theory of *atimia* and constitute noneconomic variables of the integration process.

First, it may be stated that supranational economic integration is very closely linked to political factors. Economists themselves have recognized the primacy of these factors over purely economic elements.[43] These political factors may be synthesized by stating that supranational economic integration, being the most adequate framework for economic development, is a means to raising the economic status of the participating nations and, in consequence, a means to raising the power status. Undoubtedly European economic integration was primarily a result of political aims related to military defense[44] rather than basic economic needs.[45]

In the Latin American case, political factors have also been present in the formation of the common market. As Professor Urquidi so accurately points out, after World War II the concept of economic co-operation among countries of a similar level of development was considerably strengthened. It was evident that the post-war period brought a new constellation of power into the world and that the situation of the weaker countries, independent of the degree of their participation in the armed conflict, would deteriorate if their efforts were not united.[46]

In this way, the need for reinforcing the position of their power status brought, as a consequence, the need to strengthen their economic status. As President of Brazil Juscelino Kubitschek wisely observed, Latin America cannot claim a more important role in power politics without first confirming its capacity for action through development,[47] and the common market is an indispensable condition to the adequate acceleration of economic growth in Latin America.[48]

The creation of the Latin American Common Market—as ECLA has indicated—answers two great needs: that of industrialization, and that of lessening the external vulnerability of these countries.[49] The problem involves the attempt to achieve for these nations a greater degree of economic independence in the relative sense previously defined. It is obvious that greater economic independence will increase the power status of these countries in the rest of the world.

The second noneconomic element in supranational economic integration is of a cultural nature. Supranational economic integration is a process that cannot operate in a vacuum. As is the case in all social processes, it develops within a play of interactions that obey certain patterns of behavior. A mutual compatibility of cultural values allowing a considerable predictability of behavior is required among the national groups seeking integration. The existence of this cultural compatibility explains why the initiative for a common market has come from areas with similar cultural backgrounds—European, Latin American, and Arabic.

With the foregoing established we may now analyze what indicators may be considered sufficient to qualify a system of international action as integrationist or nonintegrationist. Is it possible, in reality, to qualify the international actions of the Latin American countries and the Arabic nations as integrationist in character?

The "take-off" image, used by Rostow to mean the beginning of the evolution of a country towards a self-sustained economic development, can also serve to indicate the moment at which the process of integration acquires sufficient scope for the international actions of the participating countries to be qualified as "integrationists."[50]

We may consider that the member states of the Latin American Free-Trade Area and of the Central American Free-Trade Area have already initiated the "take-off" stage towards supranational integration. The indicators involved in this process are the following: (1) the governments of the participating countries have officially acceded to the corresponding international agreements to create areas of free trade; (2) the agreements have been ratified by the parliaments, which means that the majority of the political parties therein represented have manifested a favorable attitude towards integration, notwithstanding the attitude of certain pressure groups that are opposed to integration because of vested interests; (3) supranational administrative bodies have been established to promote the aims of the areas of free trade and these bodies, by virtue of their supranational character, may not receive orders from any government nor from any national or international entity;[51] and (4) the application of the international agreements will progressively bring about the creation of supranational groups of mutual interests, whose pressure on governments and the leaders of the participating countries will in turn reinforce the trend toward integration—a good example of this type of mechanism is the process leading to the complementarity of the economies of member countries provided for in the Montevideo Treaty.

The application of these indicators to the Arab countries leads to the conclusion that these nations have not yet entered the "take-off" stage. Granted that the idea of the creation of a common market has been approved by the governments, this approval is only in principle, implying the will to consider positively the idea of integration but with no obligation for its realization. The situation is similar to that which existed in the Latin American countries in 1957 when the Economic Conference of the OAS, whose functions are similar to those of the Economic Council of the Arab

League, stated the advisability of establishing a Latin American regional market.

The preceding analysis demonstrates that if a rational policy of planning for economic development should lead to the supranational economic integration of underdeveloped nations whose population is less than 50 million inhabitants, only a few—the Latin American nations we have mentioned—have initiated the "take-off" towards integration. In the other nations, the policy of induced economic development is evolving within the traditional framework of the nation with consequent structural limitations.

(b) *Atimia, international action, and the problem of instability of the primary commodity market*

The second point of the analysis of international actions related to the satellite character of the economies of the underdeveloped countries refers to the market fluctuations of their basic export commodities.

As we have pointed out, the solution to this problem may be brought into focus by a long-term structural view: the achievement of diversification of the economy by development and, as a consequence, the decrease of the percentage of raw materials in total exports. The solution may also be examined from an immediate point of view as demanded by the urgency and gravity of the problem. The first is implicit in the discussion of "supranational integration." We shall now consider the second.

The Economic and Social Council of the United Nations, in its Eighteenth Session held in July, 1959, proposed to make a study to determine what international measures might be adopted to combat these market fluctuations, which indicated the need for a more thorough examination of the possibilities for moderating or alleviating their damaging effects by national or international measures.

To this effect, on October 30, 1959, the Secretary General of the United Nations sent a brief questionnaire to all the members of this organization and to the governments of the states participating in the work of the Regional Economic Commissions of the organization. Fifty-two governments responded; the answers constitute the first empirical material with which to undertake a classification of the various types of international action in the under-developed countries with respect to the problem under considera-tion. The most general dichotomy appeared between countries openly favoring measures to combat the fluctuation of raw material prices and those adopting a more reserved attitude in this respect.

The great majority of underdeveloped countries answering the questionnaire fall into the first category. Among the countries that would be placed in the second we cite Ceylon, Ethiopia, and Burma. The response of Ceylon, producer of tea, rubber, and coconuts, stated that the country could not take any special meas-ure, at the moment, to reach an international agreement regarding mechanisms for price stabilization of its principal basic export com-modities. Ethiopia considered that the establishment of quota systems for coffee export would operate contrary to its interests as it proposes to increase its exports in the future. Burma simply stated that it had no comment to make.

Among the countries that adopted a favorable attitude toward combating price fluctuations of raw materials, various degrees of adherence to the policy can be observed, ranging from a simple ex-pression of agreement with the advisability of such a policy to a desire for actual participation in international agreements designed to regulate the trade of a given commodity.

The classification made by the United Nations on the basis of the survey sets forth the following types of international measures: (1) international agreements on basic commodities and other simi-lar agreements; (2) long-term contracts; (3) global plans; and (4) international compensatory measures.

The developed countries also fall into this classification, not only because some of them are also producers of raw materials, but also because they represent the most important consumer markets for basic commodities. A proper study of the problem of basic commodities demands, therefore, a consultation of the attitude of the producing countries as well as the consuming countries.

The principal purpose of international agreements on basic commodities is to avoid excessive price fluctuations to prevent overproduction or underconsumption and prejudicial speculations. The ideal goal is to achieve a stabilization at the highest figures of production and consumption. This stability is not rigid; generally price scales are established in the expectation that price fluctuation can be kept within the limits of the scale.[52]

The survey shows that of the several international measures, countries responding to the questionnaire preferred to enter into international agreements on various commodities taken separately. Agreements of this type established under the proper conditions are supported in principle by industrialized countries (such as Austria, France, Italy, Japan, the Netherlands, and the United Kingdom), by exporting countries of basic commodities (such as Australia, Canada, Ecuador, the Malay Federation, and New Zealand) and by countries of centrally planned economies (such as the Soviet Union).[53]

Long-term contracts consist of international agreements of long duration that tend to stabilize the markets of basic commodities. The sugar agreement between the United Kingdom and the countries and territories of the British Commonwealth is an example; France, in answering the questionnaire, suggested that this agreement be studied in view of the possibility of applying it to other commodities in a different geographical environment.

Global plans consist of general measures, such as the creation of an international agency of stabilization reserves or a monetary system backed by basic commodities. Countries favoring this type of agreement, as did Holland, are found at opposite poles from those favoring "commodity by commodity" agreements.

Lastly, several countries felt that a study of the various types of international compensatory measures should be continued. Sweden, for example, stated that "the granting of loans—by international organizations or by various countries—to mitigate the effect of the fluctuations of income from exports could be expanded and established in a more permanent institutional framework. It concretely suggested that some international organization could grant compensatory loans guaranteed by inventories of raw materials."[54]

A group of experts, designated by the Secretary General of the United Nations in agreement with a resolution of the fourteenth session of the General Assembly, has recently studied the problem of international compensation for fluctuations in primary commodity trade.[55] In its conclusions the group of experts pointed out the compensatory role the International Monetary Fund plays at present and the program it could carry out in the future; however, they expressed serious doubts that the activities of the Fund, present or future, would constitute a complete answer to the problem. "This applies particularly to the underdeveloped countries in view of the special importance of maintaining continuity in their developmental expenditure."[56] The compensatory effect of long-term financing through the transfer of capital by loans or grants is judged in the same light. These measures are considered useful but insufficient.

The previous considerations explain that the main part of the report of the experts is dedicated to the analyses of a general system of compensation that would function as a complementary mechanism to the existing instruments of compensation.

The system proposed is an insurance system. Under this system two previous formulae would be discarded: that of insuring the risks only of countries vulnerable to fluctuations, and that of redistributing profit and loss so that countries suffering a loss in a given period would be compensated by those benefiting from the same price movements. The first formula is discarded principally because it would demand contributions of considerable volume from those countries that are not in a position to give them, and the second may be dismissed because of the practical difficulties that an arrangement of this nature implies and because, under such a system, monetary transfers from undeveloped countries to developed countries would occur, which would be difficult to justify.

The proposed system has the characteristics of a social security system and presupposes the will of the economically advanced countries to contribute to the solution of the problem with the understanding that their direct benefits will be lower than their contributions. Their participation would constitute a form of multilateral aid that would operate when the risk occurred; the insured risk would be the decrease in export proceeds because of the instability of the raw materials market.

This system would create a Development Insurance Fund to which all the member states of the United Nations would pay contributions and against which members could make financial demands that would automatically be paid in given circumstances.

In accordance with the technical conditions specified in the report, the Fund would operate predominantly or exclusively for the benefit of the underdeveloped countries; its principal objective would be to protect the underdeveloped countries against adverse changes in their development policy caused by the instability of the world raw materials market. Given the complementary character of the proposed system and also in order to avoid possible abuses, the country would not receive the total, but only a part, of the losses occasioned by the market fluctuations.

An estimate of the possible quantity of requests that might be presented to the Fund was made by the experts. "Under conditions like those of recent years (1953-59) and assuming compensation equal to 50 per cent of the short fall in export proceeds adjusted by a minimum deduction ranging between 2.5 per cent and 10 per cent of the base value of proceeds, it appears that the underdeveloped countries would have claims ranging on the average between the equivalent of $466 million and $246 million yearly, and industrial and high-income producing countries between $142 million and $12 million."[57] The preceding considerations show that the problem of price fluctuation of raw materials cannot be solved except by large-scale international co-operation.

The solution to the problem is as crucial for the underdeveloped areas as the problem concerning the contribution of foreign capital necessary for development. To deal with the two problems separately is to create illusory solutions. Referring to this point in the case of Latin America, Ambassador Stevenson has pointed out the effect that price fluctuations of the coffee market have had on fourteen Latin American countries: "The change in the price of coffee by half a cent per pound can wipe out all the economic assistance that we could hope to give them for a long time."[58]

In spite of this fact, if a comparison is made of the degree of maturity in international action adopted by the underdeveloped countries as they respond to the *atimic* process, a significant difference is observed: while attempts to achieve "supranational integration" in counteracting small markets and in promoting economic development have become better defined in certain areas, the same degree of maturity cannot be observed in the approach to the problem of raw materials.

In effect, a study of the answers of the underdeveloped countries' governments to the United Nations survey gives the impression that if a consciousness of the magnitude of the problem truly exists, it has not yet been translated into concrete and constructive international action.

This impression is confirmed by the cool reception of the session of the United Nations Commission on International Commodity Trade (CICT) to the previously mentioned proposal of the creation of the Development Insurance Fund which seems not likely to be established in the near future.

CICT's feeling that the report had been received too late to be considered in detail did not deter it from criticizing the proposal. Criticism came from both the less developed and the industrial nations. The former complained about being expected to contribute to the Fund and about having the industrial nations share in its benefits. Their further complaint that the proposal failed to deal with long-run commodity problems may reflect a desire to find one magic cure for all commodities' headaches. When these countries think of preventing short-term instability of commodity markets, they tend to think in terms of long-run stabilization of prices, and particularly improvement of their terms of trade.[59]

(c) *Regional and nonregional formulae to obtain foreign capital and technical assistance*

We shall now consider the types of international action of underdeveloped nations in the effort to obtain foreign capital and technical assistance. This study can be made by observing a proposed dichotomy relating to the nature of international channels preferentially used to obtain foreign economic aid and technical assistance.

We shall make use of the "ideal types" method in analyzing the proposed dichotomy. On the one hand there would be the group of countries that utilize regional organizations to obtain the means for development; in this case the interested nations would establish a regional organization for the purpose of promoting the economic development of the participating countries and for obtaining the foreign capital and technical aid necessary to achieve development. The member states of the regional system would receive help solely from the organization or through it and, as a consequence, would reject any bilateral or multilateral agreement to obtain international aid outside the system. On the other hand there would be countries not affiliated with a regional organization, countries that would use only bilateral or multilateral agreements with developed countries or with a world organization to obtain foreign capital and technical assistance. It is obvious that the ideal type of regionalism does not exist and that bilateral co-operation, if it is present, does not exist as a desired aim but as a *de facto* situation that the countries, in the majority of the cases, are obliged to follow because of the lack of other formula.

We shall look first at regionalism. The basic fact seen here since World War II is the trend to create regional systems, which stands out as a characteristic of modern international co-operation. In Table XI the regional systems in which underdeveloped countries participate may be observed. Only two of these systems—the Arab League and the Organization of American States—existed at the time of the creation of the United Nations. All of these organizations are regional in a much broader sense than that proposed in our ideal type. In this broad sense, "a regional system is any long-term agreement between two or more states providing for political, military or economic action in specific circumstances, *provided* the commitment extends to a defined area and specific states. Such a system must possess permanent organs and fixed procedures."[60]

We shall now examine to what degree these organizations approximate or differ from our "ideal type." Of the regional systems included in Table XI, two—the SEATO and METO—were conceived for military defense and security and have these basic objectives as the principal aim of the organizations. Although they have attempted to incorporate the economic development of the underdeveloped participating countries into the program, financial aid and technical assistance have been granted through bilateral or multilateral channels outside the system.[61] Consequently, they do not constitute regional systems from the point of view of international co-operation for development.

Of the remaining systems in Table XI, one, the Conference of Independent African States, created in 1958 at the meeting of ACCRA, pursues the vague objective of producing "an African identity and personality in international affairs" and "providing

TABLE XI
Membership in Contemporary Pacts: 1959

Countries	AL	METO	COLOMBO	ACCRA	OAS	OCAS	SEATO
Albania					*		
Argentina					*		
Australia			*				*
Bolivia					*		
Brazil					*		
Burma			*				
Cambodia			*				
Canada			*				
Ceylon			*				
Chile					*		
Colombia					*		
Costa Rica					*	*	
Cuba					*		
Dominican Rep.					*		
El Salvador					*	*	
Ecuador					*		
Egypt	*			*			
Ethiopia				*			
France							*
Ghana				*			
Guatemala					*	*	
Haiti					*		
Honduras					*	*	
Hungary							
India			*				
Indonesia			*				
Iran		*					
Iraq	*	*					
Japan			*				
Jordan	*						
Laos			*				
Lebanon	*						
Liberia				*			
Libya	*			*			
Malaya			*				
Mexico					*		
Morocco	*			*			
Nepal			*				
New Zealand			*				*
Nicaragua					*	*	
Pakistan		*	*				*
Panama					*		
Paraguay					*		
Peru					*		
Philippines			*				*
Saudi Arabia	*						
Sudan	*			*			
Syria	*			*			
Thailand			*				*
Tunisia	*			*			
Turkey		*					

(TABLE XI Cont.)

Countries	AL	METO	COLOMBO	ACCRA	OAS	OCAS	SEATO
United Kingdom		*	*				*
United States			*		*		*
Uruguay					*		
Venezuela					*		
Yemen	*						

Symbol key to regional groups: AL: Arab League
METO: Baghdad Pact
COLOMBO: Colombo Plan
ACCRA: Conference of Independent African States
OAS: Organization of American States
OCAS: Organization of Central American States
SEATO: Southeast Asian Treaty Organization

The source for membership in regional groups indicated in the table is taken from a book written under the auspices of a United Nations Project, Center for International Studies, M.I.T.; see Thomas Hovet, Jr., *Bloc Politics in the United Nations* (Cambridge, Mass.: Harvard University Press, 1960). The number of members listed in each group includes only those members of the group who are also members of the United Nations.

The following regional groups were not included in the table for the reasons indicated below:
1. The Balkan Alliance and the Warsaw Pact, since the nature of these pacts is mostly political.
2. The Bandung Conference, since this is not a permanent organization.
3. The Arab Development Fund, created in mid-January, 1959, because it is part of the Arab League. The institution is designed to function along the lines of the International Bank, which helped to set it up. This fund can be effective in improving the nature of the Arab League as a regional channel for socio-economic development of member states. For further information, see "Economic Development Aids for Under-developed Countries" in *International Review Service*, ed., A. G. Mezerick, Volume VII, No. 63 (1961). See also, "Economic Assistance as a Cooperative Effort of the Free World," U.S. State Department, 1960.
4. The Commonwealth countries were not included as a separate regional pact, as all the underdeveloped countries who are members of the Commonwealth are also members of the Colombo Plan included in the list, with the exception of African states members of the Commonwealth. "In late 1960 the British Commonwealth countries initiated a new assistance plan for Africa—The Special Commonwealth African Assistance Plan (SCAAP)." See Mezerick, *International Review Service* and *The Times* (London), September 22, 1960.
5. The French Community of Nations was not included in the table because of its recent development after the last reform of the French Constitution, which changes the status of member states. The French Community is, indeed, a regional group with concern for socio-economic development, but for the reason previously mentioned it is difficult to indicate the present scope and nature of this regional group.

It should also be pointed out that the European Common Market has created a fund of $581.25 million U.S. (for 1958-63) for the economic development of French, Belgian, Italian, and Dutch colonies, particularly in Africa. "Negotiations toward making this fund available to newly independent African countries, former colonies of these countries, were under way in early 1961," quoted from Mezerick, *International Review Service*, p. 35.

machinery for the prompt exchange of views on problems affecting Africa as a whole and on international problems so that the 'mind' of Africa may be quickly mobilized, i.e., to ensure that an African 'personality' in international affairs may become a reality."[62]

Although the African bloc has demonstrated extraordinary solidarity in the United Nations when subjects related to economic and social development are discussed, there is no evidence that the new-born agency created under the leadership of Ghana has functioned as a channel of regional co-operation for economic development.

The four other systems—the OAS, Organization of Central American States, the Colombo Plan, and the Arab League—may in turn be reclassified into two groups depending on whether or not they are formed exclusively of underdeveloped countries. The Arab League and the OCAS constitute regional systems formed exclusively by underdeveloped countries while the OAS and the Colombo Plan include countries with a high degree of development within these organizations.

This difference is fundamental, since it is precisely the fact that developed countries belong to a system that allows the system to operate as a channel of international co-operation in obtaining foreign capital and technical aid. The OCAS and the Arab League carry out activities of technical assistance on a limited scale to the extent that the small budgets of the two organizations permit them to do so; in any case, there is no doubt that the major portion of foreign aid is received by the member states of the system through channels outside the regional organization.

The Colombo Plan and the Inter-American System, some similarities.—Therefore, of the regional systems in the broad sense, only two—the Inter-American System and the Colombo Plan—fall within the concept of regionalism defined in its pure state by the proposed "ideal type."

Of the two, the Colombo Plan is closer to the "ideal type" because it is an organization exclusively pursuing the economic and social development of the underdeveloped member states and was created for exactly that purpose. In contrast, the Inter-American System existed before the problem of economic and social development became a matter of concern to the member countries; moreover, the political objectives of the system are found to be closely linked to the promotion of economic and social development. As Professor Haas has justly observed, the regional organizations have failed in their intent to become regional communities of co-operation because none of them "is self-sufficient in terms of the aspiration of some of the member states."[63]

Only the Colombo Plan and the Inter-American System—and this last just recently—have been able to approach the goal of regional self-sufficiency. In the case of the Colombo Plan, the United States and the developed countries of the Commonwealth have carried the heaviest financial burden; similarly, in the Inter-American System, it is the United States that has assumed the largest share of the responsibility. However, both systems are far from being self-sufficient: the Colombo Plan, from the time of its initiation in 1950 recognized the fact that the resources of the

Commonwealth were not sufficient for the aims of the system. In
this regard the "White Paper" stated, ". . . the task of providing this
financial support for the development of South and Southeast Asia
is manifestly not one which can be tackled by the Commonwealth
alone. The need to raise the standard of living in South and South-
east Asia is a problem of concern to every country in the world, not
only as an end in itself, but also because the political stability of the
area and its economic progress are of vital concern to the world."[64]
Consequently, one of the tasks of its authors was to establish "how
much of the development work could be financed by the Asian
countries themselves, from their internal resources; how much from
the major Commonwealth countries; and how much from countries
outside the Commonwealth or from interested international agencies."[65] It was realized that the burden might be borne chiefly by
the countries themselves.[66]

The Inter-American System—in its most recent expression contained in the Bogotá Act and the Charter of Punta del Este establishing the Alliance for Progress—has also recognized the need of
aid from countries outside the System, especially from Western
Europe and international sources. Notwithstanding the lack of
self-sufficiency, the Colombo Plan and the Inter-American System
are regional systems of economic co-operation in the sense of our
"ideal type" because the foreign aid required for economic development is, in an appreciable or significant measure, channeled through
these systems.

A second fact that should be emphasized, with respect to the
financing of economic development plans that the member countries
of both systems propose to carry out, concerns the sources of external financing. The Colombo Plan, on enumerating the possible
channels of external financing, concludes that the traditional sources
are not sufficient and that it will be necessary to resort to government to government finance. "It seems certain, therefore," states
the "White Paper," "that a substantial element of government to
government finance will be required, particularly in the early stages
of the development programmes."[67] It may be noted that the
United States, radically changing its position with respect to Latin
American development, recognized the primacy of this type of
financing at Bogotá and at Punta del Este.

The Colombo Plan, as well as the Inter-American System, directly relates the need of promoting economic development to the stability of the political systems of the member countries and the importance of the achievement of this aim to the rest of the world. The official report of the Consultative Committee of the Commonwealth that established the Colombo Plan states with regard to South and Southeast Asia:

> Changes have been taking place [in this area] on a scale hardly precedented in world history. Independent governments have come into being supported by democratic institutions and imbued with enthusiasm for the future welfare of their countries. The horizon of thought and action in the economic as well as the political field has been greatly extended, and governments are grappling with the problem of promoting the economic development which is indispensable to social stability, and necessary to strengthen their free institutions. It is of the greatest importance that the countries of South and Southeast Asia should succeed in this undertaking. The political stability of the area, and indeed of the world, depends upon it, and nothing could do more to strengthen the cause of freedom. . . . The political stability of the countries of the area is possible only in conditions of economic progress, and a steady flow of capital from more highly developed countries is essential for this purpose.[68]

The Inter-American System, through the Act of Bogotá, recognized that "the preservation and strengthening of free and democratic institutions in the American Republics requires the acceleration of social and economic progress in Latin America adequate to meet the legitimate aspirations of peoples of the Americas for a better life and to provide them the fullest opportunity to improve their status. . . ." The last paragraph of the Act established that, in approving the document, the delegations, "convinced that the people of the Americas can achieve a better life only within the democratic system, renew their faith in the essential values which lie at the base of Western civilization, and re-affirm their determination to assure the fullest measure of well-being to the people of the Americas under conditions of freedom and respect for the supreme dignity of the individual." The Charter of Punta del Este also stressed this relation.

The differences existing between the two regional systems come from various sociological and historical factors pertinent to the group of nations in which each system has arisen.

The Colombo Plan, principal features.—The Colombo Plan is known throughout the world as the answer of the Commonwealth to the need for economic development in South and Southeast Asia. Contrary to a generalized idea, the initiative for the plan was not British—although from the beginning it had the support of the United Kingdom—but the result of an Australian concern for its future political, economic, and military relations with the Asiatic countries when the European colonial empire began to dissolve in Asia. "As soon as the European tide began to ebb from Asia, the Australian government began to show their willingness to help friendly Asian governments. As an example, the Colombo Plan is, in essence, an Australian invention. . . . The experience of being a donor in the Colombo Plan has had notable effect. Apart from the fact that it indicates a certain maturity in Australia's development as a sovereign state, it has also meant that Australian governmental, educational and industrial authorities have been brought, for almost the first time, directly in touch with Asians and Asian ways."[69]

The Plan owes its name to the fact that it was initiated in Colombo, the capital of Ceylon, in January, 1950, when for the first time the countries of the Commonwealth met in an Asian country. By an Australian motion, a Consultative Committee of the Commonwealth was created, composed of governmental representatives, to establish a co-operative development plan for South and Southeast Asia. The committee first met in Sydney, Australia, in May, 1950; it was decided that each country of the area would prepare a six-year plan of economic development. "To help the participating governments in preparing their statements and to ensure that their answers were more or less comparable, the Committee evolved a questionnaire based on one circulated to Marshall Plan countries by the Organization for European Economic Cooperation in the early stages of planning for European recovery. This questionnaire was subsequently sent to the governments of India, Pakistan, Ceylon, the Federation of Malaya, Singapore, North Borneo and Sarawak. It was intended to indicate the practical things to be done over a six-year period beginning July 1, 1951."[70]

The meeting of the Consultative Committee of the Plan, held in London in the same year, co-ordinated the plans proposed by the countries in a single six-year economic development plan. The final report was published in a "White Paper" entitled, "The Colombo Plan for Co-operative Economic Development in South and South-East Asia."

It is a detailed analysis of the region's problems, and, in particular, those of India, Pakistan, Ceylon, The Federation of Malaya, Singapore, North Borneo and Sarawak. The report also gives individual development programs proposed by these seven countries and presents a careful estimate of what is required in terms of trained manpower and capital if the six-year plans are to succeed. Three preliminary chapters describe the importance of the area, the effects of the war and its aftermath, and the urgent need for development. The Report then takes each country's program in turn, outlines briefly the problems peculiar to the region, and explains the "basis and objectives" of the relevant program. After summarizing it, the Report shows how it will be administered, the amount of government and private investment contemplated and what are the limiting factors to be expected. Finally, the proposed method of financing that particular program is analyzed. The last three chapters of the "White Paper" comprise a summary of the seven individual programs and a detailed discussion of the problems arising from the need for trained men and the need of capital in the area.[71]

Table XII shows the total cost of the Plan, its distribution by countries, and the amount of outside financing required.[72] Previous mention has been made for the lack of self-sufficiency of the Colombo Plan regarding the financing of external aid and how, at the outset, the co-operation of other developed countries outside the Commonwealth and of international agencies was considered. This co-operation was realized in 1951 with the incorporation into the Consultative Committee of the United States, the Economic Commission of the United Nations for Asia and the Far East, and the World Bank.[73] Between 1951 and 1960, United States aid has reached the sum of $7,378.1 millions[74] channeled through the Plan; except for India, the Plan constituted the principal channel through which the member countries received United States aid.[75]

TABLE XII
THE COLOMBO PLAN: SUMMARY OF EXTERNAL FINANCE REQUIRED, 1951-1957

For period, July, 1951-June, 1957	£ Million				
	India	Pakistan	Ceylon	Malaya and British Borneo	Total
Total cost of the development programme	1,379	280	102	107	1,868
Cost of capital goods imported for the programme	237	115	39	20	411
External finance needed— From sterling balances	211	16	19	—	246
From other sources	607	129	41	61	839
Total	818	145	60	61	1,084
For first year, 1951-52					
External finance needed— From sterling balances	35	10	5	—	50
From other sources	128	13	7	9	156

NOTE: The internal finance available for the programmes, on the assumption that external finance is forthcoming, would be: India, £772 million; Pakistan, £151 million; Ceylon, £61 million; Malaya and British Borneo, £46 million.
SOURCE: *The Colombo Plan for Co-operative Economic Development in South and South-East Asia*. Report by the Commonwealth Consultative Committee (London, September-October, 1950). Presented by the Chancellor of the Exchequer to Parliament by Command of His Majesty (London: 1950) His Majesty's Stationery Office, p. 58. Figures have been rounded.

Even in the case of India, the importance of the Plan as a regional channel of international co-operation was significant. (See Table XIII.)

The administrative machinery for the implementation of the Plan is simple, in that it follows the general characteristic of the Commonwealth that is distinguished by a minimum of formal structures and an effective functional collaboration among the member countries. The principal organs are "The Colombo Plan Bureau," "The Consultative Committee," and "The Council for Technical Cooperation," whose headquarters are located in Colombo. Although the Colombo Plan is a regional body, the organization serves only to channel the financial or technical aid among member countries, because finally the aid is granted bilaterally.

The Consultative Committee, as well as the bodies of technical co-operation, are co-ordinating agencies. The former meets annually to review progress made, establish future objectives, and

TABLE XIII
FOREIGN AID RECEIVED BY INDIA IN ITS FIRST DEVELOPMENT PLAN
(Rs. Crores)

	Authorizations	Loan or grant	Estimate utilization up to March, 1956	Balance available for utilization in the second plan
U.S.A.				
Wheat loan	90.3	Loan	90.3	—
Indo-U.S. Aid	102.5	Grant	70.5	32.0
Programme	39.3	Loan	7.0	32.3
I.B.R.D.	12.0	Loan	8.5	3.5
Colombo Plan				
Australia	10.5	Grant	5.3	5.2
Canada	35.6	Grant	19.5	16.2
New Zealand	1.2	Grant	0.3	0.9
U.K.	0.5	Grant	0.3	0.2
Ford Foundation	5.4	Grant	2.0	3.4
Norway	0.3	Grant	0.2	0.1
TOTAL	297.6		203.9	93.8

SOURCE: Government of India Planning Commission, *Second Five-Year Plan* (1956), p. 103. The expression "crore" signifies 10,000,000 rupees.

prepare an annual report; its functions are limited to making recommendations to the governments. The administrative machinery processes the petitions and sends them to the member states of the Plan who can give the aid.

Technical aid is organized in three channels: (a) the training of personnel from countries in the area in other suitable countries and the dispatch of missions abroad to study the latest techniques or practices; (b) the supplying of experts, instructors, and advisory missions to assist in planning, development, or reconstruction, to be utilized in public administration, health services, and scientific research, to aid in agricultural, industrial, or other productive activities, and to provide training for personnel; and (c) the providing of equipment required for training or use by technical experts in the region.[76] The program of technical assistance of the Plan does not exclude member countries from receiving aid from other organizations such as the United Nations, its specialized agencies, and Point Four (now AID).

Lastly, it should be mentioned that the Colombo Plan does not constitute a permanent organization. It was originally conceived for a six-year period and later extended for a nine-year period to end in 1961. At the Jogjakarta meeting, the Consultative Committee decided to continue the operations of the Plan until 1966, on the understanding that a further extension would be considered later.[77]

Although the amount of resources at the disposal of the countries of the Colombo Plan is far from meeting the needs of these countries, the effectiveness of the system can be measured by the fact that the sum of £839,000,000 budgeted as external financing to June, 1957 (see Table XII) has been amply met and surpassed. It is calculated that to 1960, the countries benefited have received a total of 8 billion dollars in financial aid and technical assistance.

Having established the characteristics of the regional system of the Colombo Plan, we shall now look at the differences existing between it and the Inter-American System.

The Inter-American System, principal features after the formulation of the Alliance for Progress.—The first basic fact to be emphasized is that, while the Colombo Plan has been in operation for more than ten years, the Inter-American System, considered as a regional system of co-operation for socio-economic development, only began to take form with the initiation of Operation Pan-America in 1958, the creation of the Inter-American Development Bank in 1960, and the adoption of the Bogotá Act in 1960. It is only with the Charter of Punta del Este formulating the Alliance for Progress that the system can be considered definitely established. However, the system has been in force for much longer. In Table XIV the development of the Pan-American movement can be seen from the first conference held in 1889 to the tenth held in 1954. It is not difficult to see how the movement was dominated by a concern for the political aspects of the system. Agreements among the American states were limited mainly to the condemnation of intervention in the domestic affairs of any American state, to the pacific settlement procedure of inter-American conflicts, and finally to the Inter-American Treaty of Reciprocal Assistance, or Rio Pact, in 1947.

As Professor Whitaker has pointed out, the Inter-American System is linked to the idea of the Western Hemisphere as a community of nations of the new world,[78] an idea that has undergone its brighter and darker periods. This concept reached its height

TABLE XIV
PAN-AMERICAN CONFERENCES, 1889-1959

Name	Date	Location	Countries attending	Major agenda items	Outcomes
1st International Conference of American States	Oct. 2, 1889, to Apr. 19, 1890	Washington, D.C., United States	18; all the American Republics then extant except the Dominican Republic.	Discussion of problems of mutual interest, principally questions of peace, trade, and communication.	Formation of the International Union of American Republics and the "Bureau of American Republics."
2d International Conference of American States	Oct. 22, 1901, to Jan. 22, 1902	Mexico City, Mexico	19; all the American Republics then extant.	Discussion of international legal questions, procedures for arbitration of disputes, problems of hemispheric peace.	Protocol of adhesion to "Hague Convention for Pacific Settlement of International Disputes." Treaty of Arbitration for Pecuniary Claims.
3d International Conference of American States	July 21, to Aug. 26, 1906	Rio de Janeiro, Brazil	19; all the American Republics except Haiti and Venezuela.	Consideration of problem of forcible collection of debts. Discussion of Drago and Calvo doctrines.	Conference decided to take question of forcible collection of debts to 2d Hague Conference, Convention on International Law.
4th International Conference of American States	July 12, to Aug. 30, 1910	Buenos Aires, Argentina	20; all the American Republics except Bolivia.	Consideration of various economic and cultural matters.	Decision to change name of "International Bureau of American Republics" to "Pan American Union."
5th International Conference of American States	Mar. 25 to May 3, 1923	Santiago, Chile	18; all the American Republics except Bolivia, Mexico, and Peru.	Discussion of reorganization of Pan American Union (PAU) for purpose of reducing U.S. dominance. Discussion of possible modification of Monroe Doctrine.	"Treaty to Avoid or Prevent Conflicts Between American States" (Gondra Treaty). *Decision to make chairmanship of PAU elective.*
6th International Conference of American States	Jan. 16 to Feb. 20, 1928	Havana, Cuba	21; all the American Republics.	Latin American delegates anxious to secure condemnation of American intervention in the Caribbean.	"Convention on Duties and Rights of States in the Event of Civil Strife." (Designed to prevent use of other American countries as bases for launching revolutionary activity.)
International Conference of American States on Conciliation and Arbitration	Dec. 10, 1928 to Jan. 5, 1929	Washington D.C., United States	20; all the American Republics except Argentina.	Problem of arbitration and conciliation of disputes.	General Convention of Inter-American Conciliation. General Treaty of Inter-American Arbitration.
7th International Conference of American States	Dec. 3-26, 1933	Montevideo, Uruguay	20; all the American Republics except Costa Rica.	Problem of U.S. dominance and intervention.	"Convention on Rights and Duties of States." Concerned with the principle of nonintervention.
Inter-American Conference for the Maintenance of Peace	Dec. 1-23, 1936	Buenos Aires, Argentina	21; all the American Republics.	Security of hemisphere in event of war in Europe or Far East. Principle of of nonintervention.	"Declaration of principles of inter-American solidarity and cooperation." Additional protocol relative to nonintervention.
8th International Conference of American States	Dec. 9-27, 1938	Lima, Peru	do.	Consideration of the relation of American Repub-	"Declaration of the principles of the solidarity of

(TABLE XIV Cont.)

Name	Date	Location	Countries attending	Major agenda items	Outcomes
				lics to Europe and possible German and Italian penetration of the hemisphere.	America." Established the meeting of consultation of foreign ministers.
Inter-American Conference on Problems of War and Peace	Feb. 21 to Mar. 8, 1945	Mexico City, Mexico	20; all the American Republics except Argentina.	Consideration of possible postwar problems. Hemispheric relations of Argentina.	Act of Chapultepec. Deals with acts or threats of aggression against any American republic; recommended consideration of a treaty to deal with such acts and measures to take when they occurred.
Inter-American Conference for the Maintenance of Continental Peace and Security	Aug. 15 to Sept. 2, 1947	Rio de Janeiro, Brazil	20; all the American Republics except Nicaragua.	Consideration of proposals for a treaty of mutual defense of the hemisphere.	Inter-American Treaty of Reciprocal Assistance (Rio Treaty).
9th International Conference of American States	Mar. 30 to May 2, 1948	Bogotá, Colombia	21; all the American Republics.	Discussions of means to strengthen the Inter-American System and to promote inter-American economic cooperation. Consideration of juridical and political matters, including recognition of governments and colonies.	Charter of the OAS, American Treaty on Pacific Settlement (Pact of Bogotá). American declaration of the rights and duties of man. Economic Agreement of Bogotá.
10th International Conference of American States	Mar. 1-28, 1954	Caracas, Venezuela	20; all the American Republics except Costa Rica.	Consideration of hemispheric policy respecting the intervention of communism into the Americas; discussion of possible economic assistance to Latin America.	"Declaration of solidarity for the preservation of the political integrity of the Americas against the intervention of international communism."

source: *The Organization of American States.* A study prepared at the request of the subcommittee on Foreign Relations, United States Senate, by Northwestern University (Washington: G.P.O., 1959), pp. 8-9.

with the formulation of the Good Neighbor Policy by Franklin Delano Roosevelt. At that time the isolationist position of the United States in world affairs gave the Western Hemisphere idea the character of a major framework in which American foreign policy should be developed. The period of decline began with World War II when the United States emerged in the world arena as the most powerful nation on earth and assumed the leadership of the free world.

The Western Hemisphere idea lost its meaning because the leading nation in the Americas became engaged in international politics in all the hemispheres. The idea of the North Atlantic Community of Nations—with its economic and military expres-

sions in the Marshall Plan and NATO—replaced the long-nour-
ished notion of the Western Hemisphere idea as the community of
nations of the new world. Latin America was confined to the
role of a second- or third-rank ally whose support was taken
for granted. At the same time, in the decade of the 1950's
—a major division of the world analyzed in Chapter I—the division between the developed and the underdeveloped countries began to take form. This international stratification reinforced the
idea of the North Atlantic Community, whose member nations were
primarily developed countries, and it weakened even further the
idea of the Western Hemisphere composed of one world power
and twenty underdeveloped nations.

The aid for economic development was channeled outside of
the organization by means of bilateral agreements between the

Although it seems a paradoxical statement, it was the creation
of an organization outside the Inter-American System, the Economic Commission for Latin America of the United Nations, that
began to vitalize the regional system. As the Chilean Ambassador
to the United Nations so aptly pointed out when he proposed the
creation of this agency, in spite of the existence of the Inter-American Economic and Social Council of OAS, it was not possible to
make an effective study of the economic problems of Latin America "without the resources, techniques, information, statistics and
administration of the United Nations, which however does lack
regional agencies."[79]

The words were to prove prophetic since, while ECLA rapidly
acquired Continental prestige because of the level of its economic
studies, the IA-ECOSOC, in contrast, remains at its former
mediocre level. While the Organization of American States, with
its complex machinery, showed itself incapable of channeling the
national aspirations of twenty countries for economic development
by means of technical studies, ECLA, in the meantime, accumulated the technical knowledge to make possible the realization of
those aspirations.

The Organization of American States, with a limited budget
(see figure, page 81), constituted a typical case of a regional
organization that was not self-sufficient in terms of the aspirations
of its member states.

The aid for economic development was channeled outside of
the organization by means of bilateral agreements between the

PAN AMERICAN UNION BUDGET, 1949-1960*

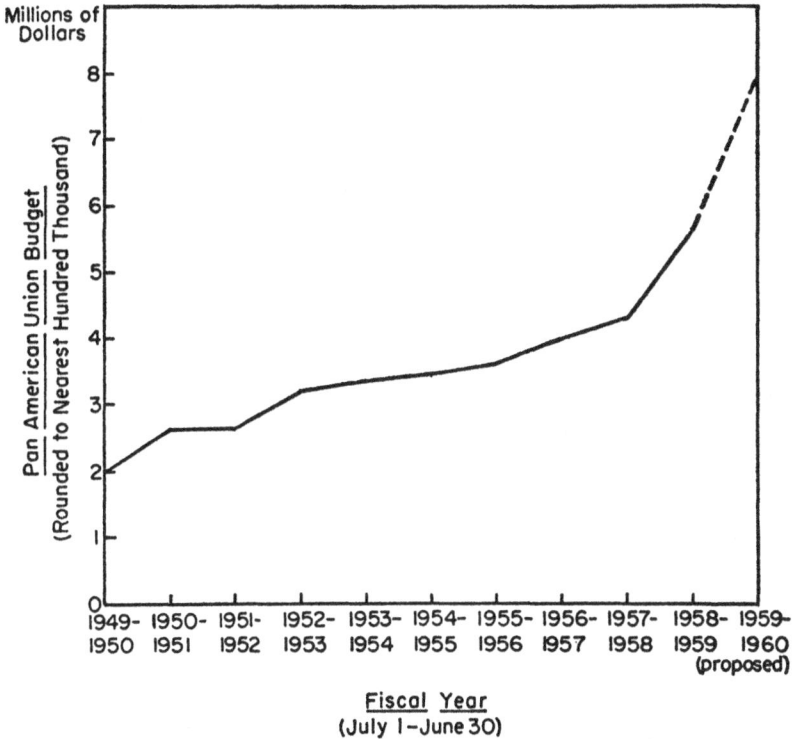

Fiscal Year
(July 1-June 30)

* Does not include expenditures for the Program of Technical Cooperation.
SOURCE: *The Organization of American States,* a study prepared at the request of the Subcommittee on American Republics Affairs of the Committee on Foreign Relations, United States Senate, by Northwestern University, p. 26.

United States and its underdeveloped neighbors to the south. The United States policymakers and businessmen believed that the flow of private capital was sufficient to ensure Latin American economic development.

In the last two years of the Eisenhower administration, this situation began to change. In the spring of 1958, public attention throughout the world was abruptly and sharply focused on Latin America as a result of the incident attending Vice-President Nixon's visit there. This was an indication that the Western Hemisphere idea had reached its lowest ebb. At this time, deep concern regarding the critical situation of inter-American relations began to grow. President Kubitschek of Brazil and President Eisenhower exchanged notes concerning the urgent need to improve the situation and there emerged the idea of "Operation Pan-America," containing a plan for joint action of the American states to fight prevailing underdevelopment in Latin America for the twenty-year period 1960 to 1980. In December of the same year, Milton Eisenhower, in his report to the President regarding United States–Latin American relations, wrote: "We are unanimous in our conviction that no area in the world is of more importance to us than Latin America, and that no other area matches us in our importance to the future of Latin America."[80] The report also emphasized the need for socio-economic development and for regional common markets, and it urged the United States to proceed as rapidly as possible to co-operate with leaders of the Latin American republics in creating the Inter-American Development Bank, which had initially been resisted by the United States.

At the same time, the United States Senate took initial steps toward planning a broad and long-range review of foreign policy toward Latin America, and in 1960 Under-Secretary of State Douglas Dillon presented to the Senate a complete revision of inter-American relations and proposed a bill to provide for assistance in the economic and social development of Latin America. These events prepared the way for a major change that took place in the Bogotá Conference of the Organization of American States in September, 1960. At that time, the United States discarded her traditional policy that private capital can achieve the necessary Latin American economic development and recognized the need for development by means of over-all national plans. A new distinction between social and economic development was made, coupled with the recognition that the effects of the economic development programs, while requiring urgent strengthening and enlargement, may be too slow in producing the social benefits necessary and that, therefore, immediate measures should be taken to meet social needs. As a result of this new trend the Bogotá Act was signed, in which a program of land reform, tax reform, measures for public health and housing improvements, and educational reform was approved.

The establishment of ECLA, the formulation of Operation Pan-America, the creation of the Inter-American Development Bank, and the adoption of the Bogotá Act had laid the bases for the transformation of the Inter-American System. To the purely political aspects of the system, it was now intended to add a series of economic and social measures designed to convert the system into an appropriate channel for the economic and social development of the member countries.

The formulation of the plan, "Alliance for Progress," made by President Kennedy in March, 1961, contains a program aimed at transforming the Inter-American System into an effective channel of regional co-operation for economic and social development.[81]

It is outside the scope of this study to make a detailed analysis of the system in all of its economic or administrative aspects. We shall merely describe it in general terms. What are the principal elements of this new concept of the regional system? First, the Western Hemisphere idea, in the new context of America's situation in the second half of the twentieth century, is characterized by an awareness of the underdeveloped condition of the Latin American countries. In the words of President Kennedy, "Our hemisphere mission is not yet complete. For our unfulfilled task is to demonstrate to the entire world that man's unsatisfied aspiration for economic progress and social justice can best be achieved by free men working within a framework of democratic institutions."

Second, the urgency of solving the problem of the underdevelopment of Latin America must be recognized because population growth is outdistancing economic growth and the low living standards are becoming further aggravated. Discontent is growing —the discontent of people who know that abundance and the tools of progress are at last within their reach.

Third, the hemisphere must become aware that the future of freedom in the Americas depends upon a successful fight against underdevelopment.

Fourth, there must be a uniform decision to meet this challenge with the proper approach—a common effort of the United States and the nations of Latin America—which is precisely what the new Alliance for Progress is, "a vast effort of a scope and magnitude sufficient to make this bold development a success, an effort comparable to that which the United States made to help rebuild the economies of Western Europe after the Second World War."

The Alliance for Progress is conceived as a vast ten-year plan to provide the Latin American people with homes, work, land, health, and schools and to create the conditions in which most Latin American nations can enter into a period of self-sustaining growth and thus can have the means to master their own progress. "These ten years will be the years of maximum effort—the years greatest obstacles must be overcome—the years when the need for assistance will be the greatest."

The doctrinal concepts contained in Operation Pan-America and the Alliance for Progress were expressed in the institutional frameworks of the OAS, ECLA, and the Inter-American Development Bank. The Punta del Este Conference, convened by the Inter-American Economic and Social Council of the OAS, was for the purpose of establishing a concrete plan of action along the general lines sketched by President Kennedy, to establish the total amount of foreign aid, and to determine the respective roles of the above institutions in the implementation of the plan.

The essential aim of the program is to achieve a substantial and sustained growth of per capita income in the Latin American countries at a rate that will produce, in the shortest time possible, a level of income capable of ensuring an accumulative development that will consistently continue to rise in relation to the more industrialized nations.

With respect to the *atimic* process, it is interesting to note that the principal aim of the program is to reduce the gap between the standard of living in Latin America and in the more advanced countries and at the same time to reduce the differences among the Latin American countries having unequal levels of development.

The objectives would be realized by means of a national program of economic and social development whereby the determined goal for economic growth would be accompanied by a social development that satisfies the aspirations of the common man. Because of this, the Charter of Punta del Este stresses the need for programs of agricultural reform, tax reform, educational reform, and health programs that will raise the standard of living of the common man.

In addition to the formulation of national development programs, which are the basic requisite of all programs of the Alliance for Progress, there are two equally important elements in the Act. The first of these is the principle of self-help. By virtue of this principle, national development plans must be based on "own effort," as was established in the Bogotá Act, i.e., the maximum use of domestic resources considering the special conditions of each country. It recognizes, as did the Colombo Plan, that the principal source of finance for these plans must come from domestic resources and that foreign aid will only supply the technical and capital resources that countries cannot themselves provide.

The Charter of Punta del Este also recognizes the need for a balanced diversification of the national economic structures to reduce dependence on a small number of basic commodities; one of the aims of the program should be to achieve stability in the prices of, or in the income from, these exports. To this end the American republics are committed to develop co-operative programs in order to avoid the damaging effects of excessive fluctuations of foreign-exchange income from basic commodities and to adopt the necessary measures for facilitating the access of Latin American exports to the world markets.

The economic and social development of Latin America is focused not only on the domestic economies but also looks toward the supranational integration of the countries. For this purpose the Charter of Punta del Este establishes the need for strengthening agreements of economic integration in order to achieve, in the long run, a Latin American Common Market that will broaden and diversify trade among the countries of Latin America and thus contribute to the economic growth of the region.

A second feature of the Charter of Punta del Este is the determination of the amount of foreign aid necessary to implement the program. It may be said that, if the agreements of Punta del Este are carried out as proposed, the Inter-American System will become a regional system approximating self-sufficiency. With the resources provided in the program, the Latin American countries could cover their needs of foreign capital and technical assistance during the forthcoming ten-year period of the Alliance for Progress. The amount of capital necessary for the economic development of Latin America had been estimated variously before the Punta del Este Conference.   In 1954 the needs were calculated at one billion dollars annually, according to ECLA estimates, of which 650 to 700 million would come from public funds invested by institutions of international credit, providing that private foreign investment did not fall below 300 to 350 million dollars annually.   At the time of Stevenson's first visit to Latin America in March, 1951, ECLA sources informed him that the aforementioned needs could be calculated at 2 billion dollars if the annual rate of the Latin American product were to be raised 3 per cent per capita.   The economic advisors of President Kubitschek calculated the Latin American need for foreign capital to achieve the goals of Operation Pan-America over a fifteen- to twenty-year period at 40 billion dollars, a figure that was fairly close to ECLA's unofficial estimate.   The Charter of Punta del Este establishes that 20 billion dollars in external financial aid should be obtained during the next ten years, the major portion of which should be public funds.   The United States stated its proposal of allotting funds which, together with those coming from other outside sources would, in kind and amount, be sufficient to achieve the aims of the agreement.   In addition to United States aid, which is the principal source of the 20 billion dollars mentioned, aid and support may be established from other capital exporting countries, from international lending agencies and institutions, and from private foreign investment.

United States Secretary of the Treasury Douglas Dillon made the following declaration with respect to the estimated 20 billion dollars required to finance the plan: ". . . the United States would provide about $1,100 million a year for the next decade, or a total of $11,000 million; the remaining $9,000 million would come from other sources.   It was hoped that private U.S. investors would put up $300 million; the World Bank, the Inter-American Development Bank (IDB), and other international agencies, another $300 million; and Europe and Japan, the final $300 million in investments to make up the necessary $900 million each year."[82]

A third accomplishment of Punta del Este concerns the role in the Alliance for Progress of the OAS, ECLA, and the Inter-

American Development Bank, the three principal organizations of the Inter-American System. These three organizations which signed a co-operation agreement in 1961 should co-ordinate their efforts in the realization of the goals of the program. One of the principal problems concerns the task of providing technical assistance to the countries needing to formulate adequate programs of development. For this purpose the three agencies will continue to reinforce their agreements to place at the disposition of the countries a group of experts in programing whose services can be utilized to facilitate the implementation of the Alliance. The key point of the whole program is the fact that foreign aid will be granted only to those countries presenting development plans that are fully acceptable from a technical point of view. To insure this highly technical level of the programs, provision is made for a nine-member group of examining experts of the highest level to be designated by the Inter-American Economic and Social Council, on the joint proposal of the Secretary General of the OAS, the President of the Inter-American Development Bank, and the Executive Secretary in charge of the Economic Commission for Latin America. These experts, who may be of any nationality, will be attached to the Inter-American Economic and Social Council; however, they will enjoy complete autonomy in the exercise of their functions and may not accept any other remunerative position during that time. They will be designated for a period of three years and may be reappointed.

Each government desirous of obtaining aid from the program, after studying a plan of economic and social development with the aid of the three agencies cited—if it considers such consultation advisable—shall then present the plan to the consideration of an *ad hoc* committee composed of a maximum of three members of the previously mentioned group of experts and an equal number of experts from outside this group. These experts will be designated by the secretary general of the OAS at the request of the interested government and with its consent.

This committee will study the development program, exchange opinions with the interested government regarding possible modifications, and, on the consent of the government, will make its conclusions known to the Inter-American Development Bank and other governments and institutions that may be willing to grant financial and technical aid for the implementation of the program. Once the government has submitted its plan in the manner indicated, the Inter-American Development Bank can take the necessary steps to obtain the foreign aid required. For this purpose the bank may organize a joint operation of lending institutions and governments disposed to contribute to the continued and systematic financing, on convenient terms, of the development program.

The harmony between the power of the *ad hoc* committee and the sovereign right of each government to determine its own national program of development is achieved first, as has been stated, because the *ad hoc* committee is composed in part of experts accepted by the interested government, and secondly, because the committee will not interfere with the right of each government to formulate its own aims, priorities, and reforms in regard to its national development plans. Each government will be interested in obtaining favorable recommendations from the *ad hoc* committee because the Act establishes these recommendations to be of great importance in determining the distribution of the public funds of the Alliance for Progress, which contributes the foreign aid provided in the programs. The recommendations of the *ad hoc* committee will especially bear in mind the fact that the national programs are conceived on the basis of achieving a self-sustained economic development and on the assumption of the 2.5 per cent annual per capita rate of growth established as one of the basic objectives of the program of the Alliance for Progress to be reached within the decade of the 1960's.

In addition to these basic objectives that constitute the central core of international administrative procedures to be followed in securing foreign aid, the Charter states that the Inter-American Social and Economic Council will examine the progress made each year in the formulation, national achievements, and international financing of the development programs and will submit the pertinent recommendations to the Council of the Organization of American States.

If the procedures of this plan are compared to those of the Colombo Plan, the outstanding difference is the extraordinary complexity of the Inter-American System vis-à-vis the relative simplicity of the administrative mechanisms of the Asiatic plan. This is the result of the fact that the program of economic and social development of Latin America was injected, one may say, into an existing international administrative structure, a structure composed basically of the three organizations previously cited: the OAS, the Inter-American Development Bank, and ECLA. To establish the plan on a proper foundation it was necessary to bring the respective roles of the three institutions into harmony. The mechanisms provided in the Punta del Este Act endeavor to accomplish this task.

It is not our purpose to evaluate the possible results that the program may achieve upon its fulfillment, but it is obvious that its success depends on several variables among which are the following:

1. The timeliness with which the United States is able to mobilize its national political system to provide the amount of foreign capital it has committed itself to contribute in accordance with the Punta del Este Act.

2. The ability and determination of each Latin American country to formulate and implement its socio-economic development program and to mobilize its national political system so that it may be possible to obtain, by democratic procedures, the necessary support for the plans of social reform.

3. The creation of the proper conditions in the Latin American countries, from the political, economic, and social point of view, to allow the flow of public and private foreign investment as a complement to the United States contribution.

4. The measure in which the three fundamental entities of the Inter-American System are able to co-ordinate their respective efforts in the execution of the Alliance for Progress and, especially, the ability of the IDB in obtaining the required financing once the various development programs have been presented by the *ad hoc* committee and the respective governments.

If we wish to synthesize the character of the Alliance for Progress, we might state that its final results depend on the interaction of the Inter-American System under the leadership of the United States and the national political systems under the leadership of the authorities of the Latin American countries. Undoubtedly this program, including rapid social development in its aims, has a revolutionary content that makes it unique in the systems of international co-operation known at this time.   Its objectives are economic, social, and political: economic, as it is attempting to realize programs of economic development with the precise goals that have been described; social, as it aspires to promote a social revolution to insure a rapid increase in the standard of living of the Latin American common man within the framework of democratic institutions; and political, because it intends to reinforce and develop the democratic structures of the countries of the continent by means of social reforms and through the creation of national economies of self-sustained economic development.

From the viewpoint of *atimia* established in this study, the program of the Alliance for Progress has particular significance, since, as has been stated, its final objective is to lessen the gap existing at the present time between the levels of living of the Latin American countries and those of the developed countries of the rest of the world.

The program is attempting, in the last analysis, to raise the real status of the Latin American nations by means of raising their economic status.   The three elements of this status—the degree of social development, the amount of gross national product, and the degree of economic development evaluated by a greater or lesser approximation to self-sustained economic growth—constitute the goals of the program.

The Alliance for Progress represents a reaction of greater scope to the *atimic* process than any previously undergone by a group of sovereign nations.

NOTES

1. Bert F. Hoselitz, *Sociological Aspects of Economic Growth* (Glencoe, Ill.: The Free Press, 1960), p. 93.

2. United Nations, "World Economic Survey" (New York, 1959), p. 80.

3. United Nations, "Measures for the Economic Development of Underdeveloped Countries," report by a group of experts appointed by the Secretary General of the United Nations (New York, 1951), p. 72.

4. *Ibid.*

5. United Nations, "Economic Survey of Latin America, 1958" (New York, 1959), p. 40.

6. *Ibid.*

7. *Ibid.*

8. United Nations, "Measures for the Economic Development of Underdeveloped Countries," p. 73.

9. United Nations, "International Compensation for Fluctuations in Commodity Trade" (New York, 1961), p. 8.

10. "The Colombo Plan for Co-operative Economic Development in South and South-East Asia," report by the Commonwealth Consultative Committee, London, September-October, 1950 (London: His Majesty's Stationery Office, 1950), p. 54.

11. Paul G. Hoffman, *One Hundred Countries: One and One Quarter Billion People* (Washington, D.C.: Committee for International Economic Growth, 1960), p. 29.

12. *Ibid.*, p. 45.

13. "U.S. Foreign Policy Goals: What Experts Propose," *Headline Series*, 142 (July-August, 1960), 53.

14. John R. E. Carr-Gregg, "The Colombo Plan: A Commonwealth Program for Southeast Asia," *International Conciliation*, 467 (January, 1951), 19.

15. This is the definition given in title four of the Foreign Economic Assistance Act of 1950 (H.R. 7797), better known as the Point Four Program, approved by the U.S. Congress on May 25, 1950, and by the President on June 5, 1950, *Congressional Record*, 81st Congress, 2nd session, vol. 96, pp. 7313-17.

16. M. Abramovitz, "Resource and Output Trends in the United States since 1870," *American Economics Review*, Papers and Proceedings, XLVI (May, 1956), 5-23, reprinted by the National Bureau of Economic Research as "Occasional Paper No. 52"; John W. Kendrick, "Productivity Trends: Capital and Labor," *Review of Economics and Statistics*, XXXVIII (August, 1956), 248-57, reprinted by the National Bureau of Economic Research as "Occasional Paper No. 53"; Jacob Schmookler, "The Changing Efficiency of the American Economy: 1869-1938," *Review of Economics and Statistics*, XXXIV (August, 1952), 214-31, cited in Charles J. Hitch and Roland N. McKean, *The Economics of Defense in the Nuclear Age* (Cambridge, Mass.: Harvard University Press, 1960), p. 36.

17. Schmookler, "Changing Efficiency," p. 244, cited by Hitch and McKean, *Economics of Defense*, p. 36.

18. Abramovitz, "Resource and Output," p. 8, cited by Hitch and McKean, *Economics of Defense*, p. 36.

19. Hitch and McKean, *Economics of Defense*, p. 36.

20. Theodore W. Schultz, "Latin American Economic Policy Lessons," *American Economic Review*, Papers and Proceedings, XLVI (May, 1956), 430-31, cited in Hitch and McKean, *Economics of Defense*, p. 36.

21. W. W. Rostow has pointed out that "the Indian effort may well be remembered in economic history as the first take-off defined *ex ante* in national product terms" in *The Stages of Economic Growth* (New York: Cambridge University Press, 1960), p. 45.

22. W. A. Jöhr and F. Knescharek, "Study of the Efficiency of a Small Nation: Switzerland," in *Economic Consequences of the Size of Nations*, ed., E. A. G. Robinson (New York: St. Martin's Press, Inc., 1960), p. 64.

23. For an explanation of the concept of external vulnerability of Latin American countries, see CEPAL, Naciones Unidas, "La Cooperación Internacional en la Política de Desarrollo Económico" (Nueva York, 1954), p. 88.

24. Talcott Parsons, "Society," in *Encyclopaedia of the Social Sciences*, vol. 14, p. 231.

25. See "The Study and Practice of Planning," *International Social Science Journal*, XI, No. 3 (1939), especially the introductory article by John Friedmann in which he analyzes the scope and content of the debate concerning planning.

26. Gunnar Myrdal, *Solidaridad o Desintegración* (México, D.F.: Fondo de Cultura Económica, 1956), p. 266.

27. United Nations, "Measures for the Economic Development of Underdeveloped Countries, pp. 93-94.

28. CEPAL, Naciones Unidas, "La Cooperación Internacional en la Política de Desarrollo Ecónomico" (Nueva York, 1954), pp. 10-12.

29. United Nations, "World Economic Survey, 1959" (New York, 1960).

30. *Ibid.*, pp. 81-83.

31. Hoselitz uses the expression "autonomous development"; we prefer to use the expression "spontaneous," which is better suited in connotation with the understanding of the basic concept of the ideal type.

32. Hoselitz, *Sociological Aspects of Economic Growth*, pp. 97-98.

33. Concerning the relation between planning and policy, see Robert A. Dahl, "The Politics of Planning," *International Social Science Journal,* XI, No. 3 (1959).

34. In this sense, see CEPAL, UNESCO, Naciones Unidas, "Informe del Grupo de Trabajo sobre los Aspectos Sociales del Desarrollo Económico en América Latina" (México, D.F., Diciembre, 1960).

35. Naciones Unidas, "El Mercado Común Latinoamericano" (México, D.F., 1959), p. 4.

36. G. Marcy, "How Far Can Foreign Trade and Customs Agreements Confer upon Small Nations the Advantages of Large Nations?" in *Economic Consequences of the Size of Nations,* ed., E. A. G. Robinson (New York: St. Martin's Press, Inc., 1960), p. 269.

37. Robinson, *Economic Consequences,* p. xviii.

38. As is well known, Brazil, in spite of her increasing population, has been seeking an expansion of her market through the Latin American Free-Trade Association (Montevideo Treaty).

39. Naciones Unidas, "El Mercado Común Latinoamericano," p. 23.

40. Lincoln Gordon, "Economic Regionalism Reconsidered," *World Politics,* XIII (January, 1961), p. 245. Colombia and Ecuador have recently entered the Latin American Free-Trade Area. Costa Rica has also recently fully joined the Central American Common Market.

41. Oded Remba, "The Middle East in 1960—An Economic Survey," *Middle Eastern Affairs,* XII, No. 3 (March, 1961), 81.

42. Myrdal, *Solidaridad o Desintegración.* Francois Perroux has pointed out a hypothesis similar to that of Myrdal in an unpublished article entitled "Depassement de la Nation": "Il est en réalité assez utopique de demander a des nations qui sont en train de se former de se dépasser. Il ne s'agit pas pour elles d'aller au dela de la forme nationale puisqu'elles n'y ont pas accédé." The same idea was expressed by Lincoln Gordon: "Desirable as they might be [the economic regionalism of underdeveloped countries], it is unlikely that many underdeveloped countries will be prepared to join in full-fledged customs unions or free trade areas. Most of these countries are not yet as mature about their nationalism as the ancient European nations," in "Economic Regionalism Reconsidered," *World Politics,* p. 248.

43. Robinson, *Economic Consequences,* p. xii; Gordon, "Economic Regionalism Reconsidered," *World Politics,* p. 246.

44. Gordon, "Economic Regionalism Reconsidered," *World Politics,* p. 246.

45. *European Organizations,* Political and Economic Planning (London: George Allen and Unwin, Ltd., 1959), pp. 11-14.

46. Victor Urquidi, *Trayectoria del Mercado Común Latinoamericano* (México, D.F.: Centro de Estudios Monetarios Latinoamericanos, 1960), p. 34.

47. See note 57 in Chapter I.

48. *Revista Brasileira de Política International,* Ano II, No. 5 (Março, 1959), 112.

49. CEPAL, Naciones Unidas, "El Mercado Común Latinoamericano" (México, D.F.: 1959), p. 4.

50. The group of political scientists and historians at Princeton University under the direction of Karl Deutsch, who are studying the supranational integration process for the formation of "security communities," have also used the concept of "take-off" to indicate the beginning of the integration process: "In studying political movements directed toward integration, we may similarly speak of take-off as a period in which small, scattered, and powerless movements of this kind change into larger and more coordinate ones with some significant power behind them. Before take-off, political integration may be a matter for theorists, for writers, for a few statesmen, or a few small pressure groups. After take-off, integration is a matter of broad political movements, of governments, or of major interest groups, often an affair of more or less organized mass persuasion and mass response, or else of the organized persuasion of large parts of the political elites or the politically relevant strata of the time. Before take-off, the proposal for integration is a matter of theory; after take-off, it is a political force."—Karl Deutsch and others, *Political Community and the North Atlantic Area* (Princeton, N.J.: Princeton University Press, 1957), pp. 83-84.

51. The Montevideo Treaty created an Executive Committee headed by an Executive Secretary and comprising technical and administrative personnel. According to Article 42, "In the performance of their duties, the Executive Secretary and the secretariat staff shall not seek or receive instructions from any Government or from any other national or international entity. They shall refrain from any action which might reflect on their position as international civil servants. The Contracting Parties undertake to respect the international character of the responsibilities of the Executive Secretary and of the secretariat staff and shall refrain from influencing them in any way in the discharge of their responsibilities."

52. ECOSOC, Naciones Unidas, Documento E/3374, p. 12.

53. ECOSOC, Naciones Unidas, Documento E/CN/13/1.69, "Medidas para combatir las fluctuaciones en los mercados de productos básicos," p. 17.

54. *Ibid.*, 19-20.

55. United Nations, E/3447-E/CN, 13/40, "International Compensation for Fluctuations in Commodity Trade" (New York, 1961).

56. *Ibid.*, 68.

57. *Ibid.*, 70.

58. *Time,* Latin American Edition, July 7, 1961, p. 18.

59. "Issues before the Sixteenth General Assembly," *International Conciliation,* 534 (September, 1961), 128.

60. Ernest B. Haas and Allen S. Whiting, *Dynamics of International Relations* (New York: McGraw-Hill Book Company, 1956), p. 492.

61. Ernest Haas, "Regional Integration and National Policy," *International Conciliation,* 513 (May, 1957), 410-11.

62. Ghana, "Draft Memorandum Conference of African States" (typewritten document, n.d.) cited by Thomas Hovet, Jr., *Bloc Politics in the United Nations* (Cambridge, Mass.: Harvard University Press, 1960), p. 94. For a study of African ideology in international affairs, see the book by the President of Nigeria, Kwame Nkrumah, *I Speak of Freedom: A Statement of African Ideology* (New York: Frederick A. Praeger, 1961).

63. Haas, "Regional Integration and National Policy," *International Conciliation,* p. 430.

64. *The Colombo Plan for Co-operative Economic Development in South and South-East Asia,* report by the Commonwealth Consultative Committee (London: September-October, 1950), p. 62. This publication is known as the Colombo "White Paper."

65. Carr-Gregg, "The Colombo Plan," *International Conciliation,* p. 31.
66. "White Paper," p. 63.
67. *Ibid.,* p. 62.
68. *Ibid.,* pp. 1-3.
69. J. D. B. Miller, *The Commonwealth in the World* (Cambridge, Mass.: Harvard University Press, 1958), pp. 167-68, 175.
70. Carr-Gregg, "The Colombo Plan," *International Conciliation,* p. 26.
71. *Ibid.,* p. 37.
72. "These calculations by the countries are based upon a number of assumptions, any or all of which may be falsified by the course of events; and the total should be regarded as representing the broad dimensions of the requirements of external finance, rather than as a forecast proposing to describe the position six years ahead."—"White Paper," p. 58.
73. "The Colombo Plan" (Ottawa: Department of External Affairs, 1954), p. 10.
74. *The Colombo Plan for Co-operative Economic Development in South and South-East Asia,* Ninth Annual Report of the Consultative Committee (London: Her Majesty's Stationery Office, 1961), p. 199.
75. Miller, *The Commonwealth in the World,* p. 246.
76. Constitution of the Council for Technical Co-operation of the Colombo Plan.
77. *The Colombo Plan,* Ninth Annual Report, p. 3.
78. Arthur Whitaker, *The Western Hemisphere Idea* (Ithaca, N.Y.: Cornell University Press, 1954).
79. Speech by the Chilean Ambassador, Hernán Santa Cruz, proposing the creation of CEPAL before the Economic and Social Council of the United Nations, Lake Success, August 1, 1947.
80. Milton Eisenhower, "United States-Latin American Relations," Department of State, December 27, 1958, p. 16.
81. The origin of the formulation of the Alliance for Progress goes back to a statement developed at the Foreign Policy Clearing House Conference at Harvard University, December 19, 1960, entitled: *Alliance for Progress: A Program of Inter-American Partnership.* Federico G. Gil, one of the participants at the meeting, coined the phrase "Alliance for Progress," and the document was passed on to President-elect Kennedy through three channels: Adlai Stevenson, Luther Hodges, and Chester Bowles. The expression "Alliance for Progress" appeared officially for the first time in the inaugural address of President Kennedy.
82. *Hispanic American Report,* XIV, No. 8 (October, 1961), 751.

CHAPTER III

INTERNATIONAL ACTION AND THE POWER STATUS OF A NATION

1. *Power politics and underdeveloped countries: some fundamental problems*

"Power politics, it has been said, is the privilege of great powers, and small ones enter into the system as passive objects."[1]   Morgenthau, after establishing the fact that international politics, like all politics, is the struggle for power, adds that the involvement of a nation in international politics is but one among many types of activities in which a nation can participate on the international scene.   All nations are not involved at all times to the same extent in international politics.

The degree of their involvement may run all the way from the maximum at present attained by the United States and the Soviet Union, through the minimum involvement of such countries as Switzerland, Luxemburg, or Venezuela, to the complete noninvolvement of Liechtenstein and Monaco. . . .   The relation of nations to international politics has a dynamic quality.   It changes with the vicissitudes of power, which may push a nation into the forefront of the power struggle, or may deprive a nation of the ability to participate actively in it.   It may also change under the impact of cultural transformations, which may make a nation prefer other pursuits, for instance commerce, to those of power.[2]

The problem that we wish to analyze concerning the underdeveloped countries can be established by taking as a point of reference the two preceding statements.   Are the underdeveloped countries small powers and, as such, do they simply constitute passive objects of international politics?   To what extent are they involved or not involved in power politics?   Or, in other terms, what are the international actions of the underdeveloped countries with respect to power politics?

The answer to these questions depends, in the first place, on the concept that we establish of *power;* in the second place, on our definition of small, middle-range, great, and world powers; and, finally, on the criteria that we use to establish the degree of involvement of any given country in power politics. In answering these questions, we shall have all of the significant elements to construct a typology of international actions of underdeveloped countries in relation to power politics.

There is no agreement among sociologists and political scientists concerning the idea of *power.* "In the entire lexicon of sociological concepts, none is more troublesome than the concept of power."[3] From the classic definition of Max Weber, who defined power as "the possibility of imposing one's will upon the behaviour of other persons," many interpretations have sprung—with greater or lesser variations on Weber's thought.[4] In this chapter, we wish to refer only to the distinction between power and influence. While, for some, these are two divergent categories,[5] for others, influence lies within the concept of power.[6]

In this study we shall stipulate the latter meaning of the term, and we shall take as our point of reference that the power of one nation upon another exists when the actions of the first are capable of changing, in greater or lesser degree, the actions of the second either by coercion or by influence. Power, in its coercive aspect, is always a latent force. In this sense, "Power . . . is the predisposition or prior capacity which makes the application of force possible. Only groups which have power can threaten to use force and the threat itself is power. Power is the ability to employ force, and not its actual employment, the ability to apply sanctions, not their actual application. Power is the ability to introduce force into the social situation; it is the presentation of force."[7] Power, in its dimension of influence, does not necessarily imply the use of the threat of force nor its introduction or presentation into a social situation. When power manifests itself as influence, subtle means of obtaining the desired change in the actions of a nation can be used. Some examples of the modes of influence may be one or more of the following: (a) conveying new information (enlightenment or clarification)—the United States may make it clear that it is not willing to provide financial help to countries that have dictatorships; (b) conveying misinformation (distortion or invention)—a certain small country can threaten to abandon a regional organization supported by a great power if some undesired action is taken by that organization, even if the country does not have the actual intention of such withdrawal; (c) advice (effective according to the prestige of the source, its presumed experience, knowledge, judgment, and good will)—a leading Latin American nation can advise the United States not to propose an international meeting of the OAS, because the circumstances are not favorable to obtain the desired aim; (d) appeal to values and sentiments—policy-makers of the British Commonwealth can make an appeal to South African leaders not to proceed in their policy of "apartheid"; (e) inducement (sometimes called exchange, offering something valuable in return for compliance)—if you do as I wish, then I can do this for you.[8]

If we put aside the reduced sphere of international relations in which, through the United Nations or other international organizations, power is in a certain form institutionalized (for example, the power of the Security Council of the United Nations to adopt certain decisions), we observe that the remaining power relationships are not guided through any institutional form. There is no legitimate authority that gives some state the right to command and others the duty to obey. On the contrary, the ideology of equalitarianism is openly contrary to such a relationship. Consequently, in order not to violate openly such an ideology, in ordinary circumstances the power of a nation will tend to manifest itself through some of the modes of influence rather than through the coercive pattern.

The concepts of *small power, middle-range power, great power,* or *world power* impinge upon the notion of power in the first of its aspects, that is to say, coercion. It is the possibility of applying force, in greater or lesser degree, as military strength that confers the title of *small power, middle-range power,*[9] *great power,* or *world power* upon a nation.

In the first chapter we have pointed out that, other factors being equal, the components of the status of power of a nation are the following:

1. Technological maturity.

2. A gross national product of sufficient quantity that a percentage of it, which fluctuates between 2 per cent and 15 per cent and is destined for the defense budget, reaches a minimum sum sufficient to permit its influencing the world balance of military power. This sum was, in 1955, one billion dollars, and according to the projections of Hitch and McKean for 1965 and 1975, it will fluctuate between 2 and 5 billion dollars.

3. A defense budget of sufficient quantity to permit participation in the technological race in military terms.

It is obvious that these components refer to the coercive aspect of power and that, as we have pointed out in Chapter I, the first factor automatically excludes all of the underdeveloped countries from participating in the world balance of military power. The other two factors only reinforce this conclusion.

What we have said is sufficient to answer the question of classifying the underdeveloped countries as small powers. But, to arrive at the limit of our analysis, we must answer the last of our questions and determine the degree of involvement of the small powers in power politics.

2. *Identifying a typology of international actions of the underdeveloped nations in relation to power politics*

Let us first point out that the underdeveloped character of these countries does not permit any one of them to weigh heavily in military power politics on a world scale, but it would be possible for them to develop a kind of power politics with participants of equal or similar capacity. Let us refer to this form of action as power politics on a local scale.

In the second place, let us point out that if the small powers remain excluded from power politics on the world scale because they lack coercive power, they still can play a role in this kind of politics using their power through the different modes of influence. This influence can have several degrees of importance according to the position of a given country within the bipolar system.

In the third place, it is possible that a country, because of its extremely small size, renounces once and for all power politics even on a local scale; and, on the other extreme, it is possible too that a country, because of its great size, which gives it the possibility of having a gross national product of significant quantity when technological maturity is reached, will aspire to become a middle-range, great, or world power. Thus we have all of the elements to construct a typology of international actions of the underdeveloped countries with relation to power politics: (1) countries that exercise political power on a local scale with participants of equal or similar capacity; (2) countries that renounce power politics, even on the local scale; (3) countries that exercise power politics as influence on a world scale; and (4) countries that aspire to become world, great, or middle-range powers.

Let us analyze each of these possibilities so that we may ascertain the degree of involvement in power politics on the part of the underdeveloped countries.

A. *Countries that use power politics on the local scale*

This political approach may be characterized by the following elements: (1) the participants who use it have an equal or similar military capacity, (2) this military capacity lacks meaning in relation to world power politics, and (3) this power is destined to establish, maintain, or augment supremacy or balance of power on the local scale.

This type of power politics is found in Latin America, Asia, and Africa. In Table XV we present the latest available data showing the burden that military budget expenditure represents in some of these nations. The great majority of nations listed in the table are expending in their military budgets more than 10 per cent of the gross domestic fixed capital formation. In one astonishing situation—that of Indonesia—the figure reaches 104.6 per cent. In many instances these military expenditures can be attributed primarily to the existence of power politics on a local scale. Latin America offers typical examples in this connection. Historically the cause may be found primarily in the conflicts concerning boundary demarcation, whose origins, in many cases, go back to the dismembering of Spanish and Portuguese colonial empires in Latin America. These conflicts erupted into five wars during the nineteenth century, and they have left latent tensions on which local power politics are based.

TABLE XV
UNDERDEVELOPED PRIVATE ENTERPRISE COUNTRIES: MILITARY
EXPENDITURES, AS STATED IN BUDGET ACCOUNTS,
COMPARED WITH OTHER STATISTICS, 1957-1959[1]

Country, period and currency unit	Military budget expenditure	Gross domestic product[1]	Gross domestic fixed capital formation	Military budget expenditure as percentage of	
				Gross domestic product	Gross domestic fixed capital formation
AFRICA					
Sudan[2] (million pounds):					
1957	3.4	—	26.2		
1958	4.9	—	42.8		
1959	5.0	—	38.2		
Average 1957-1959	4.4	—	35.7	—	12.3
Union of South Africa (million pounds):					
1957	18.1[3]	2,345.0	485.0		
1958	19.6[3]	2,411.0	544.0		
1959	21.8[3]	2,518.0	525.0		
Average 1957-1959	19.8[3]	2,425.0	518.0	0.8	3.8
AMERICA, LATIN					
Argentina (million pesos):					
1958	6,924.8[4]	318,400.0	65,610.0		
1959	15,589.4[4]	604,547.0	107,985.0		
Average 1958-1959	11,257.1[4]	461,474.0	86,798.0	2.4	13.0
Brazil (billion cruzeiros):					
1957	34.6	1,063.1	124.5		
1958	40.8	1,299.3	165.6		
1959	41.1	1,837.4	228.5		
Average 1957-1959	38.8	1,399.9	172.9	2.8	22.4
Chile (million escudos):					
1957	73.1	2,252.7[5]	247.0		
1958	82.2	2,971.8[5]	309.9		
1959	91.1	4,163.0[5]	405.0		
Average 1957-1959	82.1	3,129.2[5]	320.6	2.6	25.6
Colombia (million pesos):					
1957	288.6	17,651.0	2,630.0		
1958	306.4	20,477.0	3,350.0		
1959	274.7	22,995.0	3,919.0		
Average 1957-1959	289.9	20,374.0	3,300.0	1.4	8.8
Costa Rica (million colones):					
1957	13.4	2,302.7[6]	434.8		
1958	12.8	2,465.0[6]	404.0		
1959	13.1	2,529.8[6]	451.4		
Average 1957-1959	13.1	2,432.5[6]	430.1	0.5	3.0
Ecuador (million sucres):					
1957	289.0	12,007.0	1,561.0		
1958	282.0	12,355.0	1,586.0		
1959	273.0	12,424.0	1,553.0	2.2	17.6
El Salvador (million colones):					
1957	19.2	1,218.2[7]	—		
1958	19.0	1,249.9[7]	—		
1959	17.0	1,226.7[7]	—		
Average 1957-1959	18.4	1,231.6[7]	—	1.5[7]	—

(TABLE XV Cont.)

Country, period and currency unit	Military budget expenditure	Gross domestic product[1]	Gross domestic fixed capital formation	Military budget expenditure as percentage of	
				Gross domestic product	Gross domestic fixed capital formation
Guatemala (million quetzales):					
1957	8.9[2]	652.5	97.5[8]		
1958	9.7[2]	647.0	97.4[8]		
1959	9.9[2]	659.1	84.1[8]		
Average 1957-1959	9.5[2]	652.9	93.0[8]	1.5	10.2[8]
Honduras (million lempiras):					
1957	8.9	688.3	94.1	1.3	9.5
Mexico (million pesos):					
1957	791.7	103,000.0[9]	15,544.0		
1958	861.5	114,000.0[9]	16,282.0		
1959	971.0	122,000.0[9]	18,066.0		
Average 1957-1959	874.7	113,000.0[9]	16,631.0	0.8[9]	5.3
Peru (million soles):					
1957	1,083.8	34,342.0[5]	9,149.0		
1958	1,265.4	37,691.0[5]	8,643.0		
Average 1957-1959	1,174.6	36,016.0[5]	8,896.0	3.3[5]	13.2
Venezuela (million bolivares):					
1957	419.3[2]	23,847.0	5,950.0[10]		
1958	572.0[2]	24,585.0	5,964.0[10]		
1959	630.2[2]	24,904.0	6,721.0[10]		
Average 1957-1959	540.5[2]	24,445.0	6,212.0[10]	2.2	8.7[10]
ASIA					
Burma[11] (million kyats):					
1957	368.5	5,429.0	1,018.0		
1958	407.6	5,299.0	1,135.0		
1959	403.3	5,493.0	1,015.0		
Average 1957-1959	393.1	5,407.0	1,056.0	7.3	37.2
Cambodia:					
1957	—	—	—	4.0	—
Ceylon (million rupees):					
1957	39.9[11]	5,382.0	660.6		
1958	64.1[11]	5,662.6	682.6		
1959	72.4[11]	6,032.9	805.5		
Average 1957-1959	58.8[11]	5,692.5	716.2	1.0	8.2
China (Taiwan):					
Average 1957-1959	—	—	—	10.8[12]	—
Federation of Malaya (million dollars):					
1957	160.6	5,310.0	610.0	3.0	26.3
India[5] (million rupees):					
1957	2,828.0	114,100.0[13]	—		
1958	2,787.0	124,800.0[13]	—		
Average 1957-1958	2,808.0	119,450.0[13]	—	2.4[13]	—
Indonesia (million rupiah):					
1957	6,052.0	171,000.0[14]	7,600.0		
1958	11,085.0	180,200.0[14]	8,299.0		
1959	8,788.0	210,000.0[14]	8,895.0		
Average 1957-1959	8,642.0	187,100.0[14]	8,265.0	4.6[14]	104.6
Israel (million pounds):					
1957	197.1[3]	3,054.0[15]	829.0[10]		

(TABLE XV Cont.)

Country, period and currency unit	Military budget expenditure	Gross domestic product[1]	Gross domestic fixed capital formation	Military budget expenditure as percentage of	
				Gross domestic product	Gross domestic fixed capital formation
1958	217.1[3]	3,501.0[15]	897.0[10]		
1959	251.1[3]	4,022.0[15]	961.0[10]		
Average 1957-1959	221.8[3]	3,526.0[15]	896.0[10]	6.3[15]	24.8[10]
Korea (Republic of) (billion hwan):					
1957	112.9	1,615.7	200.9		
1958	127.8	1,706.8	219.4		
1959	141.1	1,840.0	265.0		
Average 1957-1959	127.3	1,720.8	228.4	7.4	57.8
Lebanon (million pounds):					
1957	39.1	1,503.0[13]	—		
1958	45.6	1,325.0[13]	—		
Average 1957-1958	42.4	1,414.0[13]	—	3.0[13]	—
Pakistan:					
Average 1957-1958	—	—	—	3.0[12]	—
Philippines (million pesos):					
1957	157.0[2]	10,119.0	890.0		
1958	181.1[2]	10,666.0	851.0		
1959	183.6[2]	11,161.0	901.0		
Average 1957-1959	173.9[2]	10,649.0	881.0	1.6	19.7
Syrian Arab Republic (million pounds):					
1957	140.0	2,514.0[16]	266.0	5.6	52.6
Thailand (million baht):					
1957	1,566.7	44,670.0	6,434.0	3.8	24.4
1958	1,389.7	45,458.0	6,669.0		
1959	1,439.0	49,010.0	7,334.0		
Average 1957-1959	1,465.1	46,379.0	6,812.0	3.2	21.5
Turkey (million lires):					
1957	959.1[17]	30,668.0	4,033.0		
1958	956.2[17]	38,652.0	5,278.0		
1959	1,146.1[17]	46,640.0	7,463.0		
Average 1957-1959	1,020.5[17]	38,653.0	5,591.0	2.6	18.3

1. For the concept of domestic product used see para. 2 of the annex of the Report mentioned in the source.
2. Fiscal year ending 30 June.
3. Fiscal year beginning 1 April.
4. Fiscal year ending 31 October.
5. Including a statistical discrepancy.
6. Including current international transfers.
7. At market prices of 1950.
8. Including increase in stocks.
9. Gross national product.
10. Including change in stock of livestock held on farms.
11. Fiscal year ending 30 September.
12. Ratio to net national product.
13. Net domestic product at factor cost.
14. Gross domestic product at factor cost.
15. Including interest on public debt.
16. Net domestic product at factor cost of 1956.
17. Year beginning 1 March.

SOURCE: United Nations, "Economic and Social Consequences of Disarmament: Report of the Secretary-General Transmitting the Study of His Consultative Group" (New York, 1962) pp. 58-61. The data used by the group of experts were taken from: United Nations, *Statistical Yearbook* and *Yearbook of National Accounts Statistics*, various issues, except for Cambodia, China (Taiwan), and Pakistan, the source for which is United Nations, *Economic Survey of Asia and the Far East*, 1960 (Sales No.: 61.II.F.1), table 32, p. 83.

The *atimic* process has also been evident in this field. Before the economic development of the United States, a number of Latin American countries had a military or naval capacity, if not comparable, at least of sufficient importance to prevent armed action on the part of the United States. Thus the naval forces of Chile, upon terminating the Pacific War, served as a dissuasive power in preventing United States intervention in the conflict. And in the Jeffersonian era the underdeveloped condition of both the United States and Brazil allowed the President of the United States to consider the Brazilian navy in a role similar to that of the United States as defender of the hemisphere. The memory of this lost status can be discovered in the psychological background of twentieth-century policy-makers whose international actions are inducing the Latin American countries to maintain an armed political approach.

Having said this, we shall analyze some cases that illustrate the idea of power politics on the local scale. First, let us observe the case of Chilean-Peruvian relations and that of Brazilian-Argentine relations. Second, we shall establish the relationships between total government expenditure and the defense budget in a number of Latin American countries. Third, we shall study the same relationship in selected Asian countries focusing our attention on Indonesia, and finally, we shall refer briefly to this situation in the newly independent countries of Africa.

(a) *The case of Chilean-Peruvian relations*

The complete story of the relations between Chile and Peru has as a historical background the Pacific War, which meant a loss of territory for Peru to the victorious country. At present, Peruvian officials, some of whom are descended from those families which took part in the war, know that the existence of the Inter-American System and the series of treaties that have created the peaceful solution of conflicts—under the supervisory eye of the government in Washington—make a war between the two countries impossible, a war in which Peru might recapture her old territory.

In spite of the fact that warlike action seems to have been put aside for the rational alternative of international politics, the show of more powerful weapons than those of her neighbors and the appearance to them as a military power (on a local scale) works as a psychological compensation that the Peruvian armed forces endeavor to stress. Thus they appear as the potential avengers of lost honor and national prestige, broken by a military defeat, and, taking advantage of their position as a pressure group within the Peruvian political structure, they force the government to buy arms in order to maintain this military capacity.

On the other hand, Chile, at the present time, is interested only in maintaining the frontier fixed by international treaty. At the same time, however, she recognizes the possibility of a Peruvian attack. This attitude of mistrust leads her to maintain a certain supply of arms so that she may not be left defenseless.

In this process of interaction may be found the origin of the call for disarmament of the Latin American countries, sponsored by the President of Chile in 1959, which would permit the nations to free the economic resources destined for armaments for the purpose of economic development. The idea met with continental acceptance and, significantly, the first person to echo the call was the President of Peru.

Based on a subsequent exchange of notes between the two governments relative to the plan of disarmament, the Chilean State Department supports the view that, in agreement with the traditional balance of naval forces in the Pacific, the two navies must be maintained in a proportion of 5:3. Doubtless the memory of the status of Chile in the nineteenth century as a naval power in the Pacific was present in the minds of the Chilean officials who made this statement.

(b) *The case of Brazilian-Argentine relations*

There are three factors that condition relations between Argentina and Brazil: (1) a war whose objective was the small region that later became Uruguay, a war that ended with the mediation of Great Britain and the recognition of that region as an independent state in 1828; (2) the fact that both countries aspire to the leadership of the Latin American countries; (3) the fact that these two largest countries in South America possess enormous resources and could eventually become powers.

In the contest to achieve prestige as the first Latin American power and in the effort to maintain or acquire a supremacy of power on the local scale, both countries have carried on an arms race that neither is capable of supporting. After several meetings between Argentine and Brazilian military leaders with the purpose of dealing with problems of area defense, continental defense, anti-submarine warfare, and other military topics, a conference took place between the secretaries of state of the two countries in November, 1959. A joint communiqué on cultural and economic matters was released to the public, but in diplomatic circles there was mention of a secret agreement on the limitation and balance of armaments between the two nations. This information somehow became public and provoked a disturbance in the Brazilian as well as the Argentine armed forces. Apparently they had not been consulted. In order to make peace with the military, the Brazilian Ministry of War declared that money spent on armament is not useless, and President Kubitschek stated that the modernization of the fleet "is one of our most important goals."

(c) *The relationship between total government expenditure and defense expenditure in some selected Latin American countries*

In Table XVI we can observe the relationships between total government expenditure and defense expenditure in fourteen Latin American countries. Power politics on a local scale in the cases of Chilean-Peruvian and Brazilian-Argentine relations is clearly evident in the table because of the large percentage these four nations allot to defense expenditure.

It is necessary to emphasize that, in the case of Peru, this trend is accentuated by the existence of another situation of power on the local scale with Ecuador. The origin of this conflict is the existence of a boundary dispute between the two countries.

(d) *The relationship between total government expenditure and defense expenditure in some selected Asian countries*

The study of the relationship between total government expenditure and defense expenditure in the member countries of the Economic Commission for Asia and the Far East (ECAFE), shown in Table XVII, would also permit the identification of power

TABLE XVI
GOVERNMENT EXPENDITURE OF UNDERDEVELOPED LATIN AMERICAN COUNTRIES: SELECTED COUNTRIES, 1958
(in Millions)[1]

Countries	Total	Defense		Education		Health Services		Other Social Services		Other Current Expenditure	
		Total	%	Total	%	Total	%	Total	%	Total	%
Costa Rica (colones)	314.5	12.1	3.9	61.7	19.6	7.2	2.3	74.3	23.6	159.2	50.6
El Salvador (colones)	181.0	18.5	10.3	27.9	15.4	—	—	19.2	10.6	115.4	63.7
Guatemala (quetzales)	74.5	9.4	12.6	12.5	16.8	10.3	13.8	—	—	42.3	56.8
Haiti (gourdes)	145.9	27.9	19.1	19.6	13.4	15.7	10.8	—	—	82.7	56.7
Honduras (lempiras)	76.2	9.3	12.2	7.9	10.4	5.6	7.4	1.1	1.4	52.3	68.6
Mexico (pesos)	7.776.9	877.0	11.3	1.142.0	14.7	880.0	11.3	—	—	4.877.9	62.7
Panama (balboas)	93.7	—	—	12.3	13.1	11.0	11.7	—	—	70.4	75.2
Argentina (pesos)	40.702	8.584	21.1	5.822	14.3	1.321	3.2	606	1.5	34.369	59.9
Brazil (cruzeiros)	140.257.4	38.831.9	27.7	7.529.2	5.3	7.529.2	5.3	—	—	86.366.7	61.6
Chile (pesos)	378.2	83.0	21.9	59.4	15.7	42.0	11.1	—	—	193.8	51.3
Ecuador (sucres)	1.338	289	21.6	144	10.7	44	3.3	58	4.3	803	60.0
Peru (soles)	5.309.1	1.233.0	23.2	711.1	13.4	553.7	10.4	—	—	2.811.3	53.0
Venezuela (bolivares)	5.814.4	551.8	9.5	367.7	6.3	365.3	6.3	—	—	4.529.6	77.9
Colombia (pesos)	1.673.3	306.4	18.3	145.9	8.7	135.7	8.1	—	—	1.085.3	64.9

1. All figures are given in national currency. The denomination of each currency is indicated in the corresponding languages.
SOURCE: *Presupuesto de Colombia*, 1960, Dirección Nacional del Presupuesto.

politics on a local scale. We shall refer especially to the Indonesian case. The increase of defense expenditure of the Indonesian government is primarily founded on the conflict with the Netherlands regarding the New Guinea territory that still remains under Dutch control. The Netherlands did not give it up when the rest of the Dutch East Indies gained independence in 1949. On December 19, 1961, President Sukarno of Indonesia called for the liberation of the territory and placed his armed forces on an alert. The country had been receiving quantities of arms from the Soviet bloc.

According to *New York Times* information, "President Sukarno, distracting attention from his own domestic weakness and failures, is seeking status as a champion of anticolonialism through his projected ventures in New Guinea."[10] A navy spokesman said in this connection that the Indonesian naval forces were as strong as the Dutch navy,[11] and his air force also seems to be equipped with modern aircraft. But "the 200,000 or so men of the Indonesian army are no stronger than their air or naval support."[12]

TABLE XVII

ECAFE COUNTRIES: NATIONAL EXPENDITURE ON DEFENSE,
1950-1958[1]

Country	1950	1951	1952	1953	1954	1955	1956	1957	1958
	Per cent of total government expenditure								
Burma	24	26	29	32	29	26	27	28	28
Cambodia[2]	—	24	30	35	63	45	35	28	25
Ceylon	1	1	1	3	3	3	3	2	5
China: mainland[3]	42	43	26	26	24	24	20	19	12
Taiwan	—	42	33	32	38	37	36	34	35
Federation of Malaya	2	24	25	23	21	18	15	16	16
India	20	20	19	19	17	14	13	15	13
Indonesia	—	16	19	18	16	13	14	15	20
Japan	12	9	9	9	8	7	7	7	7
Korea, southern	—	—	—	48	44	38	37	30	30
Laos[4]	—	—	—	3	5	3	4	—	—
Pakistan	39	36	32	29	26	37	31	18	20
Philippines	15	19	20	18	17	16	14	14	15
Thailand	13	15	19	18	18	15	14	22	21
Viet-Nam[4,5]	—	—	69	71	79	73	—	45	—
	Per cent of gross national product								
Burma	3.8	3.7	5.0	6.2	8.3	6.9	6.9	6.8	7.7
Cambodia[2]	—	2.8	4.2	4.7	13.5	8.8	4.4	4.0	—
Ceylon	0.2	0.2	0.3	0.6	0.6	0.5	0.6	0.6	1.1
China: mainland[6,7]	6.7	10.2	7.2	8.2	7.9	8.3	6.9	5.9	4.0
Taiwan	—	10.7	9.0	8.7	10.0	10.0	9.9	10.1	11.5
Federation of Malaya	—	—	—	—	—	3.3	2.9	3.1	—
India[6]	1.9	1.9	1.9	1.9	2.1	1.9	1.9	2.4	2.1
Indonesia	—	5.0	3.7	4.5	3.8	3.2	3.0	3.6	6.2
Japan	2.8	2.1	2.2	2.3	2.2	1.8	1.6	1.8	1.7
Korea, southern	—	—	—	6.4	7.5	5.8	5.4	6.7	7.3
Pakistan[5,6]	3.8	4.7	5.2	3.5	3.1	3.9	3.4	2.8	3.1
Philippines	1.7	2.1	2.3	2.0	1.9	1.8	1.7	1.7	1.7
Thailand	1.4	2.0	2.9	2.9	3.1	2.0	1.9	3.6	2.9

1. Defense expenditure excludes the volume of foreign assistance on which data are not available.
2. Budget estimate for 1957, and revised estimates for 1952-55. Including aid-financed defense expenditures up to 1955.
3. To the extent that heavy industries answering defense needs are also financed from investment allocation to "industry," the share of economic services has swollen, and this has been at the expense of that of general services and of defense.
4. Budget estimates.
5. Only southern Viet-Nam from 1956 on; including outlays financed by foreign aid.
6. Net national product.
7. The concept of national income differs in mainland China from the one commonly used in private enterprise economies. For a full explanation of the estimate see footnote "b" of Table 17 on page 56 of the publication mentioned in the source of this table.

SOURCE: United Nations, *Economic Survey of Asia and the Far East 1960* (Bangkok, 1961) p. 83.

(e) *Power politics on a local scale in the newly independent countries of Africa*

Indicating the sources of tension in West Africa, the well-known economist and former Deputy Director of the United Nations Special Fund, W. Arthur Lewis, stated that frontier disputes were one of the causes of conflict among African countries.

Drawing on his observation as the former U.N. economic advisor to the Government of Ghana, Dr. Lewis identified five major sources of international tension in West Africa: (1) the division of the area into British and French spheres of influence; (2) the lack of education, which helps to maintain that division; (3) the mixture of tribes and religions, which menaces the stability of each of these states; (4) boundary disputes; and (5) the federal idea, which is meant to reduce tension but which, so far, has only increased it.[13]

In analyzing the fourth cause of international tension, Dr. Lewis wrote: "Frontier disputes . . . already involve Ghana, the Cameroons, and Gambia. The metropolitan powers kept only small forces in West Africa, but there are signs that this happy state may not long persist. In view of current talk of expanding armies, this is just the right time to promote in West Africa a convention for the limitation of armaments. . . ."[14]

B. *Countries that renounce power politics even on a local scale*

The nations that enter this category are completely bordered by power politics. Costa Rica is the most typical example. The country has an area of 19,647 square miles, a population of 1,126,000; its economy is highly dependent upon the economy of the United States (more than 50 per cent of its exports go to the United States); its political system is among the most democratic in Latin America; and its educational system has the highest percentage of university students in Central America.

In 1946 President Figueres abolished the armed forces, declaring that Costa Rica had no military ambitions and, as a result, needed no army. Internal order, he felt, could be maintained by a police force of 1,000 men. Costa Rica is the only Latin American country that has adopted such a drastic measure.

For a full decade the democratic, moderately socialistic regime of Figueres and Ulate made good their claims that the army was totally unnecessary, despite invasions made by Costa Rican exiles from Nicaragua in 1949, and again in 1955. In both cases, emergency volunteer forces, aided by prompt intervention by the Organization of American States, were able to repel the attackers. Thus the armed forces were no longer decisive factors in the politics of Costa Rica. Besides giving relief from militarism in government, that nation has also avoided the huge budgetary drain that military expenditures entailed in other Latin American countries.[15]

The suppression of the armed forces has continued until the present day, confirming the assertion of Figueres that the army was unnecessary.

What has permitted Costa Rica to renounce all power politics, even in the local sphere where its Central American neighbors can be considered as equal or similar in power capacity? The international situation of Costa Rica can be defined as follows: (a) considering its small size, both in population and area, Costa Rica, even when it reaches a high degree of economic development, can hardly aspire to become a power; (b) consequently, its independence can in no case rest on its ability to defend itself; (c) the possible conflicts with its neighbors can be solved through the rulings of the OAS, as has already been demonstrated on two occasions; (d) its democratic political regime permits recourse to public opinion for a policy based on the principle of pacific coexistance among nations.

C. Countries that achieve power politics on a world scale

The third type of action for underdeveloped countries is that which is characterized by international activity that is directed toward the promotion of national interest using the world balance of power.

This type of action may be characterized as follows: (a) power politics is used not in its coercive aspect, but in its influential aspect; (b) it is based on the bipolar system of the balance of power which is evident in present international relations; and (c) the foundation of this policy is the interest that two world powers have in establishing allies in the underdeveloped areas or in preventing a nation from leaning toward the opposing bloc.

These countries have neither military capacity—or if they have it this capacity is only valid for the implementation of power politics on a local scale—nor the economic stature that they are looking for. Thus their power has no validity as a force in the world balance of power. But they can exercise their influence on the great stage of public opinion attendant upon the fluctuation of the balance of power between the two world powers. In this balance of power, from the moment the two blocs cannot prove their power (if they do not wish to destroy themselves) the greater or lesser influence in an underdeveloped nation, or group of nations, can increase its power and prestige, adding an element to tip the balance in its favor. In this way, the weakness of the underdeveloped countries becomes their strength through the subtle means of influence. As Prime Minister Nehru has stated "even a single country can make a difference when the scales are evenly balanced."

Three subtypes can be distinguished within this category: (a) neutral nations; (b) the nations that withdraw from the bloc to which they belong and use the rivalry of the two blocs as a means for this withdrawal; and (c) the nations that find themselves within the system of one of the world powers but that constitute a battlefield of the cold war.

(a) *Neutral nations*

The principal points of the position taken by the neutral nations are the safeguard of the nation faced with a quarrel between two world powers and the affirmation of the in-group values of those new, weak nations faced with the out-group values embodied in the so-called imperialistic capitalism of the West, on one hand, and the communism of the Soviet bloc, on the other. As the Prime Minister of India expressed it at the Afro-Asian conference at Bandung,

Our influence must be exercised in the right direction which has integrity of purpose and ideals and objectives. It represents the ideals of Asia, it represents the new dynamism of Asia, because, if it does not represent that, what are we then? Are we copies of Europeans or Americans or Russians? What are we? We are Asians or Africans. We are none else. If we are camp followers of Russia or America or any other country of Europe, it is, if I may say so, not very creditable to our dignity, our new independence, our new freedom, our new spirit and our new self-reliance. . . . If I join any of these big groups I lose my identity.[16]

In the second place, the existence of this group of nations is viewed as a guarantee of world peace, because "if all the world were to be divided up between these two big blocs, what would be the result? The inevitable result would be war. Therefore, every step that takes place in reducing that area in the world which may be called the unaligned area is a dangerous step and leads to war. It reduces that objective, that balance, that outlook which other countries without military might perhaps exercise."[17]

As representatives of their own values and promoters of world peace, these nations thus succeed in maximizing their international role by supplying an equilibrium between the two blocs to promote their own socio-economic development, utilizing the help of whichever nation offers the most that is of national interest in each specific situation.

It is no accident that the two leaders of neutralism in Africa and Asia, Egypt (former U.A.R.) and India, are the two countries that have received the most help from the Soviet Union.[18] Recently Pakistan, one of the firmest Asiatic allies of the United States, has expressed its resentment of the government at Washington, because India, a neutral country, has received more help from the United States than Pakistan.[19]

Guided by this underlying orientation and strategy, the neutralist ideology has been extending its influence on the international system. As can be seen on the map, page 112, fifty-five states, the majority of the nations of the world, with a total population of 903 million, have adopted a neutral attitude. From these must be excluded seven European nations that are considered developed according to the United Nations criteria, nations whose neutral position can be attributed to historical or military reasons not related to the problem of underdevelopment. The seven nations are Finland, Sweden, Ireland, Switzerland, Austria, Spain, and Yugoslavia. Forty-eight underdeveloped neutral nations thus remain, a number that has recently been increased to forty-nine by the division of the United Arab Republic into two nations. The communist bloc, with only twelve countries, has a population of 1,008 million, and includes four underdeveloped nations (North Korea, Outer Mon-

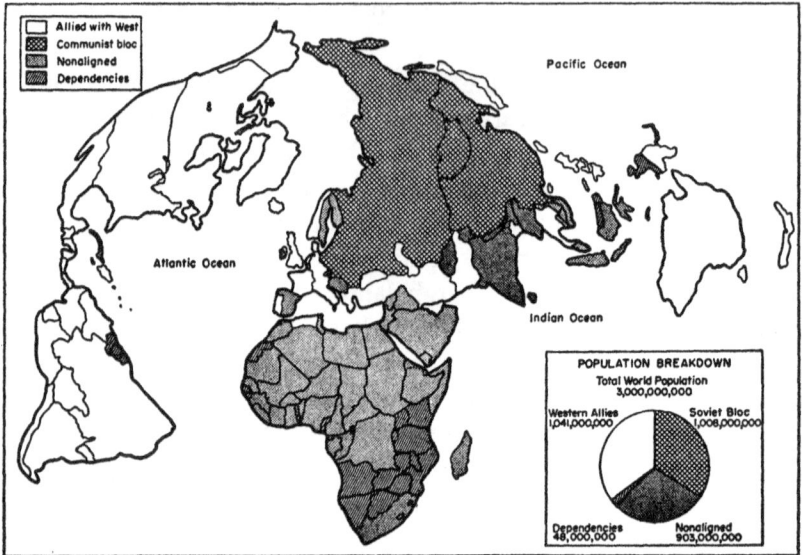

SOURCE: *New York Times,* International Edition, Weekly Review,
September 10, 1961.

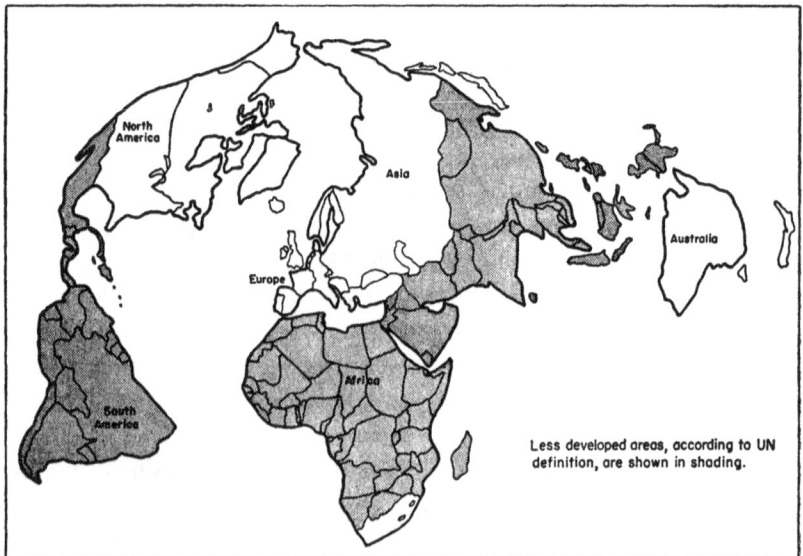

SOURCE: *New York Times,* International Edition, Weekly Review,
September 10, 1961.

golia, Vietnam, and Communist China). Communist China is subject to special classification as will subsequently be explained. The Western bloc and its allies include forty-three countries with a total population of 1,041 million and include twenty-seven underdeveloped nations, all Latin America with the exception of Cuba, plus Turkey, Iran, Pakistan, Thailand, South Korea, Taiwan, and the Philippines. From the foregoing, a high correlation is observed between neutralism and underdevelopment, since of the seventy-five underdeveloped countries, forty-nine are neutral or nonallied.

The opportunities for increasing the international influence of the underdeveloped nations appear highly attractive to the remainder of the countries that are allied to the Western bloc. In this regard, the Center for International Affairs of Harvard University observed that a trend in world opinion can be seen evolving from a norm of bipartisan bipolarity toward a more fluid tripolarity.[20] This trend is accentuated by attitudes of the leaders of the two rival blocs. In effect, important circles of United States public opinion, political as well as academic, have recommended that the United States should not discriminate, in its program of foreign aid, against nations that prefer to remain neutral. This point is established in the previously mentioned Harvard University study that was presented to the United States Senate at the request of the Committee on Foreign Relations.[21]

Furthermore, the attitude of the Soviet Union toward neutrals has evolved notoriously in the post-Stalin era. For Stalin, the world was divided into two irreconcilably opposed "camps"—capitalism and socialism—and within this concept it was impossible to admit, much less to favor, the existence of neutral nations. A declaration that Stalin formulated in 1927 to a delegation of United States workers continued to inspire Russian foreign policy until the time of his death, in spite of the fact that the characteristics and conditions of the international system had varied notably since that time.

Stalin's statement was as follows: "In the further progress of development of the international revolution, two world centers will be formed. The socialist center, attracting to itself all the countries gravitating toward socialism, and the capitalist center, attracting to itself all the countries gravitating toward capitalism. The fight between these two centers for the conquest of world economy will decide the fate of capitalism and communism throughout the whole world. . . ."[22]

One of the most important characteristics in the change in international policy in the Khrushchev era has been the new attitude towards neutral nations and the underdeveloped world in general. Stalin's rigid concept was replaced by a flexible strategy. Undoubtedly the prophecy of Lenin, formulated in several of his works between 1921 and 1923, that the poor and colonial countries would become fertile ground for Communist penetration as real or potential allies inspired the Khrushchev conception.[23] A mention of this prophecy as being confirmed by fact was made by the Soviet leader in an address to the Indian Parliament in 1955.[24]

This concept was further enriched and accentuated by the strategy of Mao Tse-tung, as laid forth in his famous work *On the Protracted War*.[25]

On the basis of this new concept of international policy, the Soviet bloc opened an offensive of economic and technical aid to the neutral and underdeveloped world. The tactics have been summarized in an official publication of the United States State Department:

> In addition to demonstrating economic progress under communism, Sino-Soviet bloc aid promotes some very immediate "cold war" objectives. The very knowledge that it provides an alternative source of economic aid will, Moscow hopes, encourage neutral states to be more demanding in their relations with the free-world nations and more sensitive to the attitude of the Communist countries. Economic assistance also provides the bloc with a political entree into countries where its role has hitherto been very limited.
>
> With independence at hand or recently achieved, local nationalist leaders are understandably worried about the future. The bloc is now able to approach these officials—in the case of African states often through the medium of the Communist party of the metropolitan power—encouraging them, with concrete offers of assistance, to look to the bloc rather than to the West, for economic and political support.
>
> Neutral states are told in turn that the acceptance of bloc economic assistance not only is consistent with a true policy of neutrality but also contributes to their ability to follow an independent policy. Those nations which have chosen to remain allies of the free world are told

that, by becoming neutral and accepting assistance from the bloc, they would receive more, rather than less, assistance from the free world.

In practice, bloc officials and their local communist agents do all they can to discredit free-world aid programs and to encourage the local government to reduce and even break off relations with the free world. Before the bloc was ready, at least in posture, to replace free-world aid, local governments could not be expected to take such an irrational step. Today the bloc hopes to persuade them that such a step is both realistic and in their best interests.[26]

Latin America is not far removed from this strong current of neutral orientation. Its position is of high strategic value in the cold war, as it is composed of the largest number of underdeveloped countries recognizing United States leadership and as it constitutes the sole group of western nations belonging to the so-called "third world." The words of President Kubitschek of Brazil, previously cited in Chapter I, define the global situation in a warning of profound political projection: "We wish to join the Free World but we do not wish to become its proletariat." A confidential report prepared at the request of the OAS and the Inter-American Development Bank has recently revealed that Latin American intellectual circles are inclined towards a neutral attitude.[27]

And as an echo to the words of Kubitschek, Brazil—the largest, the most heavily populated, and the most influential Latin American country, whose diplomatic policy was formulated by Baron de Rio Branco long ago—attempted to outline a policy of international independence close to neutralism in the fleeting government of Janio Quadros. As can be seen in the study on Brazilian nationalism published in 1959 by the Instituto Superior de Estudos Brasileiros, the matter of neutralism was a subject for discussion in the orientation of the Brazilian foreign policy some time before Quadros' rise to power. In this study the pro's and con's of neutralism are examined according to the most widely held public opinion and the views of Brazilian policy-makers.

From the bipolar-system point of departure, the study presents a "pragmatic argument" in favor of neutralism, an argument that undoubtedly was underlying the attempt of Janio Quadros to reorient Brazilian foreign policy. The argument is brilliantly put forth and the analysis is particularly relevant to our examination of the concept of power politics in its dimension of influence. It is not difficult to observe the similarities of this argument to the Afro-Asiatic ideology of neutralism.

In addition to depriving us of the advantages of exchange with the East, the "Americanist" foreign policy of Brazil places the country isolatedly in the sphere of hegemony of the United States, a fact which constitutes the most burdensome disadvantage. Led by this policy to a total dependence to whatever interest the United States may have in utilizing it as a "key country," the nation becomes a mere tool. The greatest error of such an orientation is that the very objective in view is frustrated. *De facto,* in the measure that this policy is based, as is its intent, on practical purposes and proposes not only to serve a cause considered as an ideological imperative, but also to achieve advantageous results for the country, as a nation endowed with its own destiny, the results obtained will inevitably be negative. The factor which bestows its own destiny on a country, among other conditions, is its ability for self-determination, and the effective exercise of that ability. The country may be able, in the conjuncture of inevitable relative dependence to derive benefits from functioning as a "key country" since in some, and not unappreciable measure, it will acquire conditions for achieving other functions. In such a case even though the pressure system to which a country is subject leads it to act as a "key country," the fact that it might act otherwise assures it a certain margin of self-determination and gives to the "key country role" the price that the dominant country must pay in order to ensure the desired functioning. This is typically the case of Western Germany or Japan. When, on the contrary, the role of key country is something a nation aspires to, without having other means of strengthening its international position, the burden of payment in such a case falls on the weak country and not on the dominating one. The condition of being a key country in the strategic system of the dominating country must be brought about by the future key country itself at its own expenses and thus constitutes a certain "promotion."

It is the case of Formosa in contrast to Japan. It occurs with the weaker satellites of the Soviet Union in contrast to China. And it has occurred in South America with Brazil vis-à-vis Argentina, due to the lack of force of the neutral policy of the latter. One of the most significant benefits of neutralism, independent of the advantages of exchange with the East (or with the West for countries in Soviet orbit) is an enormous increase in the ability of self-determination. Situated between two blocs, the neutral countries, and each one *per se,* possess a bargaining power corresponding to their strategic importance. In this respect, Yugoslavia, Egypt, or India may be cited. The advantages resulting from a higher bargaining power increase as a result of the acquisition of arbitral authority. Given the impossibility, outside of certain limits, of using force to solve disputes over strategic advantages, through fear of overly increasing the risks of a war which neither side wishes to explode, the super-powers are being led more and more to appeal to neutrals for the solutions of impasses occasioned by the cold war. The neutral countries thus acquire an international importance disproportionate to their positions of power. The maintenance of the balance of power between the two blocs and the impossibility of obtaining, by military victory, a definite supremacy which would compensate the catastrophic effects of total war—premises which are being confirmed with time—implies that the United States–Soviet Union conflict must turn to negotiation and compromise, which makes the role of the neutral countries increasingly important. These countries will exercise in this incipient phase of the political-juridical unification of the world, a true international jurisdiction. The position of India in this respect is highly significant. Such a position will only tend to be consolidated if countries such as Brazil, probably leading the principal powers of Latin America, adopt a third position.

Lastly, it may therefore be observed, in defense of the neutral thesis, this fact that constitutes the most relevant contribution that underdeveloped countries may make to the preservation of peace, the collective security of the two conflicting blocs, and of the world in general. In the measure that the underdeveloped countries join the line of the third position, outside of the benefits accruing from such a policy, a Third World War would become practically impossible. Such countries would constitute a world public opinion which the two superpowers could not fail to heed. The Soviet–U.S. antagonism, in lieu of taking place in an open field—with the world divided between the two powers—or increasingly leading to bellicose forms and to the concentration on the dispute for strategic advantages—would have to engage itself in the conquest of world public opinion in a world which was less compromised and more independent. Such a situation would bring the antagonism to assume more parliamentary forms, leading to its final institutionalization.

It is evident, conclude the neutralists, that as long as the Brazilian "Americanist" thesis does not presently show any possibility of practical success, such possibilities for success are found by means of the adoption, on the part of countries such as Brazil, of a position of independence and non-commitment regarding the super-powers.[28]

It is evident that, notwithstanding the fall of Quadros, the controversy concerning the possibility of Brazilian neutralism continues to exist. The fact that a part of Brazilian public opinion expressed the possibility of carrying out a "Janism" without "Janio" is significant in this regard.

(b) *Countries that withdraw from the bloc to which they be-*
long and use the rivalry of the two blocs as a means for this with-
drawal: the case of Cuba

From a legal point of view it is controversial that Cuba could
have been expelled from the OAS, because the charter does not
consider such a measure. Whatever the legal answer to this
problem may be, the political fact is that Cuba is now outside the
Inter-American System, that she has recognized herself as a member of the Soviet bloc, and that the Soviet bloc has officially accepted the new member.

No attempt will be made in this section to analyze the causes
that led Cuba to withdraw from the Western bloc. We shall con-
fine ourselves to the analysis of the Cuban Revolution within the
conceptual scheme used in this study. In effect the Cuban international attitude constitutes an excellent illustration of how an
underdeveloped country can weigh heavily enough in the balance
of world power to be of importance without any relationship whatsoever to its military capacity. Power as influence appears here
in its full meaning.

In contrast to the position of the neutral nations, it cannot be
said that the defense of the Cuban in-group values constitutes the
foundation of its international position. In effect the Manifesto
of the Revolution recognized the congruence of the ideals and
destiny of Cuba, not only with Latin America, but also with the
United States. Thus the Manifesto has adhered to the Western
Hemisphere idea. Cuba could not pretend to support its position
by the argument of the neutralist countries that they are promoting
world peace. On the contrary, its alliance with the Soviet bloc
has brought the cold war to the Western Hemisphere, and this is
now one of the sources of greatest tension in the Americas and
between the two world powers. Nevertheless, the international
position of Cuba shares with the neutral countries the use of the
bipolar system to maximize its international roles and to utilize them
for the achievement of national revolutionary objectives.

From an international viewpoint these objectives are difficult
to determine. Will Cuba increase her political and economic links
with the Soviet bloc? Do the leaders of the Soviet bloc consider
Cuba as a permanent member, or rather as a "troubled ally" who

can oppose at any time the leadership of the Soviet Union or of China? Are the Cuban leaders planning to use the Sino-Soviet dispute as a means to maintain a fluctuating pattern of international behavior and to increase their influence within the Communist bloc itself? The possibility of prediction in this matter seems to be beyond the competence of any expert. Who would be so audacious as to predict the international behavior of unpredictable Castro and Khrushchev? Nevertheless, taking into account the strong opposition of the U.S. to Cuba and the relative economic isolation of Cuba in the Western Hemisphere, one can at least attempt an hypothesis in the answer to the first two questions. If Castro wants to maintain operation of the Cuban economy, he will be forced to increase the political and economic links with the Communist bloc. In the same way, if Khrushchev hopes to retain Cuba as an example of Communist achievement in the Western Hemisphere, he will be forced to help Cuba, politically and economically, as far as is possible within the flexible Communist international strategy. Even a shift of Cuba toward neutrality could be accepted by Moscow and Peiping, if at that moment the Communist leaders' interpretation of the international situation led them to believe that this new position of Cuba fitted into their international strategy. There is no need to demonstrate the self-evident fact that Moscow and Peiping would be disposed to do anything to prevent a return of "rebel Cuba" to the community of nations in the Western Hemisphere.

The sources of Cuban international influence are two-fold. First, its international position has introduced the system of balance of power into the Western Hemisphere, which previously had been excluded from the continent for three fundamental reasons: (a) the formulation of the Monroe Doctrine that guarded the hemisphere from the intervention of extracontinental powers; (b) the existence of the Inter-American System and its ideology based on the rule of international law and not on the consideration of the size or power of the countries—the ideology of equal formal status; and (c) the obvious inequality of the real status between the United States on one hand—a world developed power—and her twenty underdeveloped neighbors to the south, which automatically inhibited equilibrium of power within the continent. Such a system could only be broken through recourse to an extracontinental power of sufficient strength to oppose the United States. Historically these traditional patterns of power relationship within the Western Hemisphere were broken when Khrushchev announced that the Soviet Union was supporting Cuba against United States intervention and that she was even disposed to use rocket artillery for this purpose. There are at present two experiments in the grand strategy of development in the Western Hemisphere. Latin American countries are following the leadership of the United States and they have created an international program—The Alliance for Progress—to demonstrate to the world that modernization, economic development, and social revolution can be achieved through peaceful and democratic means. On the other hand, Cuba, following the lead of the Communist bloc, is attempting to achieve the same ends by using the formulae, the plans, and the grand strategy of development employed in the Communist world. Thus, the cold war has been linked to the problem of underdevelopment. The Cuban experiment has forced the United States to develop a new kind of diplomacy, the diplomacy of social revolution toward the nineteen remaining members of the Inter-American System. A small country, the island of Cuba, whose alliance and economic dependence upon the United States was taken for granted, has suddenly obliged the Colossus of the North to realize that this situation is completely changed. And this traditionally dependent small country has challenged the influence, the power, and the prestige of the traditional leader of the Western Hemisphere before the rest of Latin America. The Cuban situation has demonstrated that the most powerful nation of the world, because of lack of planning by its policy-makers and through misinformation supplied by its intelligence service, is capable of committing such an error as the frustrated Cuban invasion.

These two sources of influence resulting from the Cuban Revolution are now being used as weapons to continue to weaken the prestige of the United States in Latin America. In spite of the fact that Cuba has become an ally of the Soviet bloc, the Cuban policy-makers, through all means of propaganda, continue to express and disseminate the idea that the Cuban Revolution has particular characteristics and features that can successfully be followed as a model by the rest of Latin America. As Raúl Castro expressed it, Latin America extends before the Cuban Revolution like a dry plain that at any moment may be consumed by the revolutionary flame of Cuban example. This danger is so real, so dramatic that it can be said without exaggeration that American and Latin American policy-makers must take it into account in every instance of formulation of foreign policies. Through these modes of influence the Cuban Revolution has broken the traditional framework in which Latin American foreign policies were formulated and shaped. Even if the Alliance for Progress strengthens the Inter-American System, the trend of Latin American foreign policy is no longer confined to the Western Hemisphere but to the international system as a whole. The neutralist trend of Latin American countries, analyzed in another section of this chapter, is an indicator of this new situation. The Inter-American System is no longer a "closed system" but rather a regional system open to all types of interaction with the rest of the world. Through the Cuban Revolution, Latin American countries have become involved in world politics. This achievement has provided Cuba with influence and prestige in Latin America, and no responsible policy-maker could fail to recognize the fact.

(c) *Nations that find themselves within the system of one of the two world powers but constituting a battlefield of the cold war*

The case of these nations may be well illustrated by the situation of Bolivia with respect to tin. Bolivia forms a part of the Inter-American System with all of the attendant obligations, including those of the Rio de Janeiro Treaty of 1947 relative to hemispheric defense.

The Bolivian economy is highly dependent on the export of minerals, among which tin occupies a predominant place. The structure of its trade may be seen in Table XVIII.

Because of the rise to power of the National Revolutionary Movement in 1952, the government undertook a plan of economic development, based on strong state intervention, to industrialize the country, decrease as far as possible the dependence of its economy on tin exports, nationalize the principal means of production, and initiate a vast plan of agrarian reform. The nationali-

TABLE XVIII

STRUCTURE OF BOLIVIAN FOREIGN TRADE IN 1959
(in millions of dollars and percentages)

Exports[1]		%		Imports			%	
Minerals		69.2	89	Food stuffs		16.0	25	
Tin	52.9			Essential articles	14.6			
Wolfram	1.3			Others	1.4			
Lead	4.9			Raw materials		5.0	7	
Zinc	0.9			Semi-processed				
Silver	4.1			goods		3.0	4	
Antimony	1.5			Manufactured goods				
Copper	1.7			for industrial and				
Other minerals	1.9			mining use		4.2	6	
Other exports		8.5	11	Capital goods		24.2	37	
Petroleum and				Machinery	12.6			
deriv.	3.1			Transp. equip.	4.6			
Chestnuts	1.3			Tools	2.8			
Rubber	1.3			Other capital				
Hides	0.8			goods	4.2			
Lumber	0.4			Non-foodstuffs		9.1	14	
Coffee beans	0.6			Non-perishables	5.7			
Other exports	1.0			Perishables	3.4			
				Other imports		3.5	7	
TOTAL EXPORTS		77.7	100%	TOTAL IMPORTS		65.0	100%	

1. Gross value without deduction of foundry and transport expenses.
    SOURCE: Dirección Nacional de Estadística y Censo, Ministerio de Hacienda (Ministry of the Treasury), La Paz, Bolivia.

zation of the large tin mines and the subdivision and distribution of the enormous agricultural holdings among the *campesinos* were the two basic measures of the revolution.

The growing economic difficulties of the nation, aggravated by an unprecedented inflationary process obliged the United States government in 1952 to initiate a broad program of aid to Bolivia. If we add to the foregoing the fact that 34.7 per cent of Bolivian exports are destined for the United States and 44 per cent of its imports proceed from that same nation, a clear picture of the profound subordination of Bolivia to the United States is seen. It is within this economic and political context that the battle for tin has been waged, in which the two blocs competed for the favor of the Bolivian government through offers of large subsidies.[29]

Since the nationalization of the tin mines in 1952 the industry has been operating at a loss of $500,000 (U.S.) per month and has been incapable of reaching the quota set by the International Tin Council Agreement, which is composed of the principal tin producing countries and covers approximately 90 per cent of the total world production. In spite of aid given to Bolivia, the United States government has refused to support the inefficient state tin corporation (Comibol).

Recognizing the financial difficulties of Bolivia, the Soviet Union offered the government the installation of a tin smelter at a value of $10 million (U.S.) to be operated by Russian technicians. The Soviet offer was doubly attractive, for economic reasons and because it would fulfill a long-standing Bolivian desire to have its own tin smelter. Notwithstanding the fact that local Bolivian technicians considered the installation to be a poor economic venture, Bolivian Communists utilized all propaganda means to promote the Russian offer.

The situation was critical, given the fact that Bolivia occupies an important place in world tin production and the United States is one of the large consumers of that metal. Adding to this the clear intention of the Soviet Union to intervene in the world tin market, which it demonstrated by the dumping in 1958, the battle for tin between the two "world powers" was obviously important.

In these circumstances, the United States countered the tempting Soviet offer

... with a U.S. $10,000,000 offer of aid to build concentrating facilities and subsidize exploration work aimed at finding higher-grade tin deposits. The offer, however, is part of an over-all package deal made in conjunction with Salzgitter A. G., a West German government holding company and the Inter-American Development Bank. . . . The package may amount to as much as $15,000,000 including the United States' $10,000,000, but it also carries some formidable conditions. Bolivia's inefficient state mining corporation, *Comibol,* would have to streamline its operations, lay off improductive workers and accept guidance from foreign consultants.[30]

This offer, called "Operación Triangular," was accepted decisively by President Paz Estenssoro.

The foregoing data are relevant to an analysis of the international position of an underdeveloped country which, in spite of belonging to one of the systems and strongly depending on the leader of that system, became involved in world power politics.

This involvement may come from the international action of an underdeveloped country in a conscious effort to maximize its international role or from the action of one of the world powers—directly or through a member of the system—with the purpose of obtaining determined economic and/or political objectives. This last situation seems to have occurred in the case of Bolivian tin. However, in both cases, the involvement is translated in the maximizing of the international role of a small power and in a relation to the world balance of power with the obtaining of determined advantages by the underdeveloped country.

D. *Underdeveloped countries that may become middle-range, great, or world powers*

Indonesia, Pakistan, India, Communist China, and Brazil are the five countries that are outstanding because of their population and the potential or present importance of their economies regarding the possibility of becoming middle-range, great, or world powers.

Of the five, Communist China has most clearly demonstrated her ambitions of becoming a world power. The most evident indications of this fact are certain types of international action that are characteristic of a world power: the granting of technical and financial aid to other countries; a conflict with the Soviet Union over the leadership of the Communist bloc; and sufficient military strength to play a leading role in the Asiatic balance of power.[31]

Indonesia and Pakistan, because of their populations of 86,900,000 and 85,635,000 inhabitants, respectively, have a potential market for the creation of economies on which to base a status of coercive power. However, the retarded economic and social development of these countries is still so evident that any hope of a high power status—should such a desire exist, and there is no empirical evidence of the fact—would be mere wishful thinking even in the distant future.

With respect to India and Brazil, as we shall see in a subsequent chapter, the aspiration for a high power status has been circumscribed to date by manifestations of international leadership. Those in charge of formulating Indian and Brazilian foreign policy seem to have comprehended that whatever the future of these nations may be in the (coercive) power aspect, the low level of living and the present economic difficulties prevent these countries from

TABLE XIX

MAJOR COMPONENTS OF POWER STATUS OF FIVE UNDERDEVELOPED
COUNTRIES (INDONESIA, PAKISTAN, INDIA, COMMUNIST CHINA, AND
BRAZIL) COMPARED WITH A MIDDLE-RANGE POWER (CANADA)
AND A WORLD POWER (U.S.A.)

Country	Stage of Economic Growth According to Rostow's Theory[1]	GNP ($ U.S. million)[2]	Government Expenditures[3]			
			Total Government Expenditure[4]	Defense Expenditure[4]	Defense Expenditure as a Percentage of Total Government Expenditure	Expenditure Devoted to Participate in Technological Race of Special Military Interest (U.S. million)
Indonesia	Pre take-off	9,165.4	35,313	11,085	31.4	0
Pakistan	Pre take-off	5,612.6	2,730	696	25.5	0
India	Take-off	29,600.1	16,032	2,828	17.6	0
Communist China	Take-off	57,844.0	41,666	5,000	12.0	?
Brazil	Take-off (underway)	18,082.0	140,257	38,832	27.7	0
Canada	Maturity and high mass consumption	37,506.0	7,469	1,745	23.4	0
U.S.A.	Maturity and high mass consumption	515,000.0	109,941	45,013	40.9	2,000-6,000[5]

1. W. W. Rostow, *The Stages of Economic Growth* (New York: Cambridge University Press, 1960), pp. 44, 45, 127, and table.
2. The GNP figures were taken from the study of P. N. Rosenstein-Roden "International Aid for Underdeveloped Countries," *The Review of Economics and Statistics*, XLIII, No. 2, (May, 1961). All figures are estimated for 1961.
3. Government expenditures correspond to the following fiscal year: Indonesia (1958), Pakistan and India (1957-58), Communist China (1958), Brazil (1958), Canada (1958), U.S.A. (1958). Government expenditures for the following countries are expressed in millions of national currencies: Indonesia (rupiah), Pakistan (rupees), India (rupees), Brazil (cruzeiros), and Communist China (yuan). For Canada and the United States, expenditures are expressed in U.S. dollars.
4. With respect to currencies expressed see note 3. For total and defense expeditures of Indonesia, Pakistan, and India see United Nations, *Economic Survey of Asia and the Far East, 1959* (Bangkok, 1960), pp. 152-53. For Brazil, see Table XVI of this book. For Canada and the U.S.A. the data were taken from the *U.N. Yearbook of National Accounts Statistics 1959*, New York, 1960, pp. 44 and 264. For Communist China the data on defense expenditure were taken from United Nations, *Economic and Social Consequences of Disarmament: Report of the Secretary-General Transmitting the Study of His Consultative Group* (New York, 1962), p. 62, Tables 2-3. The percentage of defense expenditure in total government expenditure was taken from United Nations, *Economic Survey of Asia and the Far East, 1960* (Bangkok, 1961), p. 83, Table 32. Total government expenditure was calculated upon the two already mentioned data. The defense expenditure of India must be interpreted with caution because total government expenditure indicated in the table represents only expenditure of the central government. For the same fiscal year (1957-58) total expenditure of the states was 9,634 million rupees.
5. Charles Hitch and Roland McKean, *The Economics of Defense in the Nuclear Age* (Cambridge, Mass.: Harvard University Press, 1960), p. 246.

giving a practical meaning to these hopes in their existing stage of development.

Table XIX shows the three constituent elements of the power of these nations (in its coercive dimension) as described in Chapter I. Various conclusions may be drawn from this table. By definition, none of the underdeveloped countries included has achieved the necessary technological maturity to participate in world power politics in its coercive aspect. According to Rostow it is probable that within forty to fifty years India and China will have reached such a stage, in which case the amount of their gross national product will enable them to become full world powers.

However, it may be stated that even while Communist China has not reached the stage of technical maturity, the amount of its gross national product is higher than that of a country of middle-range power such as Canada, and the military budgets of both nations are approximately equal. These circumstances explain the fact that while Communist China is not technically speaking a world power as it has not reached technological maturity, the size of its economic potential—measured in terms of gross national product—permits it to act as if it were, allowing it to supply economic and financial aid to other countries.

Brazil and India, which have reached the take-off stage in differing degrees, still have an insufficient gross national product (lower than Canada) to allow them a high status of coercive power. However, as has been previously observed, both countries definitely translate their aspirations of a higher power status through acts constituting international leadership, that is, by acts tending to confirm their participation in world power politics in the dimension of influence. Power politics, in its coercive dimension is manifested at the present time on a local scale. Of the Brazilian national budget, 27.7 per cent is allotted for military expenditures and India dedicates a high percentage of its total budget to the same item.

Indonesia and Pakistan not only have not achieved technological maturity but are still in a stage previous to take-off. Their participation in world power politics (in the coercive aspect) is limited to a local scale.

NOTES

1. W. F. Knapp, review of Amory Vanderbosch, *Dutch Foreign Policy Since 1815: A Study in Small Power Politics* (The Hague: Martinus Nijhoff, 1959). The review was published in the *American Political Science Review*, LIV, No. 2 (June, 1960), 574.

2. Hans J. Morgenthau, *Politics among Nations* (3rd. ed.; New York: Alfred A. Knopf, 1960), p. 28.

3. Robert Bierstedt, "An Analysis of Social Power," in *Sociological Theory*, eds., Lewis A. Coser and Bernard Rosenberg (New York: The Macmillan Co., 1957), p. 152.

4. For the Weberian concept of power and its influence in sociological theory, see Peter Heintz (ed.), *Sociología del Poder* (Santiago de Chile: Editorial Andres Bello, 1960) published under the auspices of the Latin American Faculty of Social Sciences (FLACSO).

5. *Ibid.*

6. Bierstedt, "An Analysis of Social Power," in Coser and Rosenberg, *Sociological Theory,* pp. 154-55.

7. *Ibid.,* p. 157.

8. Harry M. Johnson, *Sociology: A Systematic Introduction* (New York: Harcourt Brace and Company, 1960), pp. 317-18.

9. For the definition of Canada as a middle-range power, see Hugh L. Keenleyside and others, *The Growth of Canadian Policies in External Affairs,* (Durham, N.C.: Duke University Press, 1960).

10. *New York Times,* International Edition, Paris, January 13, 1962.

11. *Ibid.,* December 30, 1961.

12. *Ibid.,* January 13, 1962.

13. W. Arthur Lewis, "Causes of Tension in West Africa, *Current,* 6 (October, 1960), 9-11.

14. *Ibid.,* p. 10.

15. Edwin Lieuwen, *Arms and Politics in Latin America* (New York: Frederick A. Praeger, 1960), p. 97.

16. Excerpts from the speeches made by Prime Minister Nehru, chief spokesman for the neutralist position, at the Asian-African Conference in Bandung, Indonesia, 1955, as quoted in David S. McLellan, William C. Olson, and Fred A. Sonderman (eds.), *Theory and Practice of International Relations* (Englewood Cliffs, N.J.: Prentice-Hall, Inc., 1960), pp. 323-24.

17. *Ibid.*

18. *New York Times,* March 5, 1961.

19. *Ibid.,* July 16, 1961.

20. *Ideology and Foreign Affairs,* a study prepared at the request of the Committee on Foreign Relations, United States Senate, by the Center for International Affairs, Harvard University (Washington, D.C.: G.P.O., 1960), p. 61.

21. *Ibid.,* p. 76.

22. Cited in, *Communist Economic Policy in the Less Developed Areas,* United States Department of State Publication, No. 7020, July, 1960, p. 5.

23. *Soviet World Outlook,* United States Department of State Publication, No. 6836, pp. 175-76.

24. *Ibid.*

25. For a study of Communist international policy based on the strategy of the prolonged conflict, see Robert Strauss-Hupe and others, *Protracted Conflict: A Challenging Study of Communist Strategy* (New York: Harper & Brothers, 1959).

26. *Communist Economic Policy in the Less Developed Areas,* pp. 8-10. For a historical analysis of the new international Communist policy toward the underdeveloped countries see David J. Dallin, *Soviet Foreign Policy after Stalin* (New York: J. P. Lippincott Co., 1961).

27. *El Mercurio,* Santiago de Chile, 1 de Julio de 1961.

28. Helio Jaguaribe, *O Nacionalismo na Atualidade Brasileira* (Rio de Janeiro: Instituto Superior de Estudos Brasileiros, 1958), pp. 252-55.

29. "U.S. and Soviet Battle Over Bolivian Tin; Two Powers Compete Through Offers of Big Subsidies," article by Peter Bart published in the *New York Times,* January 22, 1961.

30. *Ibid.*

31. John M. Lindbeck, "The China Problem Today," *Contemporary China and the Chinese, The Annals,* Vol. 321 (January, 1959). See also A. Doak Barnett, *Communist China and Asia: Challenge to American Foreign Policy* (New York: Vintage Books, 1961).

CHAPTER IV

INTERNATIONAL ACTION AND THE PRESTIGE STATUS OF A NATION

1. *International stratification and the prestige of a nation*

The intention of this chapter is to identify the types of international action that an underdeveloped country may select to raise its prestige status. Our task here is more complex than that in the previous chapters in which we identified types of international action in the economic or power patterns. In those cases we dealt with the objective aspects of stratification. We must now analyze the pattern of prestige that is particularly related to the subjective aspects of stratification. As we pointed out in Chapter I, status is always a product of the social evaluation of certain differences between individuals or groups; status is created by the opinions that rank these differences. This is the subjective aspect of stratification. If the values, in agreement with which the social evaluation is produced, coincide with the factors that produce the differences, we have a coincidence of *the image of the nation* and *what the nation is in reality.* We stated that it is highly improbable that such a coincidence would occur *in toto,* but given the fact that wealth and power are the predominant values in the world today, we might at least expect to find a high correlation. We added that this correlation would be higher if a larger amount of information were available to the groups or persons evaluating the differences.

The analysis of the information factor gives us the possibility of penetrating deeper into the subjective aspects of international stratification. Before the space flight of Colonel Glenn, empirical research was done in the United States to measure world reaction to its space programs and those of the Soviet Union. This research has shown that not only the political or intellectual elite of developed and underdeveloped countries but also the mass of public opinion have an image that is not substantially different, one from the other, regarding certain fundamental facts and beliefs. This image is composed of the following elements:

1. The strong conviction is held in the world audience that the United States and the Soviet Union are antagonists in a general global rivalry.

2. Sputnik I and its aftermath produced a drastic revision in the general world image of the U.S.S.R. In this reassessment, it came to be viewed as a power capable of offering a credible challenge to the U.S. and with the scientific and technological resources necessary to support that challenge.

3. Space developments appear likely to continue to offer to the public mind and imagination a convenient and compelling index or symbol of important aspects of national achievement. These include scientific and technological levels of achievement as well as the national capacity for mobilizing both human and material resources. Furthermore, in an obscure but psychologically important way, space programs apparently take on a manifest significance of the confident projection of national destinies into the future. In this latter sense, space programs give a society "the forward look," a type of index of national vision, confidence, aspiration, or ambition.

4. Intimately linked to the previous factor, research shows a certain decline in general opinion regarding the capacity of the United States for world leadership; parallel to this, "the credibility of Soviet claims for its system have been enhanced, and especially among underdeveloped nations that system appears to have gained attractiveness as a way of rapidly achieving technological productivity."

5. A substantial segment of world opinion appears to believe that the U.S.S.R. will emerge as the stronger military power in the next few decades.

The differences of opinion between the masses and the more sophisticated groups are apparent only at two points. "The U.S. still enjoys, especially among sophisticated and informed audiences, a superior standing in terms of over-all scientific and technological development and leadership; this appears to rest in part on the widespread traditional image of the U.S. eminence in these fields, in part of the strongly held image of the U.S. as a society in which the products of science and technology are widely diffused, and in part on the recollections of the U.S. as the source of vast material outpourings in two world wars." The other point of difference concerns the impact of space competition on the image of military strength. "On military strength over-all popular opinion in Western Europe believes the U.S.S.R. to be superior to the U.S. although more sophisticated opinion may see them as about equal." Elsewhere opinion is most often divided regarding military strength.[1]

However, these differences are notably less significant than the areas of agreement between the two classes of opinion. This fact brings us to the conclusion that within international relations there exists a certain field of world public opinion and that the modern mass communication media have reached such magnitude and intensity—at least in certain areas of information—that the creation of similar images can occur simultaneously in various regions of the globe. We stated in Chapter I that these same media have made a comparison of living standards possible between developed and undeveloped countries, producing the "revolution of rising expectations" that will grow with the greater utilization of these mass media in the underdeveloped countries.[2]

The fact that a universally disseminated image exists of the U.S. and the U.S.S.R. is easily understandable since both countries have the highest real status on the international scene and are leaders of the two rival blocs. The images of both nations differ little in the mind of the elite and of public opinion in general.

However, such a coincidence would be highly improbable if the mass communication media did not provide the necessary information for evaluation of the inequalities in real status. The world image would be reduced in the common public opinion to a much smaller world than the actual one[3] and would show a lack of accord between the image and reality because of a lack of sufficient information. Stereotyping and prejudice would fill the gap. For example, if we question an average man in Latin America regarding his "image" of Canada in terms of economic and military power, his answer, because of a lack of adequate background information, would undoubtedly place Canada in a lower position than that which she actually holds.

The common man will not know the great extent of Canadian financial aid to the underdeveloped countries, the considerable amount of its military budget, etc. Consequently, Canada's prestige, insofar as this depends on the synthesis of her economic and power status, will necessarily rank lower to the average man than it would if he were properly informed.

The image of a nation consequently will depend on the amount of information existing about it at the different levels. The policy-makers of a given nation, who have information at their disposal regarding the different nations that does not reach the masses, will therefore have a different image from that of the average man, if these additional data are significant.

Public opinion can control the foreign policy of a nation to a greater or lesser degree according to the characteristics of the national political regime, but the policy-makers, as long as they exist as such, will, by definition, formulate international action and decide the country's position with respect to the other nations of the world. As the international system is composed of the interactions of national groups and such actions are determined by policy-makers, it is their image of the stratified system that is important for our analysis.

In Chapter I, we have seen that the prestige of a nation is the image that is impregnated with social esteem, honor, or admiration. Our hypothesis is that the prestige of a nation is basically determined by two factors: (1) the synthesis of power and economic status of a nation; (2) the degree of agreement between the international behavior of a nation and the value-orientations of the international system.

As we now attempt to establish the international efforts of an underdeveloped country to raise its status in prestige, our analysis will first be directed to the study of the component parts of prestige, since these elements will indicate to the policy-makers the course of action to be followed in increasing the nation's prestige within the international system.

The status of a nation in the economic and power patterns constitutes the institutional bases of prestige; the stability of prestige in time rests, in great part, on these components. In other words, the prestige of a nation is firmly founded when it is based on its real status in the economic and power patterns. Its foundation is weaker when institutional substance is lacking and the basis for prestige is found merely in the agreement of the international behavior of a nation and the value-orientations of the system.

We may add a new element to our analysis if we consider the study of power in the previous chapter. There we stated that power, in its dimension of influence, may exist without being based on coercion and that in this manner it was possible for an underdeveloped nation to enjoy power without its proceeding from the real status in the economic aspect. Power, whether it be coercive or influential, is a source of prestige. Therefore, if a nation acquires influence, she is achieving prestige through means not linked to the real status.

Consequently we may state that there are two types of sources of a nation's prestige: (1) those derived from institutional bases that make it possible for a nation to have a high real status from the economic and military power point of view; and (2) those derived from the nation's behavior in the international system, whether this be to achieve a conformance with the value-orientations of this system or to obtain an influential position not related to its military might.

We have thus far examined the static aspect of prestige, as though it were something which once earned is never lost. We shall now consider the dynamic aspects in order to broaden the field of our analysis and thus determine new elements or factors that may serve as a source of prestige.

2. *The dynamics of the prestige of a nation*

In the dynamics of prestige, the image of a nation is the result of interaction among the traditional image, the present image, and the future image. We shall first describe what we may call the self-generation of prestige. "Prestige helps to build itself. Once acquired it tends to be far easier to augment it than it is to acquire it in the first place. Conversely, once a person [or a group] achieves a low prestige rating his actions tend to be seen as justifying the initial low rating and his public opportunities and powers are shaped in accordance."[4]

When the traditional image of a nation is impregnated with prestige, the prestige can then generate itself—persist when the causes that served as its basis have disappeared. Hans Morgenthau has wisely observed,

> One can safely say that in the two most critical periods of its history Great Britain owes its salvation, at least in part, to its prestige. When, in 1797, all of Europe was at Napoleon's feet and France concentrated all its efforts upon the destruction of Great Britain, a mutiny broke out in the British fleet. For a time two loyal ships were all that stood between the continent and the British Isles. In the winter of 1940-41, Great Britain was, for however different reasons, similarly helpless. In both situations, the awe in which the British name was held was one of the factors deterring its enemies from an attack that the distribution of material power greatly favored.[5]

In both cases it was the traditional image of British prestige derived from its invincible naval power that generated a prestige actually without basis.

In the example described, the achievement of the past has succeeded in creating a present image of prestige. Let us now examine a case in which this image emerges from achievement of the present, destroying the traditional image and projecting a recently acquired image towards the future. On October 5, 1957, the Soviet Union, "a nation which most Westerners had dismissed as industrially and scientifically backward,"[6] launched Sputnik I and achieved a drastic revision of the image the world held of her; the traditional image of a retarded country was rejected and in its place appeared the present image of a nation capable of producing the highest technology and of facing what at the time appeared to be the invincible United States power. The fact that its traditional image was associated with backwardness in many Western eyes served to increase the prestige derived from its surprising advance in the technological field. In effect, since the nation had appeared "retarded," its successful undertaking was the more laudable because it meant a strong dedication to a national purpose, a high level of aspiration and ambition, a capacity for adaptation to change, and a vision of the future that was associated with great capacity for realization. Overcoming the traditional image, the present image emerged and the projection of the future image resulted from the interaction of the first two. As the previously cited United States survey showed, "a substantial segment of world opinion appears to believe that the U.S.S.R. will emerge the military stronger power over the next decades . . . space programs appear to take on significance as manifesting the confident projection of national destinies into the future."[7]

In like manner the traditional image of United States prestige, as the most powerful nation of the world until the time of the launching of the Sputnik, was altered. If, in spite of all its power, the United States had been incapable of out-distancing the Soviet Union, this meant that its dedication to a national purpose, its level of aspiration, its vision of the future, and its ability to make use of national resources showed a certain decline. The former image of its prestige was lowered and this loss also affected the future image of the prestige of the nation in world opinion.

Let us now examine a third example of interaction of the images of past, present, and future prestige. The traditional image of Communist China as a retarded, underdeveloped nation has been slowly changing because of its recent social and economic achievements.

China and India are roughly comparable in terms of their historic stages of economic growth and in resources; but China's rate of economic growth in 1958 was at least three times as high as India's. Especially in agricultural development and food production, where India's performance has been sagging, the Chinese record carries great appeal to under-developed Asian nations uncertain of which economic route they should follow. . . . For the first time in modern history a government appears to have found a way—however brutal its human defects—to solve the problems of large peasant under-employment and labor surplus. The mobilization of the unemployed mass of Chinese rural workers through economic communes, cottage industry, small pig-iron schemes, and all the rest is an achievement whose political and intellectual impact in less developed areas is bound to be immense.[8]

In this case the traditional image of China as an underdeveloped country of great misery is being changed, not by a spectacular impact on public opinion such as occurred with the Sputnik, but by a slow process of economic realization.

Success marks the present image of China's prestige, and this fact equally influences the future image of what that nation would become—with its population of more than 600 million inhabitants —when it will be able to develop fully from the economic point of view and raise the living standard of its inhabitants. The future image of its real status in power and in economic patterns in part determines the present image of its prestige. Its potential real status projects its prestige in the world today.

The present situation of the African and Asian countries which have acquired independence recently provides us with a further illustration of the dynamics of prestige. Anyone who has participated in a United Nations meeting in the past few years has observed the halo of prestige accompanying the action of those countries which have just acquired the position of member states in that world organization.[9] To what may this nascent prestige be attributed, a prestige that is not based on spectacular or hard-won achievements? How can it be explained that these nations have more prestige, in the eyes of many observers, than the Latin American nations, in spite of the fact that the Latin American nations have a higher level of economic development, political organization, and educational advance—in short, a higher real status.

In an international system composed of nation-states, these peoples have succeeded in acquiring the formal status of nation. They have established themselves in international life with a great sense of cohesion, constituting a majority Afro-Asiatic bloc, and they are trying to define their international personality by neutrality. They represent the principal area of conflict in the cold war between the two world powers; they are a new factor, not yet defined, on the international scene. Their prestige does not come from a traditional image, since they did not previously exist as nations, but is based in part on their formal status as independent states. The latter allows them to effect political maneuvers because of their number and particularly because of the image of their future prestige, which depends on their capacity for future achievements and their ability to influence world power politics. Here again it is the image of future potential that projects its prestige on the image of today.

The preceding observations on the dynamics of prestige have shown: a certain resistance of the image to the process of change, as in the example of British prestige analyzed above; the possibility of an abrupt and radical change, as in the case of Sputnik I; or a slow and less drastic change occurring in Communist China. We have also seen the existence of an image of potential prestige or future image. "The image contains not only what is, but what might be. It is full of potentialities as yet unrealized"[10] that have sufficient effectiveness to reflect on the present image and impregnate it with prestige.

The case of British prestige illustrates an instance of self-generation of prestige. Here that image is characterized by a phenomenal capacity for internal growth and development quite independent of the outside world.[11] In the other cases the image of prestige changes as a result of an external fact. The characteristics of this external prestige-generating fact find their origins in the capacity of national groups to develop something in the present or future capable of provoking admiration and esteem or awakening sentiments of honor. The capacity may consist of dedication to a national purpose that requires organization and sacrifice for its fulfillment, of the ability to exercise the functions associated with leadership, of the aptitude to adjust to change and to adapt the behavior of the nation to certain shared values, and of competence in reaching a high economic or power status. The greater the difficulty in executing projected accomplishments, the greater the knowledge needed for them; the fewer the number of countries having been able to achieve them, the more decisive the impact on the previous image of that nation. If one examines the causes for the radical change in prestige achieved by the Soviet Union in the launching of the Sputnik, it will be seen, as the above-cited United States research has proved, that the image of Soviet prestige emerges directly or indirectly from the various factors we have just mentioned.

Except in the case of self-generation, the dynamics of prestige cannot operate except by the acquiring of information, since this constitutes the channel through which external facts influence the previous image. We have seen that modern mass communication media are of sufficient scope to obtain the universal dissemination of certain images. We now wish to analyze another conduit for the dissemination of information—propaganda.

Propaganda has acquired particular importance with the beginning of the cold war, since this new type of conflict "has been fought primarily with the weapons of prestige"[12] and propaganda has been utilized effectively to influence the dynamics of prestige.

"Propaganda is the management of collective attitudes by the manipulation of significant symbols."[13]   If we state the strategy of propaganda in terms of culture, we may say that it involves the presentation of a concept in a culture in such a manner that certain cultural attitudes will be organized toward it.   The problem of the propagandist is to intensify attitudes favorable to his purpose, to reverse the attitudes hostile to it, and to attract the indifferent or, at least, to prevent them from assuming a hostile bent.[14]

The object of propaganda, in relation to the dynamics of prestige, is the manipulation of the significant symbols to achieve a change in the past, present, or future image of the prestige of a nation.   If the Soviet Union wishes to destroy the traditional prestige image of the Western European nations held by the underdeveloped nations, its organs of propaganda utilize certain values that are particularly esteemed in those countries—such as independence, the self-determination of peoples, and social justice— and tries to stress contrary values in the image of the European nations—"colonialism" and "capitalistic exploitation."   Conversely, if the U.S.S.R. desires to strengthen its own image of prestige, it will stress its own rapid rate of economic growth, its military power, its opposition to colonialism, and its position as standard-bearer of social justice.   Similarly, the United States tries to increase its prestige by stressing its role as protector of liberty, its respect for weak nations, the excellence of its economic system, and its democratic regime; it attempts to decrease the prestige of the Soviet Union by emphasizing the characteristics of the Soviet system that operate against liberty, democracy, and the principle of nonintervention.   In the same manner a nation like Egypt, in order to affirm its leadership in the Middle East, will utilize all the most significant values associated with that area in its propaganda: nationalism, the need of an Arab bloc to counter attempts at intervention by the world powers, and the capacity of Egypt to champion the cause of Arab unity.

The application of symbols associated with prestige may be directed toward the emphasis on aspects of the real status of a nation from an economic or military power point of view, or it may point out achievements, acts, or potentialities related to other sources of prestige not directly related to the real status in the aspects mentioned.

3. *Underdeveloped nations and the means to acquire prestige*

Morgenthau has pointed out that "a policy of prestige is an indispensable element of a rational foreign policy."[15] We might add that for the underdeveloped nations this point is not only indispensable but also basic in the elevation of their real status.

Atimia, or its consequences, for the underdeveloped nations, has meant a loss or the nonexistence of the institutional bases upon which prestige in the international system may be founded. As we have seen, such bases are formed by institutions that make it possible for a nation to reach a high status from an economic and military power viewpoint. We have also seen that these nations occupy the lowest category in both respects, which means that the degree of prestige, in general, is minimal.

If prestige is represented by an image of admiration, esteem, and honor, how can the underdeveloped nations, which are the "retarded" nations in the international system, be accredited prestige in a world dominated by the values of wealth and power, when by definition they do not possess such attributes? How can their condition of underdevelopment, characterized by subordination and dependence within the international system, awaken admiration and social recognition by other nations? How can poverty and the lack of achievement evoke the feelings associated with prestige?

The nationalism of the underdeveloped countries represents simultaneously a reaction and an answer to this low classification in national prestige. The existence of the nation rests on a group conscience, on the feeling of belonging to the national body, on the importance of in-group values vis-à-vis the values of the out-group. This ethnocentric feeling, in accordance with which the values of the in-group are superior to those of the out-group, provides a compensatory mechanism regarding the lack of international prestige within the system in which the nation moves. As a reaction to the insecurity and inferiority that the people of undeveloped nations feel as a consequence of the lack of international group prestige, ethnocentrism appears as a defense mechanism that establishes national cohesion and identification with the group values. The policy-makers of underdeveloped countries find support in this emotional reaction and at the same time an impulse for the quest of an international policy of prestige.

Since economic development as the prime component of real status represents the master key to a rise in the real status of the nation, a development policy is considered a source of national prestige; therefore one of the characteristics of nationalism in the underdeveloped countries is a growing concern for the problem of economic development and the desire to promote it.[16]

However, the acquisition of prestige by means of a rise in economic status presents a serious problem to the policy-makers desirous of obtaining a higher national prestige. The slowness of the process of economic development is the primary difficulty. The process of economic growth is slow and gradual even within a policy of integral planning such as that of India. Taking the first five-year plan (1951-56) as a point of departure, it is calculated that per capita income during that time (281 rupees) can be doubled with the fifth five-year plan (1971-76) and thus will reach 562 rupees,[17] or a little over a hundred dollars (one rupee: $0.21 U.S.).

The Latin American countries, according to Brazilian calculations of Operation Pan-America will have an average per capita income of $480 U.S. in 1980 if the plan is successful.[18] Although some countries will have passed the take-off stage by 1980 and be self-sustained in economic development, their progress will nevertheless be relatively small in comparison with that of the developed countries in the same period.

Except in the case of the nations with a very high population, which are an infinite minority within the underdeveloped world, the rest of the countries will never achieve an economic status sufficient to serve as a basis for military power. Consequently, the prestige derived from a high real status in the economic and power aspects will always be limited to the economic pattern of their status.

However, regardless of the limitations, difficulties, and slowness that the process of economic development implies, it continues to represent the sole means by which the underdeveloped countries can establish the institutional basis by which prestige in the international scene is created.   Furthermore, for those nations which, because of their great populations and resources, may arrive at a high gross national product, this development also constitutes the economic support necessary for military power and the consequent access to other sources of prestige.   Finally, a sustained and rationally oriented national dedication towards economic development can supply a certain degree of prestige to a nation by the sole fact of the effort implied.   In this case the source of prestige does not come from an aim accomplished but from the feeling of esteem awakened upon observing a group dedicated to a national goal that is highly valued in the international system.

The acquisition of prestige through channels other than economic development presents two considerable advantages to the policy-makers of the underdeveloped countries—the rapidity and relative ease in contrast to the gradual and total effort that a development policy demands.   The common characteristic of all these sources of prestige is that they are not related to a rise in the real status of the economic and military power patterns.   We may then, in accordance with the preceding analysis, identify those sources: (a) the conformity of a nation's behavior with the value-orientations of the international system, (b) the creation of a power situation in its dimension of influence, (c) the achievements of a nation in the field of a specific activity, and (d) the exercise of the role of leader in a group of nations.

The first two situations have been previously described.   We shall now study the last two cases.   Concerning the fact that a nation can acquire prestige by having been outstanding in a specific activity, Machiavelli long ago pointed out, "Nothing brings a prince more prestige than . . . striking demonstrations of his personal abilities."[19]   The reputation of having achieved something that is highly valued acts as a base for prestige.   Morgenthau has called it "reputation for performance."[20]   The most outstanding "per-

TABLE XX
ATTAINMENT OF LATIN AMERICAN REPUBLICS IN HIGHER EDUCATION

Country	Census Year	Percentage Having Completed Higher Education[1]
Argentina	1947	1.4
Bolivia	1950	1.0
Brazil	1950	1.4
Chile	1952	3.4
Colombia	1951	1.0
Costa Rica	1950	2.0
Cuba	1953	1.2
Dominican Republic	1950	0.2
Ecuador	1950	1.2
El Salvador	1950	0.8
Guatemala	1950	0.8
Haiti	1950	0.1
Honduras	1950	0.3
Mexico	1950	1.8
Nicaragua	1950	0.9
Panama	1950	1.4
Paraguay	1950	0.7
Venezuela	1950	1.7

1. In general, persons having completed four years or more of higher education. The exceptions are: Bolivia, Brazil, Chile, Costa Rica, Guatemala, Panama, and Venezuela (which include persons having completed an unstated number of years at this level). Mexico: Persons having completed 13 or more years of schooling.

SOURCE: *Basic Facts and Figures: International Statistics Relating to Education, Culture and Mass Communications, 1959*, United Nations Educational, Scientific and Cultural Organization, Paris, 1960, 196 pages.

formance" of the past decades in the technological field was the launching of Sputnik I, and we have seen how this fact completely changed the prestige image of the Soviet Union. But this capacity required high economic status; we are now interested in establishing types of performance that can be accomplished outside the economic field. One of the areas in which a nation can distinguish itself is in the field of education. Although the educational level is limited by the degree of economic development of a country, variances can be observed in this field among countries in similar stages of development. Within a given region those countries which have been the highest in educational achievements will be credited with a higher prestige.

In Latin America two countries have distinguished themselves in the category of higher education, Chile in South America and Costa Rica in Central America. In Table XX it may be observed that these two countries have the highest percentage of university-educated persons in Latin America. This situation has been recognized outside the area; the *New York Times,* in describing the causes that have given Chile "a special historic position on the continent," mentions "her leadership in higher education and in cultural affairs."[21]   Similar statements might also be cited with respect to the advance of higher education in Costa Rica in comparison with her neighbors on the Central American isthmus.

Has there been a deliberate search for prestige through educational achievements by Chile and Costa Rica?   Have the policy-makers been more or less clearly aware that, given the resources and the population of these countries, the excellence of education might be a reason for an outstanding position in the region?   Or has it simply been a policy carried out on a national level, without intentional interest in international repercussions, which has later reflected on the international scene?   The answer to these questions would undoubtedly necessitate historic sociological research that is not within the purpose of this study.   The fact remains that a part of the prestige enjoyed by both countries today can be attributed to their distinguished level of higher education and that consequently educational achievement is one route to the acquisition of international prestige.

This brings us to the central point of the analysis of the relation between prestige and international action.   This point is that the conscientious search for an international policy of prestige is linked to the policy-makers' perception of the country's position within the dynamics of prestige in its three dimensions of past, present, and future image.

A policy of acquiring prestige is instituted when the present prestige (present image) or past prestige (traditional image) does not correspond, in the eyes of the policy-makers, to the prestige that the nation can or should have in the future (future image). The international objective of the policy-makers is to achieve, in the future, a coincidence of the nation's image in the international system with the image that they anticipate.   The search for international prestige arises therefore from a lack of unity between the images in the judgment of the policy-makers.

4. *The real status of a nation, leadership, and prestige*

Leadership of a group of nations may also operate as a possible means for acquiring prestige in a way not necessarily associated with economic status or military power. We shall illustrate this situation by three examples, two of which, Brazil and India, share a certain correspondence between the capacity of the nation and the form of leadership chosen. In the third case, Peronist Argentina, no such relationship exists.

A. *A policy of prestige corresponding to the real status of the nation: the case of Brazil*

Let us first examine the Brazilian case. In inter-American politics, Brazil has always aspired to a special place as leader of the Latin American nations. Its importance as a key nation in the inter-American policy of the United States has always been recognized. From what has this permanent aspiration of leadership arisen? Certainly not from its degree of economic development; Brazil is an underdeveloped nation with a per capita income of a little over one hundred dollars and with a lower gross national product than Sweden, in spite of the fact that its population is nine times larger than that of the latter country. Its armed forces are of little significance in international power politics, and its economy is highly dependent on other countries. It is the image of its future potentiality, of the high real status it is called to occupy within the international system, that explains its constant striving for an international policy of prestige. "Covering nearly half the surface of South America, and with half the continent's population, Brazil was the world's fourth largest nation (after Russia, China, and Canada) until the United States added Alaska. With no deserts, tundra or rugged mountains, the nation is 80 per cent rolling plateau, has the third greatest expanse of arable land on earth, more than all of Europe. . . . But Brazil's potential is not yet scratched. It has the world's greatest hydroelectric potential; 16 per cent of the world's forest; more than 1,800 kinds of edible fish swarm in Brazil's water; she has 600 million trees of rubber; the world's greatest iron deposits push through Brazilian earth in mountains of solid ore; bauxite reserves run to hundreds of millions of tons; the Amazon and Parana rivers are two of the world's largest sedimentary basins; with soil so rich that almost any crop will grow, Brazil is potentially one of the world's greatest agricultural and industrial nations."[22]

It is not necessary to go back to ancient history to find this image of future national grandeur in the vision of its policy-makers. Upon the inauguration of Brasilia—called the Capital of Hope, the symbol of the creative capacity of Brazil—President Kubitschek exclaimed, ". . . from this Central Plateau, from this lonely spot that in a short time will be the nerve center of a nation, I once more regard the future of my country, and I look into that dawn with unwavering faith and unlimited confidence in its great destiny." This statement was published in the Brazilian magazine *Manchete,* in an issue that emphasized the determination of the president to construct Brasilia and "awaken the giant." It is the same image of future prestige that President Janio Quadros perceived on returning from his world tour before assuming office: ". . . from a distance I became more convinced that Almighty God destined us to become a great people. . . . Through its immense size, its natural riches and the dedicated efforts of its seventy million people, Brazil is now asserting herself as a great nation. We have created, beyond any doubt, man's most successful civilization in the tropics."[23] He affirms that Brazil will be tomorrow a great power; Brazil is leading a revolution "against nagging Latin American feelings of inferiority before the world. . . . This rebellion is invincible," says Quadros, "it is a state of mind, a collective spirit, a fact of life that has already filled the nation's conscience and that no one will compromise or paralyze."[24]

Neither Kubitschek nor Quadros—the modern interpreters of the traditional Brazilian policy in the acquisition of prestige— overlooks the present real status of the country that gives rise to a very different image in the prestige pattern from that envisioned for the future. The policy-makers of Itamaraty know that the basic principle of foreign policy is a balance between the international role of the nation and its real status. From the comparison of the Brazilian underdeveloped state and the future image of the nation in the pattern of prestige the policy-makers have defined an international policy. The rise in Brazilian prestige can be brought about by combatting the underdevelopment of that nation and its Latin American neighbors, a program in which Brazil will be the leader. Brazil will thus obtain the necessary resources for her development, reinforce the Inter-American System to which she has traditionally adhered, and achieve a higher prestige through her leadership.

The definition of the international situation that led to the formulation of Operation Pan-America may be analyzed as follows: (1) the underdeveloped condition of Brazil and the other Latin American countries; (2) the need of Brazil and the other Latin American countries to obtain foreign capital and technical assistance for the struggle against underdevelopment; (3) the existence of the United States, a great economic power that could provide the indispensable aid; (4) the presence of an Inter-American System that unites the United States and Latin America in an international co-operative regime; (5) the ineffectiveness of this regime in taking action against underdevelopment; (6) the growing uneasiness in Latin America provoked by frustration at not finding the means to combat underdevelopment; (7) the permanent intention of Brazil, stemming from her search for prestige, to assume leadership in Latin America; (8) the urgent need of Brazil to devise means and resources in her offensive against underdevelopment and her dependence on the United States as a potential source of supply; (9) the increase in tension between the United States and Latin America manifested by the incidents that occurred during Vice-President Nixon's tour; and (10) the necessity that the United States find a solution to this conflict that will reaffirm her prestige in Latin America and make it possible for her neighbors to procure the required foreign aid.

The Brazilian policy-makers propose Operation Pan-America as a solution to the problem and as a means by which Latin America can obtain outside support to fight underdevelopment. Through this plan the United States can strengthen the Inter-American System, and Brazil can realize her aspiration of leadership in Latin America by focusing the attention of the group on herself as the nation that pointed the way. The prestige of Brazil thus emanates from the demonstration of her capacity for leadership.

Along this same line, the intention of President Janio Quadros to lead Brazil towards a policy of independence approaching neutrality may also be interpreted as a new effort to reinforce the leadership of Brazil by showing the possibility of a different international attitude to Latin America.

B. *A policy of prestige corresponding to the real status of the nation: the case of India*

The case of India shows certain similarities to that of Brazil. First, as in the case of Brazil, there is a definite awareness of the underdeveloped state of the nation: the fact that India has one of the lowest standards of living in the world is clearly perceived by the policy-makers. Along with its present image appears the profile of the future image that arises from its immense geographic area (India is the seventh largest country in the world, ranking after the U.S.S.R., China, Canada, the U.S.A., Brazil, and Australia); from its enormous population (India with its 400 million inhabitants is second only to China); and from its vast mineral and agricultural resources. The importance of its position in world affairs, derived from its size and geographic location, has been described by Nehru, "Look at the map. If you have to consider any question affecting the Middle East, India inevitably comes into the picture. If you have to consider any question concerning South-East Asia, you cannot do so without India. So also with the Far East. While the Middle East may not be directly connected with South-East Asia, both are connected with India. Even if you think in terms of regional organizations in Asia, you have to keep in touch with the other regions. And whatever regions you have in mind, the importance of India cannot be ignored."[25]

But in the case of India, a further element that is particularly characteristic of that country enters into the image that the policy-makers have of the nation. This image comes from the many centuries in which the civilization isolated by the Himalayas developed an emphasis on the cultural values of spirituality, religion, and philosophy. Indian school books point out that "one result of the immense wealth of the country and the fondness of the people for spirituality and philosophy was that they never felt any desire to bring neighboring countries under subjection. The Hindus did colonize foreign lands and spread their culture abroad but they were never an *imperial nation*" (italics in the original).[26]

"Today our civilization is not much different from what it was in the remote past."[27]   The creations of this civilization, which the University of Oxford has synthesized in its publication *The Legacy of India,* may be considered a valuable cultural contribution to the world.

The philosophy of Gandhi, which inspired the Indian movement for independence, "bases itself firmly on a reformed and enlightened version of the traditional culture," "stressing duty, self-sacrifice, non-violence and anti-materialism."[28] The concept of nonviolence gave the liberation movement its own particular meaning —the movement adopted the Indian traditions of the past that stressed the role of pacific means, and this proved an effective instrument in the struggle that won independence.   Nehru has stated that the Indian leaders were "aware that India had found its own strategy, its own means. . . .   It was not a question of a frustrated search for the proper road. . . .   We knew we were right. . . ."[29]

From the traditional image of India as a centuries-old civilization oriented by a peaceful vocation of spiritual and religious values, from its future grandeur born of its material and political potentialities, and from the successful strategy of nonviolence arises the need of presenting an original Indian contribution to world affairs.   How can India express its contribution in a world characterized by the existence of two rival blocs, the possibility of a nuclear war, the differentiation of the nations in terms of military power and economic status, and the breakdown of the colonial system in Asia and Africa?   "India had not only to present a characteristic image of herself to the world; she had also to make that image an effective one by diplomatic action, and to see that the interests she pursued were consonant with that image and effectively pursuable within the context of world affairs."[30]   Nehru expressed this need emphatically: "What does independence consist of?   It consists fundamentally and basically of foreign relations."[31]   The title of his book, *Independence and After* stresses the need for looking toward the future.

The fundamental characteristic of any independent international policy is concern for the national interest, but this concern may be conceived in various ways according to Nehru: "Some people may think of the interest of their country regardless of other consequences, or take a short-distance view. Others may think that in the long-term policy the interest of another country is as important to them as that of their own country. The interest of peace is more important, because if war comes everyone suffers, so that in the long-distance view, self-interest may itself demand a policy of co-operation with other nations, good-will for other nations, as indeed it does demand."[32]

The preservation of her independence in the international system demands that India be completely free of subjection to either of the rival blocs. This is the only means of maintaining her identity and promoting her national interest, both of which are based on the higher principle of peace. This position is also mandatory for the other newly independent countries of Asia and Africa, as well as for India. Neutralism leads to the creation of "areas of peace" that will tend to decrease the tension and conflict created by the two rival world blocs.

National interest, so conceived, should also include earnest efforts to ameliorate other conditions causing international conflict, e.g., colonialism and racial discrimination. Anticolonialism, together with the affirmation of peace, gives a dynamic sense to the Indian independence movement, projects it to the continents of Asia and Africa, and relates it to all movements for national liberation. Opposition to racial discrimination stresses the value of human equality, expresses at the same time the Asian and African demands regarding the apparent sources of both evils—the West— and contributes to the cohesion of the Afro-Asiatic bloc.

In this way Indian international policy amalgamates the values of peace and nonviolence, which surge from the cultural tradition of the nation, with the needs of national interest and independence based on the promotion of peace. The transfer of this concept to the international level leads to neutralism or the creation of areas of peace, to anticolonialism, and to the struggle for racial equality. India has thus become the interpreter for a great number of the Asiatic and African countries and formulates a proper policy for movements toward national liberation, which simultaneously express the universal orientation of its culture.

In the previous chapter we analyzed this same policy from the viewpoint of its practical effect of maximizing the international role of the nation by enhancing her influence through a neutral position. We have now considered it from the angle of leadership which, while it is closely related to the former point of view, is yet different.

Both expressions of the policy merge to create prestige, one emanating from the influence acquired by a neutral position and the other from leadership of a group of nations who identify themselves with the international attitudes of the leader.

In the international policies of both Brazil and India there is careful accord between the means employed to acquire prestige and the real status of the nation characterized by underdevelopment. The type of leadership exercised is not opposed to the global interests of the foreign policy of the nation, rather it strengthens them. In the example of Brazil, Operation Pan-America is the channel by which the country hopes to procure the financial and technical resources necessary for its policy of economic development; it is at the same time a procedure to reinforce the Inter-American System and the growing relationship between the United States and Brazil. In the case of India, there is perhaps an even greater awareness. Nehru has stated, "Ultimately, foreign policy is the outcome of economic policy, and until India has properly evolved her economic policy, her foreign policy will be rather vague, rather inchoate, and will be groping."[33]　The type of leadership exercised by India is not incongruent with its underdeveloped condition; on the contrary, the power and prestige that its position gives also serve to enhance its influence on the international system and facilitate the acquisition of financial and technical resources needed for its development.

C. *A policy of prestige not conforming to the real status of the nation: the case of Peronist Argentina*

The case of Peronist Argentina is distinguished, conversely, by a complete lack of correspondence between the type of leadership desired as a basis for acquisition of prestige and the capacity of the nation—its real status in the economic and military power patterns—to exercise that leadership. We shall now analyze the manner in which the international policy of prestige was constructed in Peronist Argentina.

Such a policy cannot be understood without placing it in the context of Argentine history from which certain outstanding elements emerge: the traditional image that the Argentines have held of themselves as a nation and, as a consequence, their traditional aspiration of holding a leading role on the Latin American continent.   Let us first examine the Argentines' image of themselves and then how this image is perceived by the outside world.

Sarmiento, one of the great figures of Argentine letters, described the manner in which the Argentines see themselves as follows: "Argentines of whatever class, civilized or ignorant, have a high opinion of their own worth as a people.   The other American people throw this vanity in their faces and act offended at their presumption and arrogance.   I believe that the charge is not unwarranted, but I am not concerned about it.   God help the people who do not have faith in themselves!   Great things have not been wrought for them!"[34]

As if echoing Sarmiento, Marcelo T. Alvear, President of Argentina from 1922 to 1928 and a member of the aristocracy of the country, stated,

Argentines refuse to accept any truth which makes them inferior to anyone else.   Theirs is the greatest city in the world, their frontier mountains the highest and their *pampas* the widest; theirs the most beautiful lakes, the best cattle, the richest vineyards, and the loveliest women.   They accept no qualifications nor the fact that there might be some other country which surpasses them in anything . . . perhaps it is this overwhelming pride of the Argentines that leads them to believe they can live aloof from any interdependence of nations; that they are self-sufficient without possessing even elementary industries; and they need have no fear of whatever changes may come.[35]

This image of their own national grandeur has been confirmed by observers from other Latin American nations and from Europe who come in contact with the Argentine people.

It is sufficient to cite Ortega y Gasset: "The Argentine people are not content to be one nation among many; they require an exalted destiny, they demand of themselves a proud future, they have no taste for a history without triumph and are determined to command.   They may or may not succeed, but it is extremely interesting to witness the historical trajectory of a people called to empire."[36]

What is the basis in present or historical reality of this Argentine self-image? What has been the importance and the role of Argentina in inter-American relations? A reading of the *Memoirs of Cordell Hull,* secretary of state in charge of implementing Roosevelt's Good Neighbor Policy, suffices to prove the outstanding role of Argentina in hemispheric international policy. Such well-known authorities as Professor Whitaker have also stated that

. . . politically, the Argentines have long played a leading role in South America and one which, making allowances for their country's much smaller size and resources, is comparable to that of the United States. They have aspired to play it more effectively, for they are the most dynamic of the South American peoples and are often called, not without reason, the Yankees of South America. As a result, they have resented the rise of the United States to leadership in the whole Western Hemisphere and its consequent intrusion into their sphere of influence, and many of them still denounce "Yankee Imperialism" with a fervor reminiscent of the days of Big Stick and Dollar Diplomacy. This state of mind lies at the root both of much of the antagonism that has marked the relations between the two countries in the past half century and also the coolness Argentina has almost always shown, under whatever regime, towards the Pan-American System.[37]

The image of themselves, consequently, if not fully shared, is at least supported in part by Argentina's role in inter-American relations and in general by the opinion that exists in informal circles of their particular traits.

This self-image, partially confirmed by the outside world, provides the historical and sociological background upon which Perón constructed his international policy of the acquisition of prestige. Let us examine the characteristics of the Argentine self-image as visualized by the Peronist policy-makers.

First, they acknowledge this self-image of the Argentine people that emanates from their historical context and their aspirations as a national group; second, the self-perception of the nation's status is further strengthened, not only by its partial recognition in the outside world, especially the Western Hemisphere, but also by the extraordinary wealth of the Argentine economy. This wealth is particularly evident in agriculture and livestock, and from this fact arises an image, almost a myth, regarding the inexhaustible richness of the Argentine soil.   Third, this self-perception of status seems fully confirmed by the enormous amount of foreign exchange accumulated at the time of Perón's assumption of power. Argentina had emerged from World War II with a credit of $1,700,000,000 in London and New York.   "This amount accounted for 62% of the available gold and foreign exchange reserve of all of Latin America.   Sixteen million Argentines, therefore, had the same means of payment abroad as seventy-two and a half million inhabitants of Brazil, Cuba, and Mexico, the three countries following Argentina in this regard."[38]

Such an image might have been at least partly tempered by a consciousness of the underdeveloped state of the country, but this awareness had not yet matured.   In the international system the world had not yet been divided into developed and underdeveloped countries, and the Argentine policy-makers were far from considering Argentina a backward country on the road to development. How could a consciousness of underdevelopment have been reconciled to the traditional self-image of aspirations of grandeur and apparently indestructible economic prosperity?   Furthermore, how could Perón and his advisors be intimidated by the economic future, given Perón's concept of economic affairs?   For him—as he once stated in a letter to the President of Chile—when a chief magistrate seeks to improve the standard of living of the workers, "everyone attempts to frighten him with the phantom of the economy.   It is all a falsehood.   Nothing is more elastic than this economy, which they all fear so much, simply because they are not acquainted with it."[39]

Upon this traditional self-image, fortified by the elements we have described, the international policy of Perón was constructed. The international program of the Peronist Revolution had been synthesized in the manifesto of the Group of United Officials a few days before the seizure of power:

> Comrades! war has plainly demonstrated that nations cannot defend themselves alone, whence comes the play of alliances that mitigate but do not correct the evil.   The era of the Nation is slowly being substituted by the era of the Continent.   Yesterday the feudal holdings united to form the nation and today nations unite to form continents.   This

is the purpose of war. Germany made a titanic effort to unify the European continent. The largest and best equipped nation should rule the destinies of the continent in its new formation. In Europe it will be Germany. In North America the leading nation will be the United States, for a time. But in the South there is no nation sufficiently strong to be the undisputed tutor. There are only two to assume such a charge: Argentina and Brazil. Our mission is to make our tutorship possible and undeniable. . . . Conquering all the power, our mission will consist of being strong—stronger than all the other nations together. We must arm ourselves—overcoming all obstacles, fighting against internal and external circumstances. Hitler's struggle in war and peace will serve as our guide. Alliances will be the first step; we already have Paraguay, we will have Bolivia and Chile. These four nations can exert pressure on Uruguay and it will then be easy to attract Brazil, because of its form of government and the large nucleus of Germans in the country. And with Brazil the continent will be ours. Our leadership will be grandiose, unprecedented, achieved by the political genius and heroism of the Argentine army. . . . Our generation will be a generation sacrificed on the altar of a higher ideal: the Argentine fatherland, which in future generations will shine with an unequaled light for the good of the continent and for all of humanity.

In the study of the development of this policy, let us first consider how the Argentine self-image is projected in Peronist propaganda by a content analysis of Peron's speeches and then examine how this policy was achieved in practice. Finally we shall examine the consequences of policy of prestige based on a false perception of real status.

We shall observe the manner in which Peronist propaganda utilized all the usual symbols of prestige to project the Argentine self-image of grandeur at home and abroad.

Excerpts from Perón's Speeches[40]	*Symbol of National Prestige Utilized*
The Argentine people have an extraordinary destiny to fulfill in the future history of humanity, and this history will be for better or worse in the same measure that our people comply with their historic duty.	Extraordinary destiny and mission of Argentina in the history of humanity.
We might define our attitude by stating that we desire to aid humanity without losing sight of	

the fact that we must help ourselves. . . . For two years we have
been sending supplies to Europe
and if Italy and France have been
saved from communism, a certain
credit must be given to the help
that we sent them. The same is
true with respect to Spain.

And I thank God that I am
president of such a people as ours
at this moment (in humanity)
when their reality is perhaps the
last hope of the world.

When I think that we have been
the first to announce this solution
to men (that of the third position
of "justice")[41] and when I see that
we have been the first to provide
it, I cannot but confirm my faith
in the high destiny that God has
wished to give our fatherland,
and my soul is shaken with emo-
tion on reflecting that the day is
not far distant when humanity, to
find a star shining in its darkest
night, must fix its eyes on the national emblem of Argentina.

The Argentine economy is the
freest in the world today. But
something has been forgotten by
the economists who now appear
everywhere, and that is the fact
that political economy has totally
changed because the world has
changed. From a selling world
we have become a buying world.
. . . The characteristics of political economy must be influenced
accordingly. . . . (Argentina must
produce—but in accordance with
her own needs and possibilities
and of those of the buyers. . . .)

Argentina's ability to adapt to
change. Full economic independence of Argentina.

I state only, but solemnly, that we are economically free! Ladies and gentlemen, I believe that this simple affirmation, if it were no more than a mere affirmation, would not have cost us the ill-will and hate of the economic forces of capitalism that we mutilate in order to have our economic independence precisely more than a mere "slogan" of political propaganda. Argentine economic independence is a vigorous reality marching onward!

Ability of Argentina to triumph over international capitalism.

Without false modesty, we state that the presence of Argentina in the world, whose importance will constitute no little benefit to this era of determined effort, also shows, as one of its immediate effects, our active contribution to the cultural world. The thoughts of our time have recently found an appropriate stage in Argentina for some of their most important crystallizations. I do not employ the word "appropriate" by chance. The peace our country offers, its distance, moral rather than geographic, from political passions, its sensitivity to all matters affecting the progress of science and the life of humanity, prefigure that stage where activities of the intellect can become abstracted in order to offer their conclusions to the world.

Cultural presence of Argentina in the world.

We now have the sufficient and necessary international personality to give opinions which constitute some hope of solution to the grave problems affecting nations. Estranged as we are by our na-

World leadership through the third *justicialista* position.

tional doctrine [*justicialismo*] from the ideological extremes of humanity, our voice has the character of serene and steadfast authority which is necessary for it to be heard respectfully by those extremes (the capitalist nations and the socialist nations) as a voice free from compromise. Free from all material [economic] and ideological ties, the Argentine republic can speak on an equal moral plane with the rest of the countries of the world; and our third *justicialista* position allows us to seek and always find the necessary compromises so that humanity, in that third position, may find its proper road.

There is no country without a material or moral debt to Argentina.[42]

Having identified the image of Argentina that Perón wished to create as a basis for his international policy of prestige, we shall now analyze how this policy was implemented, how it was translated into action before the world. The policy may be studied by examining the following aspects: (1) actions tending to affirm the economic independence of Argentina; (2) actions tending to express the scientific and technological advance of Argentina; (3) actions tending to strengthen the Argentine military powers; and (4) actions tending to emphasize the quality of Argentine leadership as sustaining a third international position and challenging the influence of the United States.

(a) *Actions tending to affirm the economic independence of Argentina*

The monetary reserves of $1,700,000,000 that Argentina possessed when Perón came to power allowed her to realize an increase in the prestige of the country by showing that she was fully independent from the economic point of view. Of these reserves, $764,000,000 were spent to repay the foreign debt and to nationalize the foreign-owned public services—gas, telephone system, Buenos Aires streetcar lines, port installations, and railroads. As has subsequently been demonstrated, the amount utilized by Perón to nationalize the telephone system alone would have proved sufficient for Argentina to construct a steel industry without the need for foreign credit.

(b) *Actions tending to express the scientific and technological advance of Argentina*

In this field Perón conceived the spectacular project of transforming Argentina into an atomic power. To this end one billion Argentine pesos were invested to finance the Richter "atomic plant" on an island in the south of the country. The investment was a colossal failure.

(c) *Actions tending to strengthen Argentine military power*

A considerable amount of the Argentine foreign exchange reserve was spent on modernizing the army and the other branches of the armed forces. As Perón himself declared, "The achievements in the field of National Defense constitute a brilliant chapter in the history of my government."[43]   In his message to Congress in 1951, he stated that military aeronautics "not only had created a national air consciousness, but had also carried out enormous material tasks so that the nation should be on a par with the rest of the world in this activity."[44]   For this purpose a national aeronautical industry was organized to give the country an *infraestructura aérea* that was the basis of the "national air consciousness" according to Perón.

(d) *Actions tending to emphasize the quality of Argentine leadership in sustaining a third international position and challenging the influence of the United States*

Clearly referring to the United States, Perón stated in 1952 that the Argentine people "had for many years been subject to the forces of capitalism, enthroned in an oligarchic government, and had been manipulated by international capitalism, which ruled here as in her own domain through the venial servants of the plutocracy. Weary of animal-like treatment under the yoke of iniquitous exploitation, an anti-capitalistic reaction fermented in the minds of our people and was seized upon by the servitors of communism to open the road to a new slavery."[45] From this description of Argentine reality and the polarization of the world between "Western individualism" and "collectivist conception" comes the establishment of the third *justicialista* position. The "third position," said Perón, "is a philosophy that unites doctrine and theory in the political, economic, and social sense; it is substantially different from capitalistic individualism and from collectivism in any of its forms" and it may be applied to the solution of political, social, and economic problems of the contemporary world.[46]

In order to impose this new international position on Latin America and the world, the Perón government converted the Argentine Embassies into propaganda centers for the dissemination of *justicialismo*, at the same time equipping them with "worker attachés," since a proper international policy, according to Perón, should be aimed not only at governments but also at people. A vast network of publicity services was organized, among which was the "Latin Agency," the first and only international news agency owned by a Latin American country, and the International Radiophonic Service of Argentina.

The Argentine diplomatic corps was put at the service of the Peronist aspiration of making Argentina a continental power. To this end Perón attempted to influence the internal politics of several Latin American countries in order to establish governments favorable to *justicialismo*. All the weapons of modern propaganda were employed, and Argentina, in her new role as an economic power, even resorted to granting loans to her neighbors in order to project the image of an "economically free" country with a high economic status. It has been proven that on one highly auspicious occasion the Perón government entered into an agreement with the Presidents of Chile and Brazil to integrate these nations in a great economic union with Argentina—in which, of course, Argentina would be the leading member—a project that later failed because of the opposition of the Brazilian Chancery.[47]

In addition to the third position, the greatest tonic for the international policy of Peronist Argentina was Perón's challenge of United States influence on the Continent. The entire propaganda machine was mobilized toward this effort; latent or manifest feelings in the Latin American nations against the United States were exploited by this propaganda, and to the countries of Latin America, desirous as always of obtaining financial aid from United States sources, Peronist Argentina demonstrated its "economic independence" by stating through Perón that it would never seek recourse to foreign credit. "I will cut off my hands," said the Argentine president, "or I will leave the government before signing a document for a loan which would mean the collapse of our economic independence, which I declared at Tucumán the ninth of July, 1947, interpreting the feeling and the irrevocable will of my people."[48]

As the United States was the traditional leader of the Inter-American System, was not such open and complete opposition a proof of the high status of Argentina as a nation, a proof of its independence and its capacity for leadership? Was this not an interpretation of the latent or manifest anti-United States sentiment held by all Latin America and an affirmation of Argentine prestige?

The Argentine self-image of prestige that the international policy of Perón endeavored to impose on the inter-American and international systems has been established in previous paragraphs. We have stated that this international quest for prestige, contrary to the cases of Brazil and India, was based on a false perception of the real status of the nation, particularly regarding its degree of economic underdevelopment.

The foreign exchange reserve that Argentina possessed at the initiation of the Perón government allowed it to finance for a time a national and international policy propelled by the desire to acquire prestige but this policy overlooked the true conditions of the economic status of the country. Once these reserves had been expended by spectacular nationalizations, the armament policy, cancellation of the foreign debt, and the other measures intended to prove the total economic independence of Argentina, the hard reality of the true status of the country reappeared to demonstrate the fragile quality of the entire system.

It is not the purpose of this study to analyze the bankruptcy of the Argentine economy in the last years of the Perón government. We shall only point out the most obvious indication of collapse in the carefully constructed policy: the radical change in the position of Argentina toward the United States which Perón was obliged to effect when the economic situation of the nation acutely demanded it. If the Soviet Union had been interested in Latin America as a zone of active penetration at that moment, perhaps Argentina could have applied to that extra-continental power for support and maintained its antagonistic position towards the United States. But international circumstances of the moment did not permit this. Perón was obliged to resort to the United States for a 125 million dollar loan from Eximbank; in a sensational about-face he became reconciled with the government of Washington; and by ratifying the Rio de Janeiro Treaty on Reciprocal Aid, Argentina automatically became a military ally of the United States. In August, 1953, an "investment law" was promulgated, designed to attract the foreign capital to Argentina that had previously been repudiated by the policy of nationalization. In December, 1954, the Argentine Ambassador in Washington announced that "relations between the two governments had reached the 'peak of cordiality.' "[49]

Before a year had passed after this declaration, the Perón government was overthrown, and the economic expert Raúl Prebisch, appointed by the provisional government to report on the economic situation of the country, stated, "Argentina is in the most acute crisis of its history; more critical than when President Avellaneda adjured, 'saving by hunger and by thirst,' more so than in the crisis of 1890 and that of a quarter of a century ago in the midst of a world depression. At these times the country's productive forces were intact. Today this is not the case: the dynamic factors of the economy have been seriously damaged and an intense and persistent effort will be needed to re-establish its vigorous rate of development."[50]

NOTES

1. "The World Reaction to the United States and Soviet Space Programs," text of confidential U.S. survey on prestige rating abroad, *New York Times,* October 29, 1960.
2. *Possible Nonmilitary Scientific Developments and Their Potential Impact*

on *Foreign Policy Problems of the United States,* a study prepared at the request of the Committee on Foreign Relations, United States Senate, by Stanford Research Institute (Washington, D.C.: G.P.O., 1959), p. 70.

3. William Buchanan and Hadley Cantril, *How Nations See Each Other,* a study in public opinion prepared under the auspices of UNESCO (Urbana, Ill.: University of Illinois Press, 1953).

4. John W. Bennet and Melvin M. Tumin, *Social Life* (New York: Alfred A. Knopf, 1952), p. 109.

5. Hans J. Morgenthau, *Politics among Nations: The Struggle for Power and Peace* (New York: Alfred A. Knopf, 1960), p. 83.

6. Chester Bowles, *Ideas, People, and Peace* (New York: Harper & Brothers, 1958), p. 1.

7. "The World Reaction," *New York Times,* October 29, 1960.

8. John F. Kennedy, *The Strategy of Peace* (New York: Harper & Brothers, 1960), pp. 48-49.

9. These reflections are based on observations of the author at the Eleventh General UNESCO Conference held in Paris in November-December, 1960, which the new states attended for the first time. The author participated in the conference as a member of the Chilean delegation.

10. Kenneth E. Boulding, *The Image* (Ann Arbor, Mich.: University of Michigan Press, 1961), p. 26.

11. *Ibid.*

12. Morgenthau, *Politics among Nations,* p. 80.

13. Harold D. Laswell, "The Theory of Political Propoganda" in *Reader in Public Opinion and Communication,* eds. B. Berelson and Morris Janowitz (enl. ed.; Glencoe, Ill.: The Free Press, 1953), p. 177.

14. *Ibid.,* p. 178.

15. Morgenthau, *Politics among Nations,* p. 80. The book *France, Troubled Ally* by Edgar S. Furniss, Jr. (New York: Frederick A. Praeger, 1960) is an excellent case study of international policy of prestige of a developed nation. See especially pp. 476, 478, 491, 492, and 508.

16. See *Ideology and Foreign Affairs,* a study prepared at the request of the Committee on Foreign Relations, United States Senate, by the Center for International Affairs, Harvard University (Washington, D.C.: G.P.O., 1960), p. 37.

17. Government of India, Planning Commission, "The Second Five-Year Plan," 1956, p. 11.

18. Address of the Brazilian delegate to the Committee of the 21 of the OAS, quoted in *Revista Brasileira de Politica International,* Ano II, No. 5 (Marco, 1959), p. 101. It is evident that these calculations were made before the Alliance for Progress.

19. Niccoló Machiavelli, *The Prince,* trans. George Hull ("Penguin Books"; Baltimore, Md., 1961), p. 119.

20. Morgenthau, *Politics among Nations,* p. 81.

21. *New York Times,* April 2, 1961, p. 14.

22. *Time Magazine,* Latin American edition, June 30, 1961.

23. *Ibid.*

24. *Ibid.*

25. Jawaharlal Nehru, *Independence and After: A Collection of Speeches 1946-1949* (New York: The John Day Company, 1950), p. 231.

26. Vishwanath and Jagannath Grover, *Golden History of India* (Jullundur City: Kashmiri Lal and Sons, Publishers, 1953), p. 3.

27. *Ibid.,* p. 2.

28. *Ideology and Foreign Affairs,* p. 42.

29. Tibor Mende, *Conversaciones con Nehru* (Santiago de Chile: Editorial del Pacífico, 1956), pp. 23-24.

162   *International Stratification and Underdeveloped Countries*

30. J. D. B. Miller, *The Commonwealth in the World* (Cambridge, Mass.: Harvard University Press, 1958), p. 138.

31. Nehru, *Independence and After*, p. 237.

32. Jawaharlal Nehru, "Speeches," Ministry of Information and Broadcasting (New Delhi: Government of India, 1958), I, 207-8.

33. Nehru, *Independence and After*, p. 201.

34. Allison W. Bunkley (ed.), *A Sarmiento Anthology* (Princeton, N.J.: Princeton University Press, 1948), p. 116.

35. James Bruce, *Those Perplexing Argentines* (New York: Longmans, Green & Co., 1953), p. 7.

36. José Ortega y Gasset, *Obras de José Ortega y Gasset* (Madrid: Espasa Calpe, S. A., 1943), I, 661.

37. Arthur P. Whitaker, *Argentine Upheaval* (New York: Frederick A. Praeger, 1956), p. 129. The statement of Professor Whitaker undoubtedly does not apply to the Frondizi government which has fully co-operated with the Inter-American System. Professor Whitaker's book was written previous to the Frondizi government.

38. Alejandro Magnet, *Nuestros vecinos justicialistas* (10th ed.: Santiago de Chile: Editorial del Pacífico, 1955), p. 110.

39. Letter from Perón to President Ibáñez of Chile, published in *El Mercurio*, June 21, 1956.

40. All references to the Perón speeches which appear in the text, unless otherwise indicated, have been taken from the official publication *Los Mensajes de Perón* (Buenos Aires: Ediciones Mundo Peronista, 1952), pp. 477, 145, 241, 144-45, 417, 213, 244-45, 248.

41. The "third position," called *justicialista* by Perón, was a rather vague and empty "philosophy" of neutrality vis-à-vis the controversy of capitalism *vs.* collectivism, especially communism. We shall hereafter refer to this term in the Spanish words *justicialista* (the adjective) and *justicialismo* (the noun) to avoid an awkward translation.

42. Magnet, *Nuestros vecinos justicialistas*, p. 109.

43. *Los Mensajes de Perón*, p. 464.

44. *Ibid.*, p. 390.

45. *Ibid.*, p. 410.

46. *Ibid.*, p. 411.

47. For detailed information on this subject, reference may be made to the excellent study of Alejandro Magnet on the Perón regime in two works, *Nuestros vecinos justicialistas* and *Nuestros vecinos argentinos*, both publications of the Editorial del Pacífico, Santiago de Chile, 1953, and 1956, respectively. Further excellent works on the Perón regime are George I. Blanksten's *Perón's Argentina* (Chicago, Ill.; University of Chicago Press, 1953) and the analysis made by William W. Pierson and Federico G. Gil in their book *Governments of Latin America* (New York: McGraw-Hill Book Company, Inc., 1957). The Argentine sociologist, Gino Germani, has made a penetrating study of the Perón regime from the viewpoint of the irrationality of the Argentine working class in *Integración política de las masas y el totalitarismo* (Buenos Aires: Colegio Libre de Estudios Superiores, 1956).

48. *Los Mensajes de Perón*, p. 352.

49. *El Mercurio*, Santiago de Chile, December 29, 1954.

50. Raúl Prebisch, "Informe preliminar acerca de la situación económica," Octubre 24, 1955, Secretaría de Prensa y Actividades Culturales de la Presidencia de la Nación, Argentina.

PART THREE

A MODEL OF RATIONAL INTERNATIONAL BEHAVIOR
OF AN UNDERDEVELOPED NATION

THE METHODOLOGICAL FOUNDATION
OF THE MODEL

Part III has a dual purpose: (1) to build a model of a system of rational action for the international behavior of an underdeveloped nation that attempts to raise its real status in reaction to the *atimic* process; and (2) to compare the model with international reality for the purpose of pointing out various possible deviations with respect to the model. Chapter V will be concerned with the methodological foundation of the model; Chapter VI will construct the model itself and compare the model with reality.[1]

Before entering into the analysis, and for reasons indicated later in this chapter, the fact must be established that the model applies only to underdeveloped nations outside the Soviet orbit, i.e., those underdeveloped nations adhering to the Western bloc and to the neutral countries.

1. The classification of social action and the meaning and purpose of a model of rational international behavior

Why should we attempt to build a model of rational international behavior? The purpose of the model is to introduce greater rationality in decisions for action—to improve the efficiency of the system of means-ends relations in the formulation of the foreign policy of underdeveloped nations. This greater efficiency can only be reached by rationality of action.

The foregoing statement will be more readily understood if we consider the problem from a broader perspective by asking the following question: What are the various types of international action that a nation may adopt? International action is only one of several classes of social action. Therefore we can apply the conceptual scheme that sociology has constructed to classify social action to the classification of international action. For this purpose we shall adopt the classification that Max Weber has proposed in his classic work *The Theory of Social and Economic Organization,* not as an exhaustive classification, but as pure conceptual types constructed for the purposes of sociological research. Real action will more or less approximate these types or more frequently will result in a mixing of them. Max Weber states:

Social action, like other forms of action, may be classified in the following four types according to its mode of orientation: (1) in terms of rational orientation to a system of discrete individual ends (*zweckrational*), that is, through expectations as to the behaviour of objects in the external situation and of other human individuals, making use of the expectations as "conditions" or "means" for the successful attainment of the actor's own rationally chosen ends; (2) in terms of rational orientation to an absolute value (*wertrational*), involving a conscious belief in the absolute value of some ethical, aesthetic, religious, or other form of behaviour, entirely for its own sake and independently of any prospects of external success; (3) in terms of affectual orientation, especially emotional, determined by the specific affects and states of feeling of the actor; (4) traditionally oriented, through the habituation of long practice.

1. Strictly traditional behaviour . . . lies very close to the borderline of what can justifiably be called meaningfully oriented action, and indeed often on the other side. For it is very often a matter of almost automatic reaction to habitual stimuli which guide behaviour in a course which has been repeatedly followed. The great bulk of all everyday action to which people have become habitually accustomed approaches this type. Hence, its place in a systematic classification is not merely that of a limiting case because, as will be shown later, attachment to habitual forms can be upheld with varying degrees of self-consciousness and in a variety of senses. In this case the type may shade over into number two (*Wertrationalität*).

2. Purely affectual behaviour also stands on the borderline of what can be considered "meaningfully" oriented, and often it, too, goes over the line. It may, for instance, consist in an uncontrolled reaction to some exceptional stimulus. It is a case of sublimation when affectually determined action occurs in the form of conscious release of emotional tension. When this happens it is usually, though not always, well on the road to rationalization in one or the other or both of the above senses.

3. The orientation of action in terms of absolute value is distinguished from the affectual type by its clearly self-conscious formulation

of the ultimate values governing the action and the consistently planned orientation of its detailed course to these values. At the same time the two types have a common element, namely that the meaning of the action does not lie in the achievement of a result ulterior to it, but in carrying out the specific type of action for its own sake. Examples of affectual action are the satisfaction of a direct impulse to revenge, to sensual gratification, to devote oneself to a person or ideal, to contemplative bliss, or, finally, toward the working off of emotional tensions. Such impulses belong in this category regardless of how sordid or sublime they may be.

Examples of pure rational orientation to absolute values would be the action of persons who, regardless of possible cost to themselves, act to put into practice their convictions of what seems to them to be required by duty, honour, the pursuit of beauty, a religious call, personal loyalty, or the importance of some "cause" no matter in what it consists. For the purposes of this discussion, when action is oriented to absolute values, it always involves "commands" or "demands" to the fulfilment of which the actor feels obligated. It is only in cases where human action is motivated by the fulfilment of such unconditional demands that it will be described as oriented to absolute values. This is empirically the case in widely varying degrees, but for the most part only to a relatively slight extent. Nevertheless, it will be shown that the occurrence of this mode of action is important enough to justify its formulation as a distinct type; though it may be remarked that there is no intention here of attempting to formulate in any sense an exhaustive classification of types of action.

4. Action is rationally oriented to a system of discrete individual ends (*zweckrational*) when the end, the means, and the secondary results are all rationally taken into account and weighed. This involves rational consideration of alternative means to the end, of the relations of the end to other prospective results of employment of any given means, and finally of the relative importance of different possible ends. Determination of action, either in affectual or in traditional terms, is thus incompatible with this type. Choice between alternative and conflicting ends and results may well be determined by considerations of absolute value. In that case, action is rationally oriented to a system of discrete individual ends only in respect to the choice of means. On the other hand, the actor may, instead of deciding between alternative and conflicting ends in terms of a rational orientation to a system of values, simply take them as given subjective wants and arrange them in a scale of consciously assessed relative urgency. He may then orient his action to this scale in such a way that they are satisfied as far as possible in order of urgency, as formulated in the principle of "marginal utility." The orientation of action to absolute values may thus have

various different modes of relation to the other type of rational action, in terms of a system of discrete individual ends. From the latter point of view, however, absolute values are always irrational. Indeed, the more the value to which action is oriented is elevated to the status of an absolute value the more "irrational" in this sense the corresponding action is. For, the more unconditionally the actor devotes himself to this value for its own sake, to pure sentiment or beauty, to absolute goodness or devotion to duty, the less is he influenced by considerations of the consequences of his action. The orientation of action wholly to the rational achievement of ends without relation to fundamental values is, to be sure, essentially only a limiting case.[2]

We shall illustrate this classification with several examples, in order to appreciate the scope of its application to the field of international relations.

We shall first consider a hypothetical example that, however, has obvious and dramatic empirical reference in the inter-American policy of today. We shall suppose that the Organization of American States calls a meeting of foreign ministers to decide on action to be taken with respect to the Communistic penetration in Latin America represented by Cuba and that the objective of the United States, leader of the Inter-American System, is to request the application of economic and political sanctions against the Castro regime. The Latin American ministers of foreign relations will find themselves with the possibility of several alternatives in this situation. The selection of the alternative itself represents a rational undertaking, as the position that each ministry adopts must be made after careful consideration of the objectives, means, and consequences implied in the meeting. Furthermore, the means should be rationally weighed against the objectives, the objectives with the rational consequences implied, and the various possible objectives weighed one against the other. Some of the possible alternatives are: a ministry may decide to support the economic and political sanctions that the United States proposes to secure; not to support them and openly to oppose their adoption; not to support them but to assume a passive attitude in the meeting and abstain from the final voting; or propose the adoption of moral sanctions in lieu of the sanctions proposed by the leader of the system. Let us suppose that a Latin American government has invariably voted with the United States in all OAS meetings.

Rather than making a careful consideration of all the possible alternatives and their consequences, the Latin American nation decides to support the U.S. proposal simply because it has always proceeded in this manner in the past, because this resolution is sanctified by the principle of "always having done so."

The international action adopted is typically "traditional." It is no more than an obscure reaction to habitual stimuli, which tends towards the firmly rooted tradition as described by Max Weber. Let us now suppose that one of the Latin American governments has been the object of personal diatribes from Fidel Castro; that it has been described, for example, as a "lackey of imperialism," as "being sold to United States business"; and that the policy-makers of this government, in lieu of undertaking a rational study of the policy to be adopted, are guided simply by an emotional reaction—the result of their desire for reprisals—which causes the nation to decide, solely because of this consideration, to support the proposed sanctions. The action in this case is typically affective. Let us imagine a third possibility: the case of a Latin American country with a long tradition of representative government, whose policy-makers adhere to these values in the manner of a profound and deeply rooted tradition, believing that the inter-American policy should be closely linked to these same values and that this consideration should prevail above all others. Let us suppose at the same time that this government is convinced that, with the economic and political sanctions proposed by the United States, the government of Fidel Castro will fall and the Cuban revolution would thus terminate. And lastly, let us suppose that the leaders of the country consider that, with the fall of the Castro government, the immediate danger of Communist penetration in Latin America would disappear—with a consequent decrease in United States interest to provide technical and economic aid to the development of Latin America—and that such an outcome would be damaging to the economic interests of the country. If, notwithstanding this fact, the ministry of that country decides to support the U.S. proposal, this international action will be oriented with respect to values, the defense of democratic values. This action is guided by the adhesion to the values that determine its behavior, regardless of the cost to the economic aspect of the national interests. In other words, the action is oriented purely in terms of value.

Our example, as in Max Weber's classification, is nothing more than a conceptual scheme, a methodological procedure to approximate reality but not to encompass it in its multiplicity and complexity, within which the several "types" are combined and intermixed in the infinite variety of life.

But the Weberian classification, as well as the illustrations that we have made of it, has served to define our objective in building the model within which the rationality of an underdeveloped nation's behavior can be appreciated from the aspect of rationality with respect to ends. Our model will be analytic in the sense that, by means of the determination of a rigorously rational behavior in accordance with the desired ends, real international action can be observed as influenced by all types of irrationality (affectual behavior, traditional behavior, etc.) that are deviations from rational behavior. It has been said that "the use of a model for illuminating reality has immediate value, arising from the fact that we design a model for the purpose of inferring relationships within reality from the relationship within the model."[3] We shall try to have the model *describe* the main components that make up a system of rational action, *explain* some of the relationships among these components, and attempt to *predict* various types of action. Our model will thus conform to the definition of a model established by Levy and with the basic requirements of an analytical model as established by Singer.[4]

The fact that our model is based on the rationality of the action with regard to *ends* in the simple and well-known analysis of means-end rationality expressly eliminates certain (but not all) value considerations that are found dramatically present in the international system.

In effect, within the means-end model, the end is considered as a given fact, without further inquiry into its rationality or reasonableness. Stated in other words, the term "rational" is not applied to the end the action pursues but only to the means employed to achieve it.

This clarification is vital to our analysis, since otherwise a conflict would immediately arise between rationality as regards to ends and rationality as regards to values, given the bipolar nature of the present international system. In effect, as we have seen in Chapter IV, "There is a strong conviction held among the world audience that the United States and the Soviet Union are antagonists in a general global rivalry." This rivalry may appear not only as a struggle for world power but also as an ideological rivalry between two different concepts of the social system, as a rivalry between democratic liberalism represented by the United States and totalitarian communism represented by the Soviet Union, a rivalry between the Christian civilization of the West and the materialistic, atheistic civilization of the Soviet bloc.

The ideological content of the conflict may be perceived by the policy-makers and public opinion in the underdeveloped countries in one of the following ways: (1) the policy-makers feel that the rivalry between the two blocs does not imply a conflict of values; (2) the policy-makers feel that a conflict of values exists but that this conflict is foreign to national values; and (3) the policy-makers feel that a conflict of values exists and that this conflict affects the nation.

In the first two hypotheses stated, there is no conflict between the two types of rationality we are analyzing, and the policy-makers may, in either case, decide on a course of adhesion to the Western bloc—in varying degrees—or on a neutral position.

In the third hypothesis a conflict exists between the two rationalities. We shall clarify the problem with an illustration. Let us suppose that the policy-makers of a given country, after an analysis of the several alternatives available to achieve their objectives, conclude that a neutral position is the more advisable. In this way the nation would not only increase its influential position in the bipolar system, but it would also be in a position to obtain greater technical and financial aid for achieving its economic and social development more rapidly. Let us suppose that the nation in the example is a country of Christian majority and that communism is felt to be a threat to the fundamental values of Christian civilization. The defense of this civilization is a rational attitude with respect to values; therefore, from this point of view, adherence to the Western bloc appears to be the sole force capable of opposing the threat. In this case the criterion of rationality *with regard to ends,* where neutrality is considered the means to achieve the ends more easily, interferes with the criterion of rationality with respect to values, where neutrality is considered an ethically censurable position.

To resolve the conflict between these "two types of rationality" would lead to a philosophical and ethical analysis beyond the scope of this study. This, however, does not mean that we may disregard the existence of such a conflict. On the contrary, we recognize that this fact constitutes a pressing and dramatic dilemma for the underdeveloped countries. We simply state that a consideration of this nature does not fall within the means-end rationality that we have adopted in the construction of our model.[5] We shall, therefore, accept the adherence to the Western bloc and the neutral position as given facts without pronouncing upon the "rationality" or "reasonableness" from the point of view of value orientations.

Our model is not ethical—consequently we are not postulating certain ends as "good" or "bad"; we are not attempting to indicate the necessary behavior to achieve them, nor are we concluding that underdeveloped nations should conduct themselves accordingly.

Our model is realistic. On an abstract level it attempts to capture key elements of reality that affect the foreign-policy-makers of underdeveloped nations. Our realistic approach means nothing more than the recognition of the fact that any responsible leader of a country—developed or underdeveloped—should first look to national security and national interest before other considerations.[6] As we shall see on studying the various levels of analysis, this national interest can be conceived along broad or narrow lines.

The realism implied in our model can be illustrated by use of a paraphrase and a quotation. The first is inspired by Reinhold Niebuhr, whereby we may say, "If the underdeveloped nations fail in their attempt to raise their real status, and consequently their levels of living, their failure may in part be attributed to the strategic faults of the 'idealists,' who have many illusions, when they encounter themselves face-to-face with the realists, who have very little conscience." The quotation is from Spinoza: "When I have applied my mind to politics with the same freedom of mind as we use for mathematics, I have taken my best pains not to laugh at the actions of mankind, not to groan over them, not to be angry with them, but to understand them."[7]

Although this conflict between rationality with respect to ends and rationality with respect to values—within the limits indicated —is eliminated from our model, this does not mean that the model excludes the analysis of the role of value orientations and the normative framework implied in them. On the contrary, we shall later see that they play an important role as orientations of the international stratified system and as norms of behavior for the policy-makers. This analysis will lead to a better understanding of the meaning of "realism" in our model.

2. The relationships between the level of analysis in international relations and rationality of international actions

Having established the foregoing, we may now proceed to a further stage of our analysis, some elements of which are already implicit in the preceding considerations.

Professor Singer has stated that in an examination of the problems of international relations, two levels of analysis may be employed. "The two approaches, he suggests, though not mutually exclusive, represent different emphases and lead to different types of theories and explanations."[8] He has indicated that the analyst may look at the international system as a whole which is the most comprehensive of the available levels, "encompassing the totality of interactions which take place within the system and its environment. By focusing on the system, we are enabled to study the patterns of interaction which the system reveals. . . . In other words, the systemic level of analysis, and only this level, permits us to examine international relations in the whole, with a comprehensiveness that is of necessity lost when our focus is shifted to a lower, and more partial, level."[9]

The second level of analysis indicated by Singer is the international situation viewed from the perspective of one individual state, where the latter becomes the focal point for the study of international relations.[10] The level of analysis used in our model is somewhere between the two described by Singer. In effect, while it is true that our model of international behavior is situated within the perspective of an underdeveloped nation, this perspective is also focused on the total international system studied in Chapter I and on the regional international systems to which that nation may pertain. It is precisely the high degree of stratification of this total international system and their implications for the real status of the nation which work as motivations for the actor to establish the *end* of the rational behavior, the rise of the real status of the nation within the stratified system.

Consequently, the end that the nation within the model pursues is not placed within a limited framework of reference that might result from the perspective of a single state; the consideration of the total stratified system of the international society broadens the scope of the universe of selections and decisions within which the actor moves.

The levels of analysis considered in the building of our model undoubtedly have implications from the rational point of view of action with regard to *ends*.

In effect, the rationality of the ends of an actor may be judged from different perspectives. We consider here four that are relevant to our study: (1) that of the policy-makers who formulate the international policy of an underdeveloped nation taking into account the national interest; (2) that of the regional system to which the nation belongs; (3) that of the leaders of the rival blocs in the bipolar system; and (4) that of the total international system within which the nation moves.

Some examples will clarify this classification. India at present is spending a high percentage of its national budget on its military defense plan, principally because of its conflict with Pakistan and its proximity to the Soviet Union and Communist China. The trend has probably been accentuated by the quarrel with Communist China over Tibet. This situation may be judged as irrational, given the dedication of India to a policy of rationally planned social and economic development. An evaluation of the situation may also be made from the perspective of the Colombo Plan's regional system to which India belongs and whose object is to favor the economic development of the countries of Southeast Asia; the same evaluation may be made from the standpoint of one of the world leaders, the United States, which is vigorously helping India with the financing of its five-year plans; and lastly, judgment can also be made in the light of the stratified international system, since such expenditures are hampering a rise in the real status of India in the economic pattern.

To all of these evaluations, the Indian policy-makers may answer that India, as the United States or any other nation, must be the final judge of what is necessary for her own security.[11]

Similar examples may also easily be found in inter-American relations. Let us take the case of a nation that declines to enter the Latin American Free-Trade Association (Montevideo Treaty) because of the narrow concept of national interest on the part of the policy-makers, that is, with no justifiable reasons to substantiate such a decision. This attitude would be irrational, as much from the viewpoint of the regional international system—including the United States, which favors such integration—as that of the international stratified system, since the nation is artificially creating structural limitations to its development policy and consequently hindering the rise of its real status.

For the concept of rationality used in the model, we shall bear in mind the four levels of analysis, although basically (1) and (4) will have a certain predominance. Returning to the hypothetical case just analyzed, if the nation in our example had justifiable reasons for not entering the Latin American Free-Trade Association because such a decision would prejudice its economic development, its action, within our model, would be rational from the point of view of national interest examined objectively by the leaders of that country and also from the standpoint of the total international system since that nation would be selecting the best means for the rise of its real status in the economic pattern.[12]

3. *The relationship between the level of analysis used in the model and actors in international relations*

After establishing the relations between the different levels of analysis of international relations and rationality of action, we need to determine the connections between the level of analysis selected in our model and the approach that considers the nation-state as the main focus for the study of international relations.

We stated that, according to the level of analysis chosen, our model of international behavior is presented from the perspective of the underdeveloped nation-state, but also it takes into account the total international system, considering always the regional system to which the nation may belong and recognizing the evaluation of its behavior as it may be made by the leaders of the two rival blocs.

It is perfectly clear, then, that our analysis level has as its point of departure the national state and that the model is built basically on this focus.

This approach obliges us to clarify our position with respect to a long-debated problem in the theory of international relations. Given the fact that the international system is composed of national groups—the nation-states—that interact, it must still be determined how this interaction is produced. The problem may be clarified by a few questions. Is it the nation-state as such, i.e., considered as a collective actor, that makes the decisions? Is it France, the United States, Chile, Indonesia, Nigeria, or Mexico which produces these interactions? This approach has been called the states-as-actors theory. Is it the men of these countries who act and produce the interactions? This is the "individuals-as-actors" theory as expressed in the so-called "minds-of-men" theory of international politics, and its best-known formulation possibly comes from the following principle contained in the UNESCO Charter: "Since war has its origin in the minds of men, it is from the minds of men that war must first be eradicated."[13] From this viewpoint it would be the common man—traditionally seen as the victim rather than the beneficiary of international politics—who would appear to offer a way out of conflict, war, and power politics in general.[14]

A third approach is based on the theory of decision-making that has penetrated not only the theory of international relations and the science of public administration but also political science in general.[15] This theory maintains that international relations can be described "in terms of decision-making by identifiable individuals or groups of individuals," which shows that the study is basically "the study of human behavior in a particular social setting. . . . By focusing on decision-making it is possible to devise ways of improving the chances of getting more intelligent decisions. . . . In addition, it helps us to understand the extent to which the personality and the predispositions of the decision-maker enter into his choices of action."[16]

In accordance with this theory, the preparation and technical qualifications of the policy-makers' formulating international policy will have a fundamental importance in the rationality of the decision. The ministries of foreign relations therefore must be equipped with technically qualified personnel in order to make rational decisions. The practical implications of this theory for a realistic and rational international policy are evident. If the interactions of nation-states are the product of decisions adopted by individuals of the government staff, the knowledge of the factors that influence the decisions of the policy-makers of countries with which the underdeveloped nation has relations is of basic importance in the formulation of foreign policy.

As Frederick S. Dunn points out,

> The average decision-maker tends to operate on the basis of a speculative model of the general type of decision-makers from other communities he expects to meet in international negotiations. The accuracy of the model determines in large degree his success in achieving his objectives. . . . In the past such models have tended to follow two extreme types: the "Machiavellian" character whose sole aim was the enhancement of his own power or that of his nation and who used any means, however immoral, for these ends; and the "statesman" who paid little attention to power considerations but sought the settlement of issues solely on the basis of law and justice and the good of the greater number. . . . Neither of these speculative models has been of much use in calculating action, since only a few policy-makers met in actual life resemble them to any extent. The study of decision-making should greatly improve the mental pictures which negotiators have of those whom they are likely to encounter in their negotiations.[17]

As frequently occurs in the social sciences, all theories have a certain validity and the error consists of trying to establish one component to the exclusion of the rest. We shall clarify this statement by an example. To do this, however, a valid methodological clarification must first be made previous to the adoption of any position respecting the theories mentioned.

The states-as-actors approach has the danger of leading us into that old and erroneous habit of regarding social facts or occurrences as though they were *things,* as though they were actual entities, such as persons or objects—what sociology calls "reifica-tion."[18]   In effect, it is possible that individuals within a nation or that national groups, almost as a whole, will react against a given country.   Thus, Peruvian or Venezuelan national groups may react against certain characteristics of United States foreign policy to such an extent that they develop a general hostility against that country.   (One may recall the incidents of the Nixon visit in this connection.)   In the case of this totally hostile attitude, United States foreign policy is identified with the national group *in toto,* and one may validly speak of the reaction of minority or majority national groups against a given country taken as a whole.   What is methodologically incorrect, however, is to state that Peru, as such, reacts against the United States, as such, because both are abstract entities and do not exist as things or persons.

What actually happens when one speaks of global interactions between national groups—for example, the attitude of Bolivia in regard to Chile or of Cuba in regard to the United States, and these interactions truly correspond to the expression of national ma-jorities—is that there is an identification of the national majority with the nation.   This identification occurs because the collective objectives in a mass society—those of Nicaragua, Egypt, etc.—offer possibilities for "self-realization" and "self-aggrandizement" that could not be realized by individual efforts alone.[19]

Arnold Wolfers, in a symposium of specialists on international relations organized by the Rockefeller Foundation to analyze the theories mentioned, wisely pointed out that a more profound and realistic comprehension of international relations could be ex-pected by a simultaneous application of the "states-as-actors" and the "individuals-as-actors" approaches.[20]

Almost all analysts of international politics distinguish between nations that are satisfied with the *status quo* and others that are eager to change it.   The controversial question is whether states fall into one category or the other primarily because of the differences in the ob-jective conditions in which they find themselves.   According to the states-as-actors theory which ignores the factor of possible psychological differences, objective or environmental factors alone can account for either a *status quo* or revisionist attitude and behavior.   This theory expects a nation to be revisionist if denied the enjoyment of any of its national core values, provided it has, or hopes to obtain, enough power to enable it to seek satisfaction of its objectives. Instead, an analyst who focuses on individual actors and their varying predispositions will look for an explanation of revisionist behavior primarily in such traits of statesmen as their peculiar aggressive and acquisitive appetites, their rebellious temperaments, or their subjective dissatisfactions.[21]

Wolfers' analysis allows us to see that the simultaneous application of the theories mentioned may be very fruitful in the building of our model.

As was previously stated, the model of rational international behavior that we are attempting to build presumes an end: the rise of the real status of the underdeveloped nation within the international stratified system. The need for pursuing this end derives from the imbalance between the formal status and the real status of the nation, from the patterns of interaction characterized by superordination-subordination relationships that are a part of all stratified systems. In this sense our theory is related to the "states-as-actors" approach, as it emphasizes the existence of these patterns. To use Wolfers' example, the existence of these patterns is one cause of underdeveloped nations becoming "revisionists," and it is because of these same patterns that they are oriented toward an elevation of their real status.

But at the same time, the greater or lesser disposition that an underdeveloped nation has to carry out a system of international action destined to raise its real status effectively depends on the greater or lesser knowledge that its policy-makers have of the existing stratified system. It also depends on the technical qualifications of these policy-makers to formulate a foreign policy that will efficaciously serve this purpose, that is, to implement a policy that utilizes the available means with the greatest efficiency to achieve the end. It might be said, for example, that the present policy-makers of India, Brazil, and Argentina are highly conscious of the stratified system but that in other underdeveloped nations this awareness is notably weaker. An empirical study of this factor would probably show gradations within a continuum. As a consequence, the theory of decision-making provides us with an extraordinarily valuable conceptual focus for the building of the model.[22]

On the other hand, the approach based on the "minds-of-men" theory allows for an enrichment of the model by taking another perspective. In effect, whatever the idealistic connotations of this theory may be, it is evident that it bears the merit of facilitating the understanding of international relations by indicating the relation between the movements, fluctuations, or attitudes of public opinion within a nation and the formulation of foreign policy.

The influence of public opinion on the formulation of the foreign policy depends, in our judgment, on two factors:[23] (a) the greater or lesser extent of democratization of the political system of the nation and of its institutional structures, and (b) the types of problems being dealt with in the formulation of the policy.

With respect to (a), we may state the hypothesis that the greater the degree of democratization of the political system and the more facilities offered by the institutional structures to capture the majority opinions, the greater the influence of public opinion on the foreign policy. And inversely, with a greater degree of authoritarianism in the political system, the role of public opinion will be increasingly diminished, arriving perhaps, in the case of a totalitarian dictator, at total nonexistence. At the same time, however, if an authoritarian government wishes to carry out a given foreign policy, and if it needs the help and support of public opinion—as for example in the case of the international policy of prestige of Peronist Argentina—it can manipulate this public opinion in the desired direction by means of propaganda. In this case public opinion assumes a merely passive or "manipulated" role, in lieu of commanding an active role of influence.

Concerning the second point, (b), and with the exceptions implied in the consideration of the first point, public opinion will influence actively or will be manipulated passively in accordance with the type of problem being dealt with. We might have three situations:[24] (a) the problem is of vital interest to the public for diverse reasons (nationalism, religious content, etc.); (b) the problem is of relatively slight interest to the public; and (c) the problem is of no interest whatsoever to the public. In situation (a) the policy-makers could not disregard public opinion if the political system is effectively democratic, and they may disregard it to varying degrees if the political system approaches dictatorship. For example, if one Latin-American country attempts to seize territory from its neighbor, thus resolving by force a question of boundary dispute, the decision taken by the attacked country in the face of the aggression will be of the most vital interest to the public. With respect to any problem of type (b), the degree to which the policy-makers may disregard public opinion will be greater than in the case of (a) and such disregard will increase in direct relation to the amount of authoritarianism in the political system. Lastly, in case (c), democratic as well as authoritarian policy-makers will simply not concern themselves with public opinion. A democratic government such as Uruguay and an authoritarian government such as Paraguay may in like manner make a decision with equal lack of concern for public opinion regarding their government's participation in the activities of the International Geophysical Year since this decision does not interest any significant sector of public opinion.

The three theoretical approaches mentioned will be used in the building of the model.

4. *The model as a system of action: identifying the variables of the system*

It is implicit in the preceding considerations that our model of rational behavior in the field of international relations does not refer to any given type of action—military, economic, cultural, etc. —but to international behavior considered as a whole. In other words, our model refers to a system of action and not to specific international actions within certain fields; the latter obviously are considered in the model, but only as parts of the system of action.[25]

The idea of "system of action" appears, at times, in the literature of sociology expressed in rather complex terms. It is sufficient here to refer to the semantics of the word "system," which gives the understanding of link, co-ordinate, unite, relate, and classify in order. A system of action therefore means: a body of actions that are linked together, co-ordinated, united, related, and classified in order. In a system of international action, actions of all types —economic, military, political, cultural, etc.—are interrelated in the various connotations of the word "system," which supposes a certain interdependence among them.

The semantic approach to the term "system" coincides to a high degree with the meaning that the term has within the general statement regarding some fundamental categories of the theory of action formulated by Parsons, Shils, and associates. That study states that "the antithesis of the concept of system is 'random variability,' although no implication of rigidity is intended" and the system of action is defined as "the organized plurality of orientations of action."[26]

If we relate the semantic meaning of "system" to the idea of rationality, the connections between that meaning and the Parsonian definition are evident. In fact, if a "system" means the tying together, co-ordination, relating, and ordered classification of given acts, such a meaning necessarily implies that a system of action should be an "organized plurality" of actions. On the other hand, if the system of action is rational, this implies that the internal ordering of the actions within the system (the relations of interdependence) may not vary at random but by virtue of a rational organization and equation between means and ends.

With the foregoing established, it is now necessary to determine the variables that compose our model of a system of international action based on rationality with respect to ends. No model of a system of action can attempt to cover the totality of variables that exist in the concrete reality of life, nor can it encompass the whole scene of international relations in which the aspects of reality are more complex and varied, since they include the specific variables of the international system as well as the variables of the social systems of the nation-states interacting in the international system as such.

Our model will utilize only those variables that are relevant to the analysis of the international stratified system within the context of the analysis made in the preceding paragraphs of this chapter.

We stated in Chapter I that the international system is a stratified system within which the nation-states occupy differing status in relation to their position in the economic, power, and prestige patterns. In Chapters II, III, and IV, we have identified certain types of international actions (not systems) in the three patterns described. We have also established in Chapter I that the systems of international action of the underdeveloped countries are oriented towards a given end—the raising of their real status—selected on the basis of a general definition of the situation within the stratified system and motivated by a nationalism that reacts against *atimia* and underdevelopment.[27] We therefore have three of the variables of the model: the economic, power, and prestige variables in international behavior.

The fourth variable is also derived from considerations that are implicit or explicit to varying degrees in the preceding chapters. This variable stems from the need of analyzing the political systems of the nation-states in their interactions with the international system to which they belong.

An example taken from the modern history of international relations will clarify the concept. We refer to a decision made by Franklin D. Roosevelt during World War II, which proved decisive in the success of the war in favor of the Allies and was of extraordinary importance to the future of the world: the decision of the United States to aid Russia in 1941 through lend-lease assistance. This important decision has been analyzed in a brilliant study by Raymond H. Dawson. The study describes the process of policy-making that resulted in the decision to extend lend-lease aid to Soviet Russia, showing the relation of this series of decisions concerning policy toward the Soviet Union to the broader complex of foreign policy problems that simultaneously confronted United States officials and relating the decision to supply aid to the Soviet Union to the climate of public opinion within which the policy-makers acted.[28]

The analysis shows: (a) that the decision was made by Roosevelt in the midst of frequent friction among the members of his staff; (b) that the decision was deeply rooted in the total complex of the political system and of United States public opinion in 1941; (c) that internal political forces were of great importance in the determination of the method chosen by Roosevelt to reach an understanding with the Soviet dictatorship; (d) that considerations based on military needs played a role of primary importance; (e) that the President thought in terms of the United States and Great Britain "policing the world" after the victory over Germany was secured, and that, as a consequence, its future bargaining power vis-à-vis the Soviet Union would be considerably greater than what it was in reality; and (f) that his decision implied an underestimation of Soviet strength, an opinion that was shared by the majority of American interventionist spokesmen of the day. In a letter to Admiral Leahy, Roosevelt expressed his belief that "there was no need to worry about any possibility of Russian domination of Europe after the war."[29]

The factors indicated in points (a), (b), and (c) refer principally to the political system and United States public opinion, and the remaining factors are related to the international system in which the United States acted. This classification of the factors of the decision, which we have made here for the purposes of our study, has purely analytical objectives. As Professor Dawson has observed in the work cited, ". . . the mutual interaction of foreign policy and national politics [is of such a nature] that these two elements in the totality of the political process form a continuum and . . . neither can be adequately understood in isolation."[30]

5. *The orientation of the system of action in the model*
A. *Introduction*

Having determined the variables of the system of action, their orientation must be established, that is, the direction that an underdeveloped nation within our model assigns to its international system of action in relation to its purposes and interests.[31]

The selection of the orientation of the system will be studied analyzing the relation between the underdeveloped nation and the situation, and it presumes a decision among possible alternatives, which is guided by the gratification-deprivation polarity and by value orientations derived from cultural patterns.[32]

B. *The bipolar system and the universe of international choice for underdeveloped nations: the selection of the total aim of the system and the selection of types of means*

The possibility that a nation may make a selection among diverse alternatives presumes that the international system permits such selection. For this reason, we have indicated at the beginning of this chapter that our model applies only to underdeveloped nations outside the orbit of the Soviet bloc (underdeveloped nations adhering to the Western bloc and neutral underdeveloped countries). This does not imply that a selection among several alternatives is totally impossible within the international Communist system. The case of Yugoslavia, which was able to leave the bloc, is proof of this fact, and the Sino-Soviet rivalry is further confirmation that such a selection may be made. The limits that we have indicated in our model are determined by a general and elemental hypothesis that the interactions among the underdeveloped nations within the Communist orbit and the Soviet Union itself differ completely from those studied in our model.

In our model we assume that the underdeveloped countries may make the selection, although the alternatives are fewer for the underdeveloped nations allied with the Western bloc than for the neutral countries.

We have stated previously in this study that the total end that orients the system of action of an underdeveloped country consists of the elevation of its real status, but, as we shall see, this rise in status can be carried out in several directions. The determination, *per se,* of the most adequate direction through which the desired aim may be achieved implies a prior selection.

But if a field of choice exists with respect to the total end, there also exists, in varying degrees in a continuum, a series of selections that can be made among the different types of means employed to reach the objective. We shall later return to this point, but at present we wish to give an example to clarify the idea. Technical assistance needed by a country to stimulate its development is one type of means to reach a desired objective. To procure this means, the nation may utilize different procedures: it may apply to a world international organization (United Nations, UNESCO, etc.); it may make a request of a regional organization, such as the Inter-American System; or it may select a specific agency within that system, such as the Inter-American Development Bank. This selection refers to the channel through which assistance is solicited, but the universe of alternatives may also refer to other aspects. In what field of science or technology is the technical assistance to be requested? If we were to continue the example we would see that there are other aspects or specific fields of alternatives within this *type of means* that would broaden the universe from which the selection is to be made.

The selection of the total end of the system of action depends on the general definition of the nation's situation in the international stratified system. The selection that operates regarding the *type of means* established to achieve the end depends, in turn, upon the definition of the situation in the specific field to which the type of means refers (technical assistance in the case of our previous example). But, in order that the system of action of the nation be coherent and effectively organize the plurality of orientations in the attempt to reach the total objective of an elevation of status, the selections made for *each type of means* should be duly associated and interconnected to constitute an organized plurality. Stated in other terms, the gamut of selections, constituted of the relation among the selections made in each type, should be oriented to serve with the *greatest possible efficiency,* within the general and specific definition of the situations, the achievement of the total end of the system of action of the nation.

C. *The relationship between selection and gratification-deprivation: some examples*

We have stated that the selections—at the level of the total end of the system as well as at the level of the selections in each type of means—should be made in accordance with the rules of maximum efficiency. These rules are composed of a whole that is an internally co-ordinated and hierarchical range of the gratifications and deprivations that a nation may experience on effecting its selections. In the system of rational conduct of our model, the nation, on making its selections, will try to obtain the maximum gratifications and the minimum deprivations.

What are "gratifications" and "deprivations," terms that might seem at first glance to be rather abstract? Again we make use of semantics to explain the concepts. The word "gratification" implies recompense, reward, and advantage; the term "advantage" is semantically associated with profit, utility, benefit, priority, improvement, superiority, excellence, etc. In clarifying the idea we shall fix our attention on these five meanings: benefit, profit, improvement, superiority, and excellence, and we shall further illustrate them with examples.

We first consider the concepts of "benefit" and "profit" from an economic point of view. Let us presume that a country has received a grant from a United States foundation to finance a portion of its development plan; for example, the grant received by India from the Ford Foundation to aid the financing of its first five-year plan. (See Table XIII.) Let us also suppose that the grant does not stipulate the way in which the funds are to be used but that the agreement signed between the Indian government and the Ford Foundation simply states "the grant is to be employed for those activities of the five-year plan requiring utilization of foreign exchange in the manner the Indian government considers most appropriate for the achievement of the objectives of the five-year plan."[33] The government of India therefore finds it has alternatives in applying the grant: it may be used for technical assistance to bring in foreign technicians paid in dollars; or it may be used to build a dam to irrigate dry areas, which necessitates the importation of dollar-paid machinery for the implementation of the project. In our example, the Indian government will act rationally if it selects a *given field and a given form* of using the grant that will result in the maximum gratification in terms of "benefit" and "profit" from the economic point of view, bearing in mind the total objectives of the five-year plan, the greater or smaller shortage of dollars, and a series of possible alternatives that will appear in the definition of this particular field of decision.[34]

We now look at an example related to the concepts of "improvement," "superiority," and "excellence" to observe relations to the ideas of power and prestige. It will be remembered that in Chapter IV an analysis was made of leadership that referred to the acquisition of prestige and power (in its dimension of influence) by Brazil through her leadership in the formulation of Operation Pan-America. The position that Brazil secured by this means obtained for her, through the prestige and influence thus acquired, an improvement with respect to her former international position; on becoming outstanding as a leader, she reached a situation of superiority with respect to the rest of the Latin American countries by indicating the way to a solution of the internal conflicts existing in the Inter-American System. In this manner the foreign policy of Brazil achieved an excellence compared to the other Latin American countries who had not been capable of, or interested in, seeking the means to solve the conflicts in the Inter-American System. Within the Inter-American System, Brazil earned, at that time, a high degree of gratification in terms of "improvement," "superiority," and "excellence" in its international position.[35]   She realized, at that opportunity, the maximum of her prestige with the consequent results on her international influence.

Having established the concept of "gratification," we shall now examine the meaning of "deprivation," utilizing the same method of investigating the rich variety of semantics.   The word "deprivation" implies lack, despoliation, depredation, exaction, dispossession, removal, and disadvantage.   The term "disadvantage" is associated semantically with damage, deterioration, inferiority, and depreciation.   To clarify the idea of "deprivation," we shall first concentrate on lack, despoliation, depredation, and dispossession; we shall later discuss deterioration, inferiority, and depreciation.

Let us now interpret the first group of terms from an economic point of view.   In Chapter II we have seen that the underdeveloped countries are historically affected by the unfavorable aspect of their terms of trade.   As countries whose foreign trade is concentrated on the export of one or a very few primary commodities, the underdeveloped countries have witnessed the fact that, while the prices of manufactured goods that they must import rise on the world market in the majority of cases, the prices of primary commodities have shown a tendency to drop.   As a consequence, the underdeveloped countries have faced a chronic lack of foreign exchange to pay for their imports, have undergone a depredation regarding their expectations or calculations of having foreign exchange to finance their development.   The policy-makers, and the nations as human groups, have felt a certain despoliation or dispossession, tinged with diverse value implications that are associated with the injustice of the situation.   In short, the underdeveloped countries have experienced a deprivation in the complex network of interactions of their economies and the economies of the developed world.

We now consider the second group of terms ("deterioration," "inferiority," and "depreciation"), stressing particularly the idea of "inferiority" and studying the concepts from a political point of view.

At the American Foreign Ministers Meeting called by the Organization of American States in 1960 in San José, Costa Rica, because of a series of events that had occurred in the Dominican Republic, the meeting adopted a three-part resolution. First, it energetically condemned the participation of the Dominican Republic in acts of aggression and intervention in Venezuela that had culminated in the attack on President Betancourt. Second, it agreed to the breaking of relations of all the members states of the OAS with the Dominican Republic and established the partial interruption of economic relations of all the states with the Trujillo regime. Lastly, because of a draft resolution presented to the meeting, an international supervisory commission was created at a later meeting of the OAS to control the gradual democratization of the Dominican political system.[36]

As a consequence of the application of the sanctions censuring its international interventionist and aggressive actions, which were closely linked to its dictatorial system, the Dominican Republic suffered a serious deterioration and depreciation within the Inter-American System. The sanctions described placed the country in a manifest situation of inferiority with respect to the rest of the member nations of the Organization of American States. Such measures meant a deprivation with repercussions of every possible nature in the political and economic spheres.[37]

D. *The patterns of selection in the model: an analysis of the relationships among "gratification and deprivation," "superiority and inferiority," and the real status of the underdeveloped nations*

The semantic analysis of the concepts of "gratification" and "deprivation" have shown that these two terms have diverse shades of meanings that bear, in one way or another, a connotation of superiority and inferiority. The concept of "superiority" clearly emerges in the examples of the attainment of leadership by Brazil; that of "inferiority" applies in the case of the unfavorable terms of trade on the world market experienced by the underdeveloped nations, and in the situation of the Dominican Republic as a consequence of the sanctions applied by the Organization of American States.

Therefore we may state that "gratification," from the point of view of a nation's actions, is translated as the achievement of a superiority with respect to the position held previous to the actions and that "deprivation" is translated as inferiority.

These meanings are particularly relevant in the analysis of the international system as a stratified system. In Chapter I we pointed out that the superordination and subordination variables are essential components of any stratified system and that our basic hypothesis in this study is that the systems of international action of the underdeveloped nations may be studied as a reaction to the situation of inferiority in which these countries find themselves as a result of *atimia* or its consequences.

It is evident then that the selection among possible alternatives within the system of action of our model should be carried out so as to obtain the maximum gratification—with the implications of superiority—and the minimum deprivation—with the implications of inferiority. As the real status of the nation consists of its position of greater superiority or less inferiority in the economic, power, and prestige patterns, a rise in the real status involves a selection of those alternatives that bring a maximization of superiority and a minimization of inferiority. We have thus found the key to the system of selections of the model by centering our attention on its basic orientation, which derives from the total end pursued: the rise in the real status as a reaction to the *atimic* process or to its consequences.

E. *The patterns of selection in the model and value-orientations: the Inter-American System as a case study*

With the foregoing established, we may continue to another stage of our examination of the system of selections of the model, studying the relations among the various levels of analysis of the international system previously mentioned, the implications of those relations from the point of view of their rationality, and the value-orientations by which an orientation is attributed to the system of actions.

We have stated that within the total end of the system of action of the model, the underdeveloped nation is not situated within the narrow reference framework that her own perspective would imply, because the perspective is oriented toward the totality of the international stratified system in which the nation moves. In this manner the scope of the universe of alternatives from which the selection is made is broadened. And with such an enlargement of the universe, the sphere of rationality increases.

Now the fact that the nation is thus oriented depends partially on the value-orientations that motivate it. In effect the widening of the universe of alternatives for selection, as well as the orientation towards the total international system, demands a certain type of value-orientation that makes this possible.

The value-orientations derive from cultural patterns and assume the existence of normative frameworks of action. Such orientations are components of the systems of action in the aspects related to the motivation of the actor as well as to his orientation. Value-orientations may be considered as components of the situation in which the actor is found, as well as internalized components of the actions of the policy-makers.[38]

These value-orientations can be seen as alternatives for the actor; they can be considered "as dilemmas in which the actor has to choose" and they give rise to the five "pattern-alternatives" according to the classification of Parsons and Shils: (1) affectivity *vs.* affective neutrality; (2) specificity *vs.* diffuseness; (3) universalism *vs.* particularism; (4) ascription *vs.* achievement; and (5) self-orientation *vs.* collective orientation.[39] These concepts in our opinion shed light on the analysis of international relations. Values play an important role in a system of international action from several points of view and constitute basic elements of the decisions the nation should adopt within a general or particular definition of the system. In the first place nations are human groups that are characterized by the holding of certain shared values that are expressed on the world scene as manifestations of group aspirations.[40]

Secondly, the degree to which these common values are shared by the various strata of the nation contributes to a greater or lesser internal group cohesion—to its integration. As a study by Almond and Coleman concerning the political systems of seventy-five underdeveloped nations has pointed out, the under-developed countries are characterized by a lack of integration as human groups because of the existence of diverse strata that do not share the same values—or share them in widely varying de-grees—for ethnic, religious, racial, and cultural reasons. These characteristics of the cultural pluralism of these nations can be attributed in part to the limited and unequal degree of the process of modernization that has operated in the underdeveloped world.[41] This greater or lesser integration of the underdeveloped nations influences their foreign policy, as we shall see on analyzing the fourth variable of our model.

And third, the value-orientations of the socio-cultural system of the nation act not only as components of the situation facing the policy-makers but also as value-orientations of the policy-makers as persons. In effect, when a policy-maker cannot, with-out an intense feeling of guilt, violate a moral principle, the value-orientations function as an constitutive part of his personality.[42] The moral principles derived from cultural patterns have been internalized by the policy-maker and may considerably influence the definition of the situation and consequently his decision.

In the fourth place, the value-orientations are related to the rationality of the action. From the classification of the action made in the first part of this chapter, a dichotomy arises: rational action vis-à-vis traditional action. Both are developed in a norma-tive frame; the difference lies in the fact that, while in traditional action the normative frame tends to set the behavior of a nation rigidly in a given situation, in rational action with respect to ends the normative frame provides only certain general criteria.[43] For this reason it may be said that the more consistent a nation's selections, independent of varying situations, the more traditional she becomes; the more her choices vary with the situations, the more rational she becomes.[44]

It is, therefore, not difficult to understand the implications of value-orientations for rationality of action in our model, since it is necessary to specify what type of value-orientations are relevant in order for the selections of a nation to be consistent with the total orientation of the system of action—a rise of the real status of the nation.

It must, of course, be pointed out that total orientation in the system of action of the model presumes that the values related to the three variables of the stratified system—economic stature, power, and prestige—are values that are shared by the underdeveloped nations and that they motivate the reaction to the *atimic* process or to its consequences.

The value-orientations that the variables imply necessarily stamp the system of action of the model with a given orientation. We shall illustrate this by utilizing the dichotomy of the Parsons and Shils classification that is directly related to this orientation, that of universalism *vs.* particularism.[45]

The fact that the system of action of the model is oriented towards the values on which the international stratified system rests gives it a distinct tendency towards universalism. The fact that the system of action of the model is that of one nation-state moving in the stratified system and pursuing given purposes and interests related to the rise of its real status gives it the stamp of particularism. The fact that the underdeveloped nation equally considers the leaders of the rival blocs as elements of the situation accentuates the trend toward universalism, since the United States as well as the Soviet Union—because of their real status as world powers—move in the international system in accordance with universalist orientations and strategies. Lastly, the fact that some underdeveloped nations—those of Latin America for example— belong to a regional system implies that their systems of action must be equally concerned with value-orientations that transcend their national values, but which may at the same time imply a deviation from the universalist orientation. In other words, participation in a regional system may cause a nation to become situated in an intermediate zone between particularism and universalism.

We may now apply the body of concepts stated above to the case of the Inter-American System, considering the dynamics of its evolution in accordance with the universalism-particularism dichotomy.

As we have stated in Chapter II, because of the isolationist position of the United States in world affairs before World War II, the Western Hemisphere idea—and therefore the Inter-American System—acquired the rank of a major framework in which American foreign policy would mainly be developed. The United States orientation was far from being universalist (in its political but not in its economic aspects). At the same time, the Latin American nations guided their foreign policies by a more or less particularist pattern that, in any case, was completely divorced from universalist concerns. In the Chilean case, for example, the problems or conflicts derived from given historical and geographical situations—the boundary disputes with Argentina, the tensions with Peru and Bolivia as a result of the War of the Pacific, and the relations with the "Colossus of the North"— sketched in general outlines the particularist orientation of its system of international action. Similar examples may be found in the history of international relations of the other Latin American countries.

At the end of World War II, the United States abandoned its particularist orientation and, as the richest and most powerful nation of the world, turned, perforce, towards universalism. This orientation became intensified as the rise in the real status of the Soviet Union made that nation a world power and a rival of the United States, and both countries entered an era of struggle for world domination, each attempting to implant its own values (particularist orientation) and social systems in other regions of the globe. The phrase of Ambassador Stevenson "extend our vision . . . to all mankind"[46] is a synthesis of the new universalist orientation, and nothing illustrates the new attitude with greater brilliance than President John F. Kennedy's inaugural address.

As a consequence of the new orientation of the group leader, the Inter-American System—and the Western Hemisphere idea— lost its significance. As the United States became a world leader, Latin America was relegated to the role of a second- or third-rank ally whose support was taken for granted. The United States, instead of defining a new policy within the Inter-American System in accordance with a totally new situation, followed traditionally oriented patterns toward Latin America, and as she was following these patterns in the face of a completely different international situation, her international system of action regarding her neighbors to the South ceased to be rational.

The Latin-American nations' reactions were delayed (they continued in their traditional orientation), irrationally rooted in the habits of the past. Their particularist orientation continued to persist in spite of the fact that the international system had become universal because of the rivalry of the two blocs and the stratification of the world into developed and underdeveloped nations. However, as the new situation was perceived and defined by the Latin American policy-makers, by the common man, and by those nations considered as human groups with determined aspirations, the orientation of their international systems of action began to change, to become more rational—if not in a general sense, at least in definitions of the situation adopted by specific fields.

Let us examine a number of revealing cases. The creation of an institutional framework of typically universalist content, the United Nations, constituted a broad and varied field of interaction within which certain men of vision could define given situations in universal terms. Such was the case with the Chilean ambassador to the United Nations, Hernán Santa Cruz. During the discussion of the creation of Regional Economic Commissions of the United Nations for Europe and for Asia and the Far East to study the dislocations in world economy provoked by the war and to aid in the task of reconstruction, the Chilean delegate maintained that an Economic Commission for Latin America should be established, and he immediately encountered the opposition of the great powers, including the United States. The process that later led to the institution of ECLA (Economic Commission for Latin America) was based on a typically universalist argument; in effect, it was stated that the retardation and misery existing in Latin America were comparable to the destruction created by war in other areas, and the corresponding reports of the *ad hoc* committee set up to study the creation of the new agency mentioned all of the characteristics of underdevelopment without the utilization of that term which had not yet been coined. The pressure of the Latin American group on the United States particularly, and the other powers in general, finally overcame all resistance, and the new agency was constituted.

The institution of the Inter-American Development Bank can be attributed to a similar process of decision. Although the framework within which the decision was made did not have the characteristics of universality as in the preceding case—because a regional and not a world organization was under discussion—the arguments employed by the Latin American policy-makers who participated in its creation originated in a universalist perspective. Contrary to this perspective, the resistance that the United States showed was a further demonstration that the orientation of its international system of action toward Latin America was still guided by traditional patterns.

The formulation of Operation Pan-America and the Alliance for Progress—to which we referred in Chapter II—clearly indicates that the state of the Inter-American System is now defined in universal terms. The United States abandoned its system of particularist and traditional orientation toward the Latin American countries and replaced it by a system based on a new definition of the situation, realized in world terms.

Within this process, the Cuban case, which brought the cold war dramatically and definitely within the boundaries of the regional system, only reaffirms the universalist orientation of the United States and obliges the Latin American nations to define the problem with a similar orientation.

The neutral trends now vaguely beginning to appear in the international systems of action of some Latin American countries (see Chapter III) arise from the correlation between neutralism and underdevelopment—an international situation defined in universalist terms.

Nevertheless, notwithstanding all the indications of universalist action of the Latin American international systems of action, it cannot be affirmed that their systems of action are rational. On the contrary, we have the impression that the obscure habitual reactions to completely new situations that characterize traditional action continue in evidence, and thus these systems move away from rationality and universality. The empirical study of the functioning of these systems of action would undoubtedly reveal valuable data that would contribute to the enrichment of the incipient theory of international relations.

F. *Identifying the rational orientation of the system of action*

With the foregoing established, we may now study the determination of the precise orientation of the model's system of action within the total end pursued. This end—as we have frequently mentioned—is the elevation of the real status of the nation within the stratified international system. We have also stated that within this system the nations occupy diverse positions in the three basic patterns. These positions can be ranked in terms of economic stature, power, and prestige. The real status of the nation is determined by the complex resulting from the distinct positions of these ratings, that is to say, its status set.

Considering the fact that the over-all real status, the status set, is determined by these three variables, and the total end of the system is the rise of the real status, the obtaining of this end may give rise to a system of action oriented predominantly toward any one of the three patterns mentioned. Hence the system of action of the model may be oriented in three different ways: (1) an international system of action that pursues a rise in the real status oriented *predominantly* to a rise in the economic status of the nation; (2) a system of action that pursues a rise in the real status oriented *predominantly* in the power pattern; and (3) a system of action that pursues a rise in the real status oriented *predominantly* in the prestige pattern.

What is the relation between these three possible orientations and the concept of rationality in the system of action of the model? The answer may be found in the analysis of: (1) the relation between the status in the economic, power, and prestige patterns and the components of the status set of the nation; (2) the general definition of the international situation in which the underdeveloped nation is found; (3) the gratifications or deprivations that the nation may experience in terms of a greater "superiority" or "inferiority" of its status as a consequence of the orientation of the system; and (4) of the value-orientations that influence the orientation of the system analyzed in terms of the universalism-particularism dichotomy.

With respect to the first point, we have seen that the economic status of the nation is the basic component of real status, since status in the power pattern (in its coercive dimension) depends upon it, and both provide the institutional bases of prestige on the international scene. We also established that of the three constituent elements of economic status, two—the degree of social development and the amount of gross national product—depend on a third, the degree of economic development evaluated by the position that the nation occupies in some of the stages of economic growth as described by Rostow.

It is obvious then that a system of action oriented towards economic development, as a base for social development and the increase of gross national product, provides the only possible path to the elevation of the economic status of the nation, which in turn provides the base for the raising of power and prestige status, and, in this way, raises the status set.[47]

From the foregoing, the rationality of an economically oriented international system of action is clearly seen. Within such a system, actions based on power considerations (in its coercive dimension) or on prestige (when such actions mean a deprivation that affects economic development, as in the case of Peronist foreign policy described in Chapter IV) are subordinated to actions in the economic pattern, *whenever incompatibility among them appear.* In other words, actions in the power and prestige patterns become subordinated to the total system of action that is economically oriented.

Concerning the second point, the general definition of the international situation—made in terms of *atimia* and underdevelopment—confirms the rationality of the economically oriented system, inasmuch as the reaction to the *atimic* process, or its consequences, can only be achieved by a rise in the economic status of the nation. Only in this manner is it possible to encounter the resources necessary to confront the "revolution of rising expectations." Only thus can the nation enter the stage of self-sustained development and technological maturity that will allow it to approximate, in the fullest measure possible, its formal status as an independent nation in the relative sense defined in Chapter II. Only in this way can the nation find the means and resources to cope with the population explosion.

In regard to the third point, the rationality of the economically oriented system is equally justified because such a system provides the nation with the media to obtain a superiority in its status, and at the same time it provides the necessary resources to satisfy man's aspirations through social development from a domestic point of view. A maximization of gratifications and a minimization of deprivations is thus realized.

The rationality of the system also conforms with the value-orientations from a domestic as well as an international point of view. From a domestic point of view, through social development, the system tends to satisfy value-orientations of universalist content derived from the values of human equality and justice. From the international point of view, such a system of action satisfies the value-orientations of the stratified system by tending to raise the real status of the nation; it equally satisfies the value-orientations related to a greater "national independence" derived from the equalitarian ideology analyzed in Chapter I, and it also conforms to the principles of human equality and justice for the common man which are advocated by the leaders of the rival blocs, the United Nations, and world public opinion. The universalism that such value-orientations give to the system of action at the same time permits the nation to widen its field of alternatives for selection and allows it to influence the two world leaders and the developed nations in general with demands based on the equalitarian ideology in its double dimension—national and international.

Lastly, the rationality of the economically oriented system is in accord with the value-orientations derived from the ideology and the "diplomacy of economic development"[48] that the United Nations, its specialized agencies, international institutions in general, the two rival blocs, and the neutral world have contributed to create, transforming it into the "theme of our times."

G. *The rational orientation of the system of action and its postulates*

The rationality of the economically oriented system of action assumes the existence of certain conditions, mainly in the international field, which we shall consider as postulates, the first principles upon which the rationality rests.

These postulates are the following: (1) that the system of action of the model rests on a long-term conception of rationality; (2) that the self-preservation of the underdeveloped nation (defined in the limited sense that we shall later establish) is not threatened by, nor conflicts with, the long-term rationality that the model presumes; (3) that there are no exceptional circumstances that move the nation to carry out a policy of acquisition of prestige; and (4) that notwithstanding the uncertainty derived from interactions within the stratified international system—associated with the "cold war," the possibility of a nuclear war, and irrationalities of many varieties—it is possible for a nation to have a rational behavior.

Concerning (1), it is evident that long-term rationality can constitute short-term irrationality. The relation between the two is directly related to the cost of rationality. A classic Biblical example may be seen in the story of Esau who sold his birthright to his brother Jacob for a pottage of lentils. Short-term rationality existed in this case since a pottage of lentils is a means of satisfying hunger. But the cost of that pottage—the birthright, with the consequent access to all the rights and privileges that is implied— is too high a price in ordinary circumstances. So the cost of short-term rationality makes Esau's action irrational. But suppose that Esau had died of starvation if he had not eaten the lentils, then the action would be considered rational, since the cost is not too high, assuming that we consider the value of human life to be greater than the rights and privileges of the first-born son.

Similarly, in international decisions, a nation may find itself confronted with situations that imply a selection between the two types of rationalities. The nation's choice will depend on the general definition of the international situation, the definition of the particular situation of the given case, the immediate sources of gratification and deprivation involved in the situation, and lastly on value-orientations.

Let us assume the case of a democratic Latin American government with a multiparty system which, following a policy of supranational economic integration, wishes to adhere to the

Latin American Free-Trade Association. At that moment the government is supported by a coalition of parties. Among them figures a particular party of great importance, because of its political influence and its large number of representatives in parliament, that opposes the integration policy and has stated that it will withdraw its support if the government persists in this direction. The policy-makers in the executive branch who are desirous of realizing economic integration become involved in a conflict of interests implying various value-orientations within the universalism-particularism dichotomy and various types of gratifications and deprivations. The interpretation of the national interest is at stake. If the executive branch bows to the pressure of the party in the coalition government, it interprets the national interests by subordinating a supranational interest, that of economic integration, to a subnational interest, that of the party mentioned. In this case the executive branch chooses an immediate source of gratification, the permanence of the party in the coalition government, and is oriented in a particularist sense, since subnational gratifications have been preferred to supranational gratifications and to an orientation tending toward universalism. This example, which refers to the hypothetical case of a Latin American nation, is not far from the situation that Prime Minister Macmillan encountered when England decided to enter the European Common Market, notwithstanding the internal opposition in the English political system and the opposition of some nations of the regional system of the Commonwealth. Macmillan *seems to have abandoned*, in this case, the theory of circles of value-orientations and gratifications expressed by Churchill in one of his many addresses. In accordance with the Churchillian concept, England moved within three great circles: the Commonwealth with all that is implied from a political and economic point of view, the English-speaking world, "and finally there is United Europe. . . . These three majestic circles are coexistent and if they are linked together there is no force or combination which could overthrow them or even challenge them."[49] We have italicized the expression "seems to have abandoned" because the entrance of England to the European Common Market would appear to strengthen, economically and militarily, the Western bloc that is under the leadership of that prominent member of the English-speaking world, the United States, thus giving England greater economic power to increase her capacity for aiding the underdeveloped members of the Commonwealth associated in the Colombo Plan. Only the future—a long-run perspective—can tell whether, in reality, Macmillan departed from the Churchillian concept of the three circles.

The foregoing proves the complexity of decisions involving discrimination between long-run rationality and short-term rationality.

Our model postulates that the basis of an international action system in an underdeveloped nation is the *predominance* of long-term rationality. If we state this criterion as a postulate it is because we start from the premise that only that type of rationality can lead the underdeveloped nations to that stage of self-sustained economic development and technological maturity that is essential to their future progress. The model presumes that the specific decisions in the system of action are made by the use of a compromise that weighs in a calculating manner the gratifications, deprivations, and value-orientations, taking into account the essential elements of the situation at any given moment. But it is also presumed that, whatever compromises are made in each case, those compromises are always arrived at in accordance with a long-term criterion of rationality.

In summary, our model assumes that whatever the advantages of short-term rationality in international actions may be, long-term rationality *always prevails*. Such advantages cannot supersede the benefits on the international scene that the underdeveloped countries may derive, either from gratifications or from value-orientations resulting from self-sustained economic growth and technological maturity.

We may now look at the second postulate, which supposes that the preservation of the nation, as such, does not conflict with, nor is it threatened by, the long-term rationality implied in the model. This postulate is closely linked to one of the basic objectives of all nations considered as human groups with certain beliefs, shared values, and aims.

Professors Haas and Whiting have called it the end of self-preservation. "Self-preservation implies the desire to maintain social, economic, institutional, ideological, and therefore political systems as they are at a given point in time."[50] This idea is particularly relevant for our theory, because as Haas and Whiting so aptly stated, ". . . self preservation as an aim in international relations refers to the position and status *already achieved* by nations and groups within nations" and involves, among other things, the defense of certain "ways of life" and shared values. "Those nations who would create a new set of institutions nationally and internationally in conformance with their beliefs and aspirations aim at self-extension and not at self-preservation."[51]

Taking the analysis of self-preservation and self-extension as a departure point, it is evident that the second postulate of our model cannot refer to the aim of self-preservation in as broad a sense as that described above. In effect, such an end is incompatible with the total end of the action system of the model, since the underdeveloped nation, far from being content with the status already achieved (the formal status of an independent nation in our theoretical scheme) tends to change that formal status for the real status of an independent nation (in the relative sense previously defined) which calls for an attitude of innovation and the realization of a body of actions that our model wishes to describe. In this sense the underdeveloped nation is closer to the aim of self-extension of Haas and Whiting.

Nevertheless, the concept of self-preservation interpreted in a more limited way provides us with a useful analytical tool as we shall immediately see.

In Chapter II we pointed out one of these elements of the aim of self-preservation understood in its limited sense. We stated at that time that one of the problems for underdeveloped countries is the achievement of the socio-cultural change necessary for their development without a loss of their own values, their worthy traditions and heritage. And we added that this defense of the underdeveloped in-group values with respect to the developed out-group values can be observed typically in the case of India, which pursues economic development systematically through its five-year plans and at the same time is endeavoring to bring about the change in such a way that its cultural and religious values are not lost.

The compromise between the socio-cultural change *needed* for development and the preservation of the underdeveloped nation's values is one end of self-preservation in our postulate. It is evident that the nature of this compromise and its scope will vary in different countries, according to the relationship between the two variables (the socio-cultural change *needed* and the in-group values to be preserved). The case of India, for instance, will be very different from the cases of Chile or Argentina.

The second element of the aim of self-preservation in our postulate is the conservation of territorial integrity and national security in the military sense. Obviously, if a country is concretely threatened in either of these two aspects, it will dedicate all the economic resources necessary to preserve its national integrity to the detriment of any economic development plan that may exist *if there is no other possible alternative*. This will undoubtedly be the attitude of any responsible policy-makers as long as the system of the nation-states exists.[52]

In summary, the rationality of the economically oriented system of action in the model presumes that the two ends of self-preservation mentioned are not threatened by, or in conflict with, this rationality. This postulate includes two widely divergent elements. The first element consists of the supposition that the value-orientations, beliefs, and aspirations of the underdeveloped nation as a human group are compatible with the socio-cultural change needed for the development policy, if a certain compromise between the two variables is achieved. The second element of the postulate consists of the supposition that the underdeveloped nation is not substantially threatened by external power pressures on a local, regional, or world scale.

The third postulate on which the rationality of the model's system of action rests is that there are no exceptional circumstances that move the policy-makers of the nation to attempt a rapid increase in the status of the nation in the prestige pattern.

We may illustrate this situation with a hypothetical example. We shall suppose that a regional system exists in which the member states adhere to the democratic principles of government and that the defense of these value-orientations has acquired a special relevance at a given moment as a consequence of the fact that several countries in the area have democratic governments. We shall also suppose that there are some dictatorial governments in the system that run the risk of being expelled from the regional organization if they do not adapt their political systems to the democratic concept and that this situation has become particularly critical for one of these governments which, by its international actions, has flagrantly violated the value-orientations of the system. As a consequence of these factors and of other internal factors in the dictatorship, the dictatorial government is overthrown and replaced by an interim political regime. Let us finally suppose that the policy-makers of the new government clearly perceive that, if the country does not adopt democratic norms as rapidly as possible, it will be expelled from the regional organization, which would bring about such a body of deprivations from the economic and political point of view that the internal political situation of the nation would become chaotic. Having thus defined the situation, the policy-makers decide that the international system of action should be basically oriented toward increasing the status of the nation in the prestige pattern—the policy-makers would attempt to achieve a growing democratization of the political system of the country that would allow it to be adapted to the value-orientations of the regional system based on democracy.

Now if the nation in our example has, at the time of the fall of the dictatorial government, a rationally oriented plan of economic development, the democratization of the political system as sought by the interim government may provoke a digression in the execution of the plan. In this case, the international system of action based on the acquisition of prestige will have displaced an economically oriented international system of action. Such a change of orientation in the system would not be irrational if account is taken of the interim government's new definition of the situation, based on the need of conforming to the value-orientations of the regional organization.

The elements of the situation described in the example are not totally hypothetical. Actually, all of the suppositions on which it is based bear a close similarity to the situation of the Dominican Republic after the fall of the Trujillo regime, especially to the international situation within the Organization of American States and the internal political situation faced by the interim government of President Balaguer. The democratization of the political system appeared to be an imperious need in the "salvation of the country," as much from a national as an international point of view. A special commission of the OAS had been sent to study the problem presented by the democratization of the system. The situation was dramatically described when President Joaquin Balaguer appeared before a special joint session of the Dominican Congress and demanded a vote of confidence. He said, "Either accept our resignations . . . or unreservedly support the policy of democratization which the executive power and the joint chief of staff of the Armed Forces propose as the only means of saving the country."[53]

The example coincides, with the exception of one point, with reality in the Dominican case. This one point is our assumption that the dictatorial government was pursuing a rational policy of economic development. The situation was precisely the contrary. But this last element was necessary to demonstrate how an international policy of acquisition of prestige could displace, with rational justification, an economically oriented international system of action. It is not difficult to imagine a situation in which this last element of our hypothesis might be found. Such would be the case of a "popular democracy" situated within the Soviet orbit whose government was overthrown by a popular movement that would tend toward the democratization of the political system and the inclusion of the country in the field of the neutral nations or in the Western bloc.

In summary, our third postulate consists of presuming that the functioning of the economically oriented international system of action in our model is not disturbed by exceptional situations such as those described.

The last postulate establishes that it is possible for an underdeveloped nation to exhibit rational international behavior in spite of the "climate of uncertainty" that characterizes the stratified international system. This "climate" is intimately linked with the fluctuating conditions of the cold war, the possibility of nuclear war, and with irrationalities of various types that are manifest in the interactions within the system.

The analysis of this postulate may be made by the raising of a question: Given the uncertainty and the irrationality of the stratified international system, what is the best course for an under-developed nation that is trying to act rationally in an irrational world? The answer to this question depends upon whether the irrationality of the international system the nation faces involves some predictable patterns of behavior. If so, a rational system of action is still possible for the nation.

The rational policy-makers in our model must try to discern the underlying patterns of rationality of the behavior of nations in the international system. They must discover, either in the general or the specific definitions of the international situations in which the nation is placed, whose ends that behavior is actually serving and what those ends are. Then they can decide, in view of the ends of the nation on whose behalf they are acting, how they should react to that behavior. Only when no patterns of rationality can be discovered and all acts are unpredictable—when chaos prevails—is there no rational course for policy-makers who know the ends that they are attempting to pursue.

Our postulate establishes: (1) that some patterns of rationality are predictable in the international stratified system; (2) that rational policy-makers must be able to predict roughly the behavior of other nations pursuing their own goals, of other policy-makers acting on behalf of their own nations, and of relevant groups within the nation pursuing certain goals of their own; and (3) that some ambiguity of the predictions is inevitable, but, nevertheless, rational behavior is still possible in spite of this ambiguity.[54]

NOTES

1. On the use of models in political science, see Maurice Duverger, *Méthodes de la Science Politique* (Paris: Presses Universitaires de France, 1959), particularly pp. 429-42 and the bibliography on pp. 442-44. For the application of models to the study of international relations, mention must be made of the many valuable contributions made by the *Journal of Conflict Resolution* published quarterly by the Center for Research on Conflict Resolution, University of Michigan, Ann Arbor. Recently the journal *World Politics*, published under the sponsorship of the Center of International Studies of Princeton University, has made an important contribution to this field: see Klaus Knorr and Sidney Verba (eds.), *The International System: Theoretical Essays, World Politics*, Special Issue, XIV (1961). For a general treatment of the use of models, see

Max Black, *Models and Metaphors: Studies in Language and Philosophy* (Ithaca, N.Y.: Cornell University Press, 1962). All of these studies have been of great help in the construction of the model. I am especially indebted to the study of Anthony Downs, *An Economic Theory of Democracy* (New York: Harper & Brothers, 1957); although this study does not refer to international relations, his methodological implications have provided me with a fruitful insight into the problems of model building.

2. Max Weber, *The Theory of Social and Economic Organization,* trans. A. M. Henderson and Talcott Parsons (Glencoe, Ill: The Free Press, 1947), pp. 115-17.

3. Richard E. Quandt, "On the Use of Game Models in Theories of International Relations," *World Politics,* XIV (1961), 71.

4. Marion J. Levy, Jr., *The Structure of Society* (Princeton, N.J.: Princeton University Press, 1952), pp. 29-30. J. David Singer, "The Level-of-Analysis Problem in International Relations," *World Politics,* XIV (1961), 77-92, especially pp. 78-80. About the predictive capacity of any analytical model, Singer rightly states: ". . . we may legitimately demand that any analytical model offers the promise of reliable *prediction.* In mentioning this requirement last, there is no implication that it is the most demanding or difficult of the three. Despite the popular belief to the contrary, prediction demands less of one's model than does explanation or description. For example, any informed layman can predict that pressure on the accelerator of a slowly moving car will increase its speed; that more or less of the moon will be visible tonight than last night; or that the normal human will flinch when confronted with an impending blow. These *predictions* do not require a particularly elegant or sophisticated model of the universe, but their *explanation* demands far more than most of us carry around in our minds. Likewise, we can predict with impressive reliability that any nation will respond to military attack in kind, but a description and under-standing of the processes and factors leading to such a response are considerably more elusive, despite the gross simplicity of the acts themselves" (pp. 79-80).

5. For an analysis of the relations between ethics and international politics, see Kenneth W. Thompson, *Christian Ethics and the Dilemmas of Foreign Policy* (Durham, N.C.: Duke University Press, 1959), and Ernest Lefever, *Ethics and United States Foreign Policy* (New York: Meridian Books Inc., 1957).

6. Thompson, *Christian Ethics,* p. 22.

7. Spinoza, *Tractatus Politicus,* Chapter I, paragraph 4.

8. Knorr and Verba, "Introduction," *World Politics,* p. 4.

9. Singer, "The Level-of-Analysis Problem," *World Politics,* p. 80.

10. *Ibid.,* pp. 82-89. Singer does not pretend that these two levels of analysis are the only two possible. On the contrary, he states that ". . . many others are available and perhaps even more fruitful potentially than either of those selected." He also points out that the national state level-of-analysis "is clearly the traditional focus among Western students, and is the one which dominates almost all of the texts employed in English-speaking colleges and universities."

11. In stating this example we have drawn on Chester Bowles, *Ideas, People and Peace* (New York: Alfred A. Knopf, 1954), pp. 113-14.

12. Our example does not imply any *de facto* judgment on the rationality of the international behavior of the Latin American countries who have not entered the Free-Trade Area Association nor on the real existence of the problem. A rational answer—scientifically valid—to such a question might be given by the technically qualified policy-makers of these countries and by ECLA.

13. UNESCO Charter. In this connection UNESCO has published an interesting study: International Sociological Association with the collaboration of Jessie Bernard, T. H. Pear, Raymond Aron, and Robert C. Angell, *The Nature*

of Conflict: Studies on the Sociological Aspects of International Tensions (Paris: UNESCO, 1957).

14. Arnold Wolfers, "The Actors in International Politics," in *Theoretical Aspects of International Relations,* ed., William T. R. Fox (Notre Dame, Ind.: University of Notre Dame Press, 1959), p. 85.

15. There is a growing body of literature about "decision theory." For fruitful theoretical insights and an extensive bibliography concerning this subject, see Richard C. Snyder and James A. Robinson, *National and International Decision-Making: A Report to the Committee on Research for Peace* (New York: The Institute for International Order, n.d., Program of Research No. 4).

16. Frederick S. Dunn, "The Scope of International Relations," in *Contemporary Theory in International Relations,* ed., Stanley H. Hoffmann (Englewood Cliffs, N.J.: Prentice Hall, Inc., 1960), p. 15.

17. *Ibid.,* pp. 15-16.

18. About the reification of abstract concepts, and especially of the concept "state," see Vernon Van Dyke, *Political Science: A Philosophical Analysis* (Stanford, Cal.: Stanford University Press, 1960), pp. 63-64.

19. Thompson, *Christian Ethics,* p. 20; Wolfers, "The Actors in International Politics," in Fox, *Theoretical Aspects,* pp. 86-88. Perhaps nobody has stated more clearly this identification process than Herbert Spencer, *The Study of Sociology* (Ann Arbor, Michigan: The University of Michigan Press, 1961), p. 186: "Estimation of one's society is a reflex of self-estimation; and assertion of one's own claims as a part of it. The pride a citizen feels in a national achievement is the pride in belonging to a nation capable of that achievement: the belonging to such a nation having the tacit implication that in himself there exists the superiority of nature displayed. And the anger aroused in him by an aggression on his nation is an anger against something which threatens to injure him also, by injuring his nation."

20. Wolfers, "The Actors in International Politics," in Fox, *Theoretical Aspects,* pp. 83-106.

21. *Ibid.,* p. 99.

22. In an unpublished study about the decision-making process that led to the creation of ECLA, I found the existence of a great gap between the formal mechanism of the decision (legal and institutional) and the actual mechanism through which the decision was made. The study is focused in the analysis of the relationship between the Ministry of Foreign Affairs of Chile and the Chilean Ambassador to the United Nations, who presented the proposal for the creation of ECLA. The study reveals that, although the Ministry of Foreign Affairs formally supported the proposal and the following negotiations within the United Nations, the actual decisions and negotiations were made and conducted by Chilean Ambassador Hernán Santa Cruz. A study of the autonomy that some Latin American ambassadors have in their international negotiations may reveal, I think, unsuspected aspects of the decision-making process in the formulation of Latin American foreign policy. The plausability of this hypothesis was enhanced when I conducted some interviews in 1960 with members of the staff of the OAS; in effect, those interviews showed also that the positions of certain Latin American countries have changed in important inter-American conferences because the ambassadors representing the countries were changed. Concerning the relative autonomy of Latin American ambassadors in the formulation of the foreign policy of their countries, see also Thomas Jovet, *Bloc Politics in the United Nations* (Cambridge, Mass.: Harvard University Press, 1960).

23. Our analysis does not exclude the existence of other factors. We have confined ourselves to pointing out two which we consider especially relevant for our study.

24. J. B. Duroselle, "Sondages et Science des Relations Internationales," *Sondages: Revue Française de l'Opinion Publique*, Nos. 1-2 (1958), iii-xiv.

25. For an application of the concept of "system of action" to the study of international relations, see bibliography quoted in footnote 9 of Chapter 1.

26. Talcott Parsons and Edward A. Shils (eds.), *Toward a General Theory of Action* (Cambridge, Mass.: Harvard University Press, 1959), p. 5.

27. As Parsons and Shils have pointed out, "The concept of *motivation* in a strict sense applies only to individual actors. The motivational components of the action of collectivities are organized systems of the motivation of the relevant individual actors" (Parsons and Shils, *Toward a General Theory of Action*, p. 4).

28. Raymond H. Dawson, *The Decision to Aid Russia, 1941: Foreign Policy and Domestic Politics* (Chapel Hill, N.C.: The University of North Carolina Press, 1959).

29. *Ibid.*, pp. 290-94.

30. Professor Dawson adds: "This reciprocal impact of domestic and international factors is certainly not advanced here as a novel idea. It is believed, however, that the ensuing pages will emphasize the necessity for making explicit these interactions of national and international factors if the processes of foreign policy-making are to be seen in proper perspective" (*ibid.*, p. xii).

31. Parsons and Shils, *Toward a General Theory of Action*, p. 4. We use here the concept of orientation of action in the sense defined by Parsons and Shils: "Whether the acting unit is an individual or a collectivity, we shall speak of the actor's *orientation of action* when we describe the action. . . . Action has an orientation when it is guided by the meaning which the actor attaches to it in its relationship to his goals and interests."

32. *Ibid.*

33. This clause is naturally purely hypothetical.

34. Our example refers to what Parsons calls "the levels of organization of rational action in action systems." The example is related to the second level, which "introduces considerations of economy, which consists of the process of the allocation of resources relative to a plurality of alternative goals." Talcott Parsons, *The Social System* (Glencoe, Ill.: The Free Press, 1951), pp. 549-50.

35. Our example refers to the third level of organization of rational action in action systems, which "is concerned not with economy but with the maximization of power in the political sense" (*ibid.*, p. 550). In our example the maximization of power is obtained through the acquisition of prestige which is the source of power.

36. These data are taken from an article written by the author, which appeared in the daily newspaper *La Nación* (Santiago de Chile), August 22, 1960.

37. The concept of deprivation is defined by Parsons and Shils, *Toward a General Theory of Action*, p. 9, n. 11, as follows: "Deprivation is to be understood here as subsuming: (1) the withdrawal of gratifying objects already possessed by the actor; (2) the obstruction of access to gratifying objects which the actor does not possess and for which he is striving; (3) the enforced relationship with objects which are not gratifying, e.g., physical or psychological suffering of positive pain or injury (this category includes both actively encountering and passively receiving pain, etc.); (4) the threat of any of the foregoing. Responses by the actors to each of these types of deprivation might vary considerably." Each of these items could be applied within the conceptual framework of our model, considering the national state as a collectivity of actors. However, the example of physical suffering mentioned in the third item cannot be applied. We have previously mentioned the dangers of reification of the concept of the national state.

38. Parsons and Shils, *Toward a General Theory of Action*, pp. 7-8. In the same book, p. 409, Clyde Kluckhohn and his associates have offered the fol-

lowing definition of value-orientation: "It is convenient to use the term *value-orientation* for those value notions which are (a) general, (b) organized, and (c) include definitely existential judgments. A value-orientation is a set of linked propositions embracing both value and existential elements." For an analysis of value-orientations as components of the situation, see *ibid.*, pp. 410, 411, 417, 421, 423.

39. Professor W. J. Sprott has made a deep and clear analysis of the introductory chapter, "Some Fundamental Categories of the Theory of Action: A General Statement," in Parsons and Shils, *Toward a General Theory of Action*, pp. 3-27, and that analysis appeared in an article entitled "Principia Sociologica," published in the *British Journal of Sociology*, III, No. 4 (1952), 203-22. The phrases in quotation marks are taken from this study, p. 210.

The five patterns of alternatives can be combined in a variety of ways. Parsons and Shils have presented several types of combinations. See Parsons and Shils, "Values, Motives, and Systems of Action," in Parsons and Shils, *Toward a General Theory of Action*, pp. 47-275.

The most recent study about the Parsonian theory is Max Black (ed.), *The Social Theories of Talcott Parsons: A Critical Examination* (Englewood Cliffs, N.J.: Prentice Hall, Inc., 1961).

40. For a systematic application of the concept of *shared values* to the study of international relations, see Ernst B. Haas and Allen S. Whiting, *Dynamics of International Relations* (New York: McGraw-Hill Book Company, Inc., 1956). As Professors Haas and Whiting state in the Preface, p. vii: ". . . we have attempted to synthesize the study of political behavior and social action with an analysis of international relations as one manifestation of group aspirations."

41. Gabriel A. Almond and James S. Coleman, *The Politics of the Developing Areas* (Princeton, N.J.: Princeton University Press, 1960). See especially pp. 535-36.

42. Parsons and Shils, *Toward a General Theory of Action*, p. 8.

43. Gino Germani, "Algunas Contribuciones de la Sociología al Estudio del Desarrollo Económico," paper presented at the seminar held under the joint sponsorship of UNESCO and the Latin American Faculty of Social Sciences (FLACSO), Santiago, Chile, September 22-29, 1958, mimeographed copy in the files of FLACSO.

44. Adapted from Parsons and Shils, *Toward a General Theory of Action*, p. 90.

45. The use of the other dichotomies of the classification of Parsons and Shils might be profitable in our opinion. We have not used them here for lack of space.

46. Adlai Stevenson, "Extend our vision . . . to all mankind," in John K. Jessup and others, *The National Purpose* (New York: Holt, Rinehart and Winston, 1960).

47. A rise in the economic status will not necessarily bring about a rise in the power status in its coercive dimension, if the nation lacks sufficient population, for example, as would be the case of the Central American nations and of many African and Asiatic nations, but, on the other hand, the prestige of these countries would increase. One need only think of the international prestige of the Scandinavian countries which have a small population. An increase in influence derives from an increase in prestige and, consequently, of power considered in this dimension.

48. The term "the diplomacy of economic development" is taken from the penetrating study of the former President of the World Bank, Eugene Black, *The Diplomacy of Economic Development* (Cambridge, Mass.: Harvard University Press, 1960).

49. Speech delivered by Sir Winston Churchill at Llandudno, October 9, 1948, quoted by F. B. Czernomski (ed.), *The Eloquence of Winston Churchill* (New York: Signet Key Book, 1957), p. 184.

50. Haas and Whiting, *Dynamics of International Relations,* p. 59. This term is much more comprehensive than "national security," which is most often interpreted from a military point of view. Professor Arnold Wolfers was the first to formulate the "theory of ends" of a nation in his article "The Pole of Power and the Pole of Indifference," *World Politics,* IV (1951), 39-63. For a recent study of this theory see Ronald J. Yalem, " 'The Theory of Ends' of Arnold Wolfers," *The Journal of Conflict Resolution,* IV, No. 4 (1960), 421-25.

51. Haas and Whiting, *Dynamics of International Relations,* p. 60.

52. See footnote 11.

53. *Hispanic American Report,* XIX, No. 8 (1961), 698.

54. The analysis of this postulate is based on the study of Downs, *An Economic Theory of Democracy,* who was faced with the same problem in the construction of the model proposed in his book. At times we cite textual phrases from the book, but as we have needed to adapt them to the study of the rational behavior of a group—the nation—we have not used quotation marks in the text. Downs also established the postulate that citizens behave rationally in politics, but his postulate rests on a premise that we cannot presume in our model. In effect, Downs establishes that "rational behavior requires a predictable social order" (p. 11); that "rational behavior is impossible without the ordered stability which government furnishes" (p. 11). "Thus political rationality is the *sine qua non* of all forms of rational behavior" (p. 11).

In our model there does not exist the *ordered stability that government furnishes* because there is no world government in the international system. The United Nations and international organizations, as everyone knows, are only precarious and embryonic elements of such a goverment. However, some underlying patterns of rationality exist in spite of that fact. Without pretending to make an exhaustive analysis of them we can indicate several cases. For example, if an underdeveloped country presents a request for economic aid to the World Bank, it can predict that if the request fulfills certain requirements, it may be accepted. If the Latin American nations unite in a solid bloc to confront opposition from the United States, they can predict that, in *given circumstances,* they can finally overcome that resistance. Furthermore, the patterns of economics, power, and prestige of the international system provide a field in which rational policy-makers can discover lines of predictable behavior. Many examples could be given in connection with the types of international behavior described in Chapters II, III, and IV.

CHAPTER VI

THE MODEL

1. *The basic structure of the model*

In the preceding paragraphs we have established that the model that we intend to construct is a model of a system of action. We have identified its four variables, and we have determined the system's orientation, within which we have specified that the model, in order to conform to the exigencies of rationality with respect to ends, must be economically oriented.

We shall not study the elements that constitute the basic structure of the model, the requirements that the system of action must fulfill in order to be considered rationally oriented from an economic point of view.

The first component of the basic structure of the model is the establishment of a policy of induced national development. For this it becomes necessary to formulate a plan of development that establishes the measures that will be adopted to obtain the maximum advantage from the human and material resources which the country possesses or may obtain within a determined time period. For the study of this first element it is necessary to consider that development is (1) a total process, (2) a continuous process, and (3) a process that requires long-range planning.

We say that development is a total process because it involves, in addition to economic change, socio-cultural change that makes the former possible. Consequently, an induced development policy is not only a policy for economic development but also a policy for total socio-economic change. As the Indian Government's Planning Commission has pointed out in the formulation of its Second Five-Year Plan, development ". . . touches all aspects of community life and has to be viewed comprehensively. Economic planning thus extends itself into extra-economic spheres, educational, social, and cultural."[1]

Development is a dynamic process that is characterized by a complex interaction among political, social, economic, psychological, and cultural elements.[2]

In the process of modernization involved in the passage of an underdeveloped society to a developed society, "there are three principal areas in which elements of resistance must be overcome if the modernization of a traditional society is to be carried through successfully: politics, economics, and social structure. The underlying requirement for change in these areas is the modernization of attitudes. Modernity is a style of life. The ensemble of behaviors that compose the modern style is given its coherence by a frame of mind—toward the here and hereafter, toward permanence and change, toward oneself and one's fellow men."[3]

It is more proper, consequently, to speak of national development rather than economic development. Within the concept of national development, the economy of a country is only a subsystem of the total society, and concrete economic processes are always conditioned by noneconomic factors that derive from interactions between the economy as a subsystem and the other noneconomic subsystems of the society.[4] The problem of institutional change in an economy is a very eloquent example of the process of interaction because the fundamental factors involved in this change are not economic ones.[5]

We say that development is a continuous process, because, while it is necessary to plan for a determined period, it is equally indispensable—as India's Development Plan shows—"to keep in view a more long-range perspective and to be ready to adjust and adapt the programmes in hand as this perspective becomes clearer."[6] Other development plans have also insisted upon the fact that planning or programming must not be rigid but flexible; as a typical case in this respect one could cite the Chilean National Plan for Economic Development, which states that the Plan has been drawn up taking into account the necessity for its adaptation to socio-economic alternatives which present themselves either from within or without the national borders.[7] It requires that the

Plan be frequently revised in order to accommodate new priorities that emerge periodically.

As we pointed out in the second chapter, the two existing regional systems of co-operation for economic and social development with the greatest scope—the Colombo Plan and the Alliance for Progress—establish mechanisms for the annual analysis and discussion of the gains made by the member countries in the economic and social fields in accordance with each country's plans. In the case of the Latin American nations the purpose of the annual review is also to analyze and discuss "the problems encountered in each country, to exchange opinions on possible measures that might be adopted to intensify further social and economic progress, to prepare reports on the outlook for the future, and to make such recommendations as may be considered appropriate on policies and measures of a general nature to promote further economic and social development, in accordance with the Act of Bogotá and the Charter of Punta del Este. The results of this review will be summarized in an Annual Report on Economic and Social Progress in Latin America, to be issued by the Meeting at the Ministerial Level. This report will cover the principal accomplishments and problems of economic and social development in Latin America, the future tasks that need emphasis, and the outlook for the area as a whole."[8]

From a historical point of view, the fact that national development is a continuous process which requires long-range perspective appears in evident form. In effect, what the underdeveloped countries are trying to bring about in a few decades through the medium of development plans required centuries of socio-cultural change in Western Europe, a long process of maturation that was fulfilled in a spontaneous manner over successive stages. Only the United States, through very special historical conditions in which elements resistant to change were minimal, realized the miracle of converting itself into a developed society without passing through many of the stages the countries of Western Europe had to experience.[9]

The necessity of carrying on long-range planning for economic development arises logically from the two preceding characteristics. The total transformation of the society—the change in the style of life which modernization signifies—cannot be achieved suddenly, but requires the execution of successive plans and their adaptation to new conditions that are, in part, the products of goals achieved through earlier plans.

The total character of the process of economic development implies the preparation of an over-all, integrated development plan in order to avoid a piecemeal approach. The continuous character of the development process requires a long-term approach. This permits the carrying-out of a strategy designed to overcome resistant factors, pressures, tensions, and disequilibria derived from the execution of the plan, as well as the gradual modification of the structure of the socio-cultural world of the underdeveloped society (in short, modification of the complex network of interactions in the total society and in its subsystems resulting from the total process of change).

In his penetrating book, *The Strategy of Economic Development,* Albert O. Hirschman correctly points out that underdeveloped countries "already operate under the *grand tension* that stems from the universal desire for economic improvement oddly combined with many resistances to change. . . . Much is to be said," he adds, "for breaking down this grand tension, a highly explosive mixture of hopes and fears, into a series of smaller and more manageable tensions."[10]

The strategy of national development requires that tensions resulting from the process of modernization be identified, at least in their neurological points, that measures be taken in order to manage and control them, and that these measures be utilized within the policy of the plan. It is necessary that the leaders who are implementing the plan in its different aspects, through the policy of induced development, acquire an awareness that national development is not "a limited war" (to things economic) but a "total war" that takes in the whole society, even though its primary objective may be to produce a self-sustained economy. No one can contest the contribution of economists to the formation of an awareness of the problem of development; at least in Latin America this contribution has been evident, principally through ECLA. But it is necessary to recognize now that the planning of a country's economy, which until a short time ago was viewed as the private function of economists in collaboration with diverse "technical assistants," can no longer be accomplished with the traditional independence, if at the same time plans are made for the health of the population, its education, and if a total modernization is being attempted, that is, a change in the style of life.[11]

The emphasis that economists have placed on purely economic planning, and the greater relative development of economic science in relation to other social sciences, has led unconsciously to a confusion between means and ends. The essential end of economic planning—the attainment of an economy of self-sustained development—has been confused with the means used to reach that end. It has been believed that matters could be circumscribed to a war limited to economic phenomena, without perceiving the total character of the modernization process which necessarily requires a "total war."

Economists as outstanding as Myrdal have perceived this fact in the past. "The traditional division of neatly separated disciplines in the field of Social Sciences," he wrote, "does not correspond, to reality. Concrete problems never are exclusively economic, sociological, psychological, or political. A theory of underdevelopment or of economic development that exclusively operates with economic variables is unrealistic for logical reasons and therefore not applicable."[12] An Indian economist, C. N. Vakil, reached the same conclusion in a study presented to the "Round Table Conference on the Teaching of the Social Sciences in South Asia," organized by UNESCO in New Delhi in 1954.[13]

The Economic Commission for Latin America has already begun to concern itself with the social aspects of economic development.[14] In a recent international meeting of experts in diverse disciplines within the social sciences, its director, Raul Prebisch, declared that he considered it vital that research activities in the field of economics take place in a broad sociological context. "I consider this," he said, "to be of great importance because of the indissoluble links between economic and social factors which we are forced to separate for methodological reasons only."[15]

In a study for defining the concept of planning, prepared for the Dictionary of the Social Sciences in the Spanish language which will be published under the auspices of UNESCO, the Director of the Center for Economic Planning of the University of Chile has delineated the idea's evolution. The conclusions of this study may be summarized in the following points: (1) Planning is a technic of universal character, applicable to any field of thought and human activity. Its basic mission consists of introducing greater rationality into decisions for action, that is of improving the efficiency of any system of relations between means and ends. (2) There are as many specific types of planning as there are fields of application. One may mention, for example, the traditional fields of planning such as the economic, physical, budgetary, and production planning of business enterprise, whose methods have reached an appreciable degree of development. Or there are those plans for education, health, and the development of the community which are receiving growing attention at present. Finally, at a lower level of methodological refinement, there are those of administrative planning, of labor unions, and of social change in general. (3) Until now, these technics and their use, constantly improved by technological progress and the amplification of scientific knowledge, have been developed independently under the pressure of social problems ever more urgent and complex; this fact has been brought about partly because each planning area has corresponded to a specific field, thus identifying itself, in large measure, with the exercise of determined professions. (4) As a typical case one may point out what happens in a country when simultaneous planning in the fields of economy, health, and education signifies that the objectives which society proposes in each of them compete among themselves for the use of limited available resources. The rational solution of this competition assumes the previous establishment of a scale of priorities for these different objectives. This would guarantee maximum satisfaction of the social necessities in the three fields, in accordance with the urgency of each. But it is not easy to establish the importance of a determined educational level in an objective manner, for example, compared with a possible increase in agricultural production and/or with an improvement in public health. The possible importance of education is different for an economist, a physician, a physical planner, an agent of communal action, and an educator. This diversity can be resolved in accordance with the objective values of costs and benefits provided by the economist, and it has been thus resolved in the past. But this traditional state of things proves less effective every day. The growing accentuation of extra-economic values within the group of objectives of contemporary society has contributed to this. Another reason for this has been the advance in economic investigation itself, which has permitted the establishment of the fact that quantitative values derived directly from the market price system depend, in part, upon qualitative variables not directly quantifiable. (5) In short, the independent exercise of the different technics of planning turns out to be incompatible with its central objective of introducing greater rationality into decisions for action.

The different fields and levels in which planning has been exercised in isolation are found to be related among themselves in a manner so close, in reality, that the attempt to plan independently in each one of them can lead to a state of greater disorder instead of greater rationality. This conclusion, which imposes itself in our time as the natural result of experience, corresponds directly to the general principle that establishes the interactive character of social acts and facts and cannot be ignored in the future development of planning.[16]

The problem is—as various economists, sociologists, and political scientists have recently shown in a brilliant collective study—that the social sciences have been developed in specialized form and that interdisciplinary attempts are still in their beginning stages. There is an awareness now that the process of modernization required by the underdeveloped societies is a vast network of political, social, economic, psychological, and cultural interactions. But the social sciences—whether their contributions be considered separately or collectively through the medium of interdisciplinary collaboration—have not achieved sufficient maturity to offer a satisfactory analytical focus upon the complex process of interactions that attend the transition of an underdeveloped society into a modernized society.[17]

So it is, then, that the planners—these new strategists of modernization—must operate with provisional arms and with limited equipment to carry on the "total war" of national development. Paradoxically, the underdeveloped countries must develop themselves utilizing precarious elements from underdeveloped sciences.

It is clear, therefore, that the modernization of underdeveloped societies requires not only a strategy of economic development, as pointed out by Hirschman, but also a "grand strategy" for social change.

The role of this "grand strategy" is to co-ordinate and to direct all the resources of the nation toward the achievement of a change in the style of life which makes possible the functioning of an economy with self-sustained growth. This grand strategy, when applied to lower levels, is expressed in different "specific strategies" in the educational, social, economic, and political fields within the nation as much as internationally. In turn, these specific strategies, when translated into action, give rise to numerous "tactics" intimately linked to each of them.[18]

The concept of an over-all, integrated development plan corresponds to "grand strategy"; economic, educational, and other types of planning correspond to "specific strategies" integrated in the grand strategy so that they may be mutually consistent and their relative costs and benefits are justified in terms of the two primordial ends sought by grand strategy. The concrete measures that should be adopted to direct operations within the camp of each specific strategy are the "tactics." These tactics are carried out, in large part, through the structures of government and public administration. This machinery of public administration—including relationships with local governments, decentralized agencies, and non-governmental organizations, such as labor groups, co-operatives, educational, business, and industrial organizations—constitutes the main channel to be used in carrying out the program, adapting it to changing circumstances and evaluating the progress made. The tactics necessary for carrying out the specific strategies include all the measures that will be adopted to direct operations of the public sector (educational, economic, health, etc.) and to encourage private action in all the fields of the specific strategies in support of the grand strategy of the over-all development plan.[19]

The basic structure of our model will be constructed around those elements of "grand strategy" which require a planning of the international actions of an underdeveloped country for the achievement of its primordial purposes: (1) the creation of an economy of self-sustained growth; and (2) the modernization of the style of life.

A. *Self-sustained economic growth and an international grand strategy of development*

The planning of international actions constitutes a system of action integrated within the "grand strategy" of national development and, consequently, is intimately connected with it. Put in other terms "grand strategy" has two expressions, one on the national plane, the other on the international. Relations between the two will receive particular attention when we analyze the fourth variable of the model.

Nevertheless, we now point out that they are interdependent and are connected in such a manner that only for analytical purposes are we able to separate them and say that one is subordinate to the other. In effect, if we study grand strategy—that is, the over-all, integrated development plan—from a national point of view, its international aspect appears as a group of actions destined to seek out means of an international character (technical and economic aid, etc.) which the national aspect of the strategy may require. On the contrary, if we center our attention on the international aspect of grand strategy, we shall see that it presents itself in the national field as a group of measures necessary for elevating the nation's status in the stratified international system.

Since, for the moment, our proposition is the construction of a model for rational international action, the focus of our analysis will be grand strategy in its international expressions, and in this sense grand strategy in its national expressions will appear as a group of elements that make possible the operations of international grand strategy. But this distinction—we want to insist—has only analytical validity, as we shall see in the course of our study.

Having established this, we may ask ourselves: what is the rational sequence of international actions which should be considered by policy-makers in formulating the over-all, integrated development plan and, then, in executing it?

In the very formulation of the plan or of the grand strategy, there arise two types of problems of international character: (1)

can the plan be projected without technical assistance of an international character, and (2) within what *economic unit* will the grand strategy be carried out in order to achieve a self-sustained development?

Given the fact that every national plan of integrated development requires international technical and financial assistance, we may safely assume that international technical assistance in the formulation of the plan itself is the first measure that the policy-makers should adopt. Empirical evidence confirms this. The development plans of the countries in the Colombo Plan were formulated within the framework of international co-operation of that plan; in a like manner the development plans of the Latin American countries will be formulated within the framework of the Alliance for Progress. Before this latter program existed, several Latin American governments had already required international technical assistance for projecting their plans. The case of the Chilean Ten-Year Development Plan may be singled out. In its formulation ECLA and the United Nations lent technical assistance to the administrative unit of the Chilean government (Corporation for the Promotion of Production) which was charged with planning.

The rationality of this first measure is evident if one considers that the external aid required for the execution of the plan will be obtained more easily once the plan is supported by international institutions of regional or universal character and of recognized prestige and competence.

The second step in a rational sequence of action for policy-makers is the determination of the economic unit in which the plan is to be formulated. Given the satellite position of the underdeveloped economies, the size of their populations, and the analysis presented in Chapter II, we may say that the underdeveloped countries should look for ways of broadening their markets through supra-national economic integration, if they desire to act rationally in promoting industrial economies of scale. That is, the grand strategy of national development requires, from the international point of view, that the underdeveloped countries integrate themselves within supranational economic subsystems, in order that their national economies can reach the stage of self-sustained growth.

Some regional systems of economic co-operation have specifically considered supranational economic integration as a policy officially favored by the member states. As a typical case one can cite the Program of the Alliance for Progress of the Inter-American System, in which the American republics agreed to work toward the achievement of some fundamental goals in the present decade. Among them was the goal "to strengthen existing agreements on economic integration, with the view to the ultimate fulfillment of aspirations for a Latin American Common Market that will expand and diversify trade among the Latin American countries and thus contribute to the economic growth of the region."[20]

Once the economic unit within which the development of the economic subsystem will be carried out is determined, one can design a *specific strategy* of national development in this area, a strategy of economic development as one of the elements subordinated to the grand strategy. This specific strategy must take different factors into account, factors whose implications and technical content fall to economists and whose analysis remains outside the field of this study. We only wish to point out that the specific strategy of economic development is related to several fundamental aspects of international grand strategy: (1) the amount and nature of foreign aid; (2) the amount and nature of economic aid for social development; (3) the amount and nature of the required technical assistance; (4) the determination of the type of international mechanisms that will be created or utilized in order to compensate for fluctuations in the prices of raw materials in the international market; and (5) the determination of the role of international monetary mechanisms—especially the IMF—in relation to national monetary policy.

The first three aspects require that within the international grand strategy there is assured: (a) a regular inflow of such aid; and (b) that the proceedings through which the aid is obtained imply a weakening of the subordinate relation with respect to the countries granting that help—that they contribute to increasing the economic independence of the country in the relative sense defined in Chapter II.

The last two aspects require the formulation of an active international strategy and not simply a passive or defensive one, in order that these mechanisms may adapt themselves where possible to the requirements established in the national development plans.

Some comments and examples will clarify the scope and implications of international grand strategy in the economic field. Let us first consider the requirements stated under letters (a) and (b) in relation to the first three aspects of international grand strategy.

Let us attempt to identify which are the international actions that, from a rational point of view, are required to insure a regular, normal, systematic flow of foreign aid necessary for the financing of the national development plan. In the term "aid" we include (1), (2), and (3). The dichotomy analyzed in Chapter II, which distinguishes between the utilization of regional channels and the use of bilateral or multilateral ways of obtaining aid, is not directly related to a criterion of rationality. In effect, the selection which an underdeveloped nation makes in one or another sense may be more or less efficient to achieve such aid. It will depend on several variables linked to the definition of the international situation which the policy-makers of the underdeveloped nation formulate within the grand strategy. Thus, for example, for the Latin American countries it is rational to take advantage of the existence of the Inter-American System in order to channel the required aid principally through it. Especially after the establishment of the program of the Alliance for Progress at the Conference of Punta del Este, the means afforded by the Inter-American System for the financing of aid are of such a magnitude that it would be irrational for a member state not to utilize them. The United States, within the framework of the Charter of Punta del Este, has pledged its efforts "to supply financial and technical cooperation in order to achieve the aims of the Alliance for Progress. To this end, the United States will provide a *major part* of the minimum of twenty billion dollars, principally in public funds, which Latin America will require over the next ten years from all external sources in order to supplement its own effort."[21]

But even in this case it will be necessary to resort to sources outside the Inter-American System for additional aid, since the United States will furnish only a part of the total foreign aid required. The additional portion may possibly come from Western Europe or from private sources in the United States and other capital exporting countries. The case of the aid granted to Bolivia provides an example of how resources from the Inter-American System (Inter-American Development Bank) can be combined with public funds from the United States and financial support from a Western European country (West Germany). Nevertheless, one must note that there was also an organization of the Inter-American System (the IDB) involved in this example. This agency co-ordinated efforts, and everything seems to indicate that in the future the IDB will work as a catalytic agent for structuring the different sources of aid.[22]

A similar affirmation might be made with respect to the underdeveloped member countries of the Colombo Plan, with a special qualification in relation to India. In effect, the "bargaining power" of India as a key country in the power struggle between the Soviet Union and the United States is so evident that India can expand its field of solicitations to achieve the foreign aid required for its development without recurring solely to regional channels. This has taken place in reality, because, in spite of the fact that India is a member of the Colombo Plan, it is making convenient direct arrangements. The formation of the so-called "Indian Club" is a clear example of this phenomenon. Consequently, in this case, international grand strategy is required to be designed in terms of a careful selection of sources of foreign aid in relation to the country's bargaining power. It is obvious that such a task cannot be merely the work of economists but of the policy-makers charged with the direction of India's foreign policy. Once again we face the fact that the planning of grand strategy is fundamentally the result of the definition of the international situation of a given country, couched in political terms.

We may say, therefore, that the rational manner of insuring a *regular flow of foreign aid* lies in seeking adequate ways for obtaining it according to the real status of the nation and of the international roles that it has within the stratified international system. For the underdeveloped countries that adhere to the Western bloc, such a relation depends primarily upon their *political* ties with the United States, the leader of the bloc, and secondarily upon their ties with the developed countries of the same bloc, especially with Western Europe, Canada, and the rest of the developed members of the

Commonwealth. For the neutral underdeveloped countries, the universe of possible choices for insuring the regular flow of foreign aid widens, since in such cases the bargaining power within the cold war is considerably greater.

The formulation of the Alliance for Progress is clearly connected to the unleashing of the cold war within the Inter-American System as a consequence of the Cuban Revolution. And the amount of aid to India is derived from its importance as a key country in the international strategy of the two blocs.

We must specify, now, in what manner this aid can be obtained and still contribute to a country's economic independence. Let us examine several illustrations of grand strategy in relation to economic aid.

A basic distinction fits within the analysis of economic aid: the differentiation between the *flow of foreign capital* required for development (generic concept) and *international aid as such* (specific concept). Foreign capital that reaches an underdeveloped country can come from many different sources. Let us enumerate the principal ones: (a) private investors who create foreign enterprises in the underdeveloped country; (b) private investors who lend to governments or state entities (the Bolivian case in relation to German enterprise); (c) private foreign investors who, in union with national capital, make investments of a mixed nature; (d) foreign nonprofit institutions that make donations (for example, the grant to India from the Ford Foundation) or loans; (e) international organizations that lend to governments or to private parties (international lending agencies such as the IDB); and (f) foreign governments that lend to other governments or to public entities backed by those governments (capital exporting countries of America and Western Europe).

In accordance with the concept established by Professor Rosenstein-Rodan, ". . . aid, properly speaking, refers only to those parts of capital inflow which normal market incentives do not provide. It consists of: (1) long-term loans repayable in foreign currency . . . ; (2) grants and soft loans, including loans repayable in local currency . . .; and (3) sale of surplus products for local currency payment (P.L. 480 in the U.S.)."[23] Accordingly, short-

and medium-term loans and private foreign investment should not be counted as aid. They are "trade, not aid."[24]

In agreement with the concepts enunciated above one may consider as rational—for an underdeveloped country and speaking in general terms—that policy which tends to circumscribe the flow of foreign capital to "aid" and to long-term "private investments." The reasons are obvious. In effect, "aid" includes donations, acquisition of products paid for in national currency units, and long-term loans, which in some cases may be repayable in local currency. On the contrary, "private investments" often represent short- and medium-term loans.

Consequently, a rational international policy will try to obtain the maximum of "economic aid" from governments of capital exporting countries and from international lending agencies—letters (d), (e), and (f) enumerated above. If the foreign financing required cannot be obtained through these sources, the underdeveloped nation will be obliged to resort *additionally* to the private investor—letters (a), (b), and (c) above. In this case an international strategy of development will have to establish a relationship between the kind of treatment extended to already existing foreign investments in the country and the treatment intended for those investments which the country wishes to attract. A definition of the national interest must be *specifically established* in this case, with the object of clarifying its implications for international strategy. If the underdeveloped country can in large measure do without private foreign capital, a more radical interpretation of the national interest may be formulated in relation to the private foreign investments already in place. In this case the policy-makers are able to demand more from private foreign investments in terms of the financial contribution of such enterprises to the financing of the development plan (for example, through taxation). On the contrary, if the underdeveloped nation needs to obtain foreign investments, as the general situation seems to be (see Table VIII), a different definition of national interest must be formulated. The international strategy must establish, as part of the specific strategy of economic development, the group of conditions capable (from the point of view of normal market incentives) of stimulating private foreign capital to make the required investments. We may say, consequently, that the international grand strategy of development, with respect to private foreign investment, depends upon how necessary that investment is to finance the additional part needed for the development plan.   An equilibrium must be reached, therefore, between those demands imposed by the national interest (in terms of lesser economic dependence upon the outside) and those derived from the necessity of creating the right climate in order that private foreign capital flow may be possible.[25]

Let us now analyze the aspects of international grand strategy related to monetary policy and the problem of primary materials. Both form part of the specific strategy of economic development, but, as we pointed out earlier, their international implications require decisions that enter into the field of grand strategy.

The phenomenon of chronic disequilibrium in the balance of payments, which we have pointed to in Chapter II, raises a monetary problem for the underdeveloped countries.   Two solutions have usually been presented to achieve equilibrium in the balance of payments—deflation or devaluation.   Some economists think that these "solutions" should be discarded because they are both too costly for development policy.[26]   A dichotomy has been drawn in this respect within the last few years in Latin America: the so-called "monetarist" and "structuralist" schools.[27]

The specific focus of the "monetarist"-"structuralist" controversy has been the IMF-supported anti-inflationary programs.   "Monetarists" regard them as essential for reviving economic growth.   Halting inflation and abolishing various direct controls and subsidies would, they believe, eliminate most of the imbalances and supply rigidities on which the "structuralists" lay such heavy stress.   In other words, "monetarists" believe that there is a latent dynamism in the private sector as well as untapped possibilities for attracting substantially larger amounts of foreign investment.   But to realize this potential the economies must undergo a painful but necessary anti-inflationary therapy to purge themselves of distortions and obstacles to growth induced by inflation.   Price level stability and the elimination of various direct controls seems, thus, to be viewed as virtually a sufficient as well as a necessary condition for reviving economic growth.   This may be inferred from the reduced relative role assigned in the programs to public investment.   While the latter is expected to expand in volume over time through foreign loans and a gradual increase in tax receipts, no dramatic increase of taxes is postulated either as part of the stabilization effort or of the subsequent development effort. Confidence in the latent dynamism of the private sector is also stressed in the pronouncements of key government officials, supporting business groups, editorials in the friendly press and pep talks by visiting U.S. dignitaries. Finally it is implied by the fact that domestic support for the stabilization programs has come chiefly from the Rightist parties who have an ideological antipathy to large-scale planned development programs. This is not, however, to say that the "monetarists" want a free economy in the classical sense. Terms like "free enterprise" and "competition" are bandied about in Latin America even more loosely than in the United States. They presume protection against competing imports, trade association pricing, and public industrial and infrastructure investment if complementary to rather than competitive with the private sector.

The "structuralist" dispute with the "monetarists" is thus carried on at three levels. There is disagreement as to the causes of the inflation and of the efficacy of tightened credit, fiscal retrenchment and the elimination of direct controls in checking it. There is a closely related disagreement on economic development policy. Finally, there is mistrust of the Rightist sponsorship of the stabilization programs which stems from the fact that many of the "structuralists" are partisans of the parties of the Left. The task of summarizing the "structuralist" position is made more difficult, moreover, by the fact that there are really various positions. "Structuralists" are more united as critics than as programmers. This should be kept in mind in appraising the following effort at a synthesis.

Let us begin by putting forth the "structuralist" inflationary model in skeletal form. The setting is that of a Latin American country undergoing industrialization. . . .

The model has the following basic features. There is chronic upward pressure on import and food prices. These, respectively, raise domestic costs and set off wage demands, culminating in a general rise of the cost-price level, with oligopoly pricing in industry and trade facilitating the upward price movement. Because the government operating budget tends to be inflexible in real terms, and because revenue comes largely from indirect taxes, the rise in prices generates fiscal deficits which are met by central bank borrowing. Similarly, the higher cost-price level also "forces" the banking system to provide additional private credit. While tight money could thus prevent the cost-price rise, with import and agricultural prices rising autonomously, a fall in industrial prices and wages would be required. Since both are sticky downward, a substantial drop in output and employment would be needed to force them down. Moreover, the relative rigidity of the government operating budget means that the alternative to central bank credit would be primarily a reduction in public investment. Since the low social boiling point in Latin American countries is rapidly approached when per capita output stagnates or falls and urban unemployment rises, efforts to maintain tight money are soon aborted, as has frequently been demonstrated in postwar Latin American experience.

Monetarists are thus stressing an irrelevancy when they point out that inflation cannot be sustained without a continued expansion of the money supply and can therefore be checked by halting the expansion. To do so for long without exacerbating social tensions is not possible unless per capita output and employment are expanding. Given the existing productive structure and class hostilities in Latin American countries, such a stabilization program could succeed only if external circumstances were favorable, as during a sustained export boom. Alternatively, tight money might be maintained by a strong dictatorship which is able to plug the outlets for the expression of social discontent.[28]

As is clearly deduced from the foregoing exposition, the debate between both "schools" has profound implications for the grand strategy of development, as much in its national aspects as its international aspects. The discussion is very far from academic. The common man in Latin America meets the practical consequences of this policy every day, even though he does not even realize the existence of the debate, much less understand its technical content. Inflationary pressures which may be derived from the "structuralist" position affect the price levels of articles used in everyday consumption. In this manner the common man, with his ever-increasing level of aspiration, owing to the "revolution of rising expectations," lives in permanent economic insecurity. This insecurity is the product of a combination of two factors: his low standard of living derived from the state of underdevelopment, and the psychological insecurity that springs from the lack of correlation between inflationary price rises and his salary increases.

In the wage-price spiral, wages climb the stairway, while prices go up by the elevator. When the "monetarists" come to "put the house in order," the common man sees himself confronted with all kinds of difficulties in using even the stairs. The ground is prepared, then, for all sorts of frustrations originating in the impossibility of satisfying his "rising expectations" with wages that continually lose their real purchasing power. Pressures and tensions of every order begin to form within the social system (and in the political and economic subsystems), and they slowly create a climate wherein the common man begins to think that only a "strong hand" can "put the house in order." The monetary debate, which might seem confined to the academic world and to the world of the policy-makers, projects itself into the political plane, preparing the way for the ascension to power of charismatic leaders, of *caudillos,* of dictators, and of the "saviors of the people," whose solutions are more simple as problems grow more complex. But the common man, deceived by "structuralist" policies and even more by "monetarist" policies, is anxious to accept any policy, however simple it be, that seems to offer some hope for ending his permanent psychological insecurity.[29] Authoritarian solutions of a political nature which emerge from a *purely monetary* debate involve profound international repercussions. There is but one step between charismatic authoritarian leadership and demagogy. If, as a consequence of a *purely monetary* debate, there emerges a dictator or a Marxist government of the extreme left, then, and only then, do the monetarists ask themselves if the "putting of the house in order" which they sought is, in reality, a true "order." The monetarist experience in Chile in recent years, which ended in the breaking of that policy in the first months of 1961, is a tragic illustration of this phenomenon. In less than a month the new Chilean monetary unit, the *escudo* (equivalent to 1,000 pesos, the former currency unit), depreciated in astonishing percentages. The monetary policy of the Chilean government, in first "putting the house in order," was praised by financial circles in the United States and Chile, but ended up in total bankruptcy, with the government obliged to return to monetary controls propitiated by the *heterodox* "structuralists."[30]

The practical implications of such debate for international grand strategy of development may be summarized as follows: (1) "The International Monetary Fund is the chief exponent of traditional monetary policy in Latin America and elsewhere, and a borrowing country must conform to certain IMF guidelines to be eligible for loans not only from the IMF but often also from other international and United States government agencies."[31] (2) As a consequence of the foregoing, the United States appears as a supporter of the "monetarist school," linked up after a fashion with the parties of the right in Latin America that sympathize with such policy. (3) As some American and Latin American economists have pointed out, the dividing line between the two schools is not so clear as it seems. The "structuralists" as much as the "monetarists" have tended, for political reasons, to present the dichotomy as true "ideal types" in the sociological sense. "It is obvious that the 'monetarists' would agree with much of what the 'structuralists' say and vice versa."[32] (4) The surprising fact is that "it was the International Monetary Fund which helped draw the lines of battle."[33] (5) The Economic Commission for Latin America, an agency of the United Nations, and the elite of the Latin American economists (for example, Celso Furtado), generally following ECLA's leadership, appear as supporters of "structuralist" policy. (6) Most of the parties of the center or of the left in Latin America abide by the line of ECLA and the elite of Latin America's economists. (7) In this manner the debate of the "monetarists" versus the "structuralists" takes on international dimensions directly tied to grand strategy. In effect, the "monetarist school" appears to be backed by the IMF, the U.S. government, Latin American and United States financial circles, and parties of the right; the "structuralist school" seems to be backed by ECLA, the elite of Latin America's economists, and the Latin American parties of the left and center. (8) Some parties of the right in Latin American oppose, overtly or covertly, the Alliance for Progress, or at least are not sympathetic to it. (9) The democratic parties of the left and center generally support the Alliance and are the principal public-opinion groups upon which the success of such a program in Latin American may rest. (10) The IMF is accused of attempting to encroach upon the national sovereignty and of operating "behind the scenes."

An American economist, analyzing the controversy between the two schools, writes in this vein: "The official views on development of the IMF are not available, since the IMF missions (in different countries) operate as behind-the-scenes advisers and critics of programs *which formally* are the responsibility of each government."[34]

The well-known Chilean economics journal, *Panorama Económico,* whose technical adviser and editor, Aníbal Pinto, is closely associated with ECLA circles, has incessantly emphasized this fact. In a series of issues dedicated to the analysis of the IMF's monetary policy, *Panorama Económico* has accused the Fund of establishing a veritable dictatorship in the management of monetary policy in Latin America and of violating national sovereignty in these countries by implanting a monetary policy that is resisted by the most outstanding Latin American economists and is contrary to the national interest of the Latin American nations.[35] These accusations were confirmed in the eyes of the policy-makers of Brazil in the conflict between that country and the Fund. In 1959, President Kubitschek of Brazil entered into negotiations with the IMF to obtain a loan that would serve to offset the shortage of dollars in the economy because of balance-of-payment disequilibrium. The IMF, guided by its "monetarist" policy, demanded a number of predetermined conditions from the Brazilian government that were designed to "put the house in order." These measures were resisted by Brazil, which maintained that they would be prejudicial to the country's plans for economic development. An international tension grew out of these differences. The government, the economists, and some Brazilian political parties expressed in one form or another that the IMF was encroaching upon the sovereign right of Brazil to determine its own development policy. The United States government, as a supporter of IMF policy, became involved in the conflict. Finally the Brazilian government broke off negotiations with the IMF. The *Hispanic American Report,* a journal published by Stanford University, summarized the international implications of the conflict as follows:

Early in June President Kubitschek broke off negotiations with the International Monetary Fund (IMF), declaring that adoption of the austerity program suggested by the IMF would drive the nation's living costs sky-high and foment so much internal unrest that it might turn the course of Brazil's presidential election next year. The IMF program called for tighter Brazilian bank credit, sharp cuts in government spending, and liberalization of foreign trade through removal of multiple exchange rates. At this, Kubitschek decided to seek U.S. financial aid, which meant that he was counting on the willingness of U.S. lending agencies to extend foreign aid to Brazil without IMF approval. His attitude put the United States in a dilemma, since it neither wanted to stop helping Brazil nor to change its policy of loaning money only to those countries approved by the IMF.

"Failure to yield to Kubitschek's demand," commented Joseph R. Slevin of the *New York Herald Tribune*, "could lead the Brazilian President to seek aid from the Soviet bloc—a maneuver that would give the Communists a much greater foothold in South America than the United States would like. Brazil sought from $250 million to more than $500 million to cover the servicing of foreign debts which would cost the country about $320 million this year (1959) and $350 million in 1960, amounting to 30 to 40 per cent of the nation's foreign exchange earnings. Vital oil imports would take approximately another 30 per cent ($280 to $300 million), leaving little for other imports. One possible solution was being considered by the U.S. State Department. Under it no new loan would be made, but Brazil's burden would be eased by permitting its government to postpone first scheduled debt payments for a certain period. Acceptance of the proposal would give Brazil a welcome breathing spell but would also reduce its chances of obtaining future credit. Further, the country would be obliged to pay cash for all imports. This 'solution' involved a penalty for Brazil for failing to take the needed internal reform measures. U.S. officials commented that this solution has the merit of avoiding the general embarrassment to U.S.–Brazilian relations that would result if Brazil were permitted openly to default on her debts. Further negotiations awaited the arrival in Washington of Walter Moreira Sales, the new Ambassador to the United States who was replacing Amaral Peixoto."

According to *Visao,* the cancellation of negotiations with the IMF would not have occurred if Finance Minister Lucas Lopes had not suffered a heart attack, leaving the road open for Kubitschek to play his hand unhampered by Lopes' conservative opposition. Whatever the circumstances, Kubitschek's move was generally well received. Brazil's increasingly belligerent mood was well reflected in a defiant speech by Kubitschek, who said Brazil has "come of age." The President was applauded by figures as diverse as Lott [a military leader who was candidate to the presidency against Janio Quadros] and Prestes [a leader of the Communist party for more than forty years].

Few criticized the President, although there were some charges by the opposition that the country was insolvent. Talk of renewed relations with Russia increased, but an official announcement said no such plans were being considered. However, Senator Lino de Matos spoke in favor of renewed trade relations with the Soviet bloc to solve the economic crisis."[36]

Echoing the declarations of the Brazilian president, the Chilean journal *Panorama Económico,* in an article entitled "The Facts Make Us Right," commented:

It has been demonstrated in the words of Brazil's president and government spokesmen that there are no "suggestions" in the dictums of the [International Monetary] Fund, nor are there "propositions" which should be followed by governments of a spontaneous nature . . . but rather they deal with a precise and meticulous written prescription, which governments must accept integrally and which must be "pro forma" agreed to and expounded by the [country] applicant for credit.

Everything that has been said in official, journalistic, and congressional circles [about the negotiations between Chile and the IMF] in defense of this situation does not take away one comma of what is maintained by this journal: that it implies an abuse of power and confidence on the part of the [International Monetary] Fund, whose statutes in no way authorize it to become the international dictator of the economic policies of the Western World.

On the other side, it remains to be added that such a state of things involves, on the part of governments "poured in a mold," the renunciation of the management of instruments and the adoption of decisions which are primordial parts of the exercise of sovereignty.[37]

The "case study" of the monetary debate in Latin America has shown us, once again, that a matter appearing to be *purely technical and economic* is linked directly with international patterns of superordination-subordination and that it is the disequilibrium between the formal status of the underdeveloped countries as sovereign and independent nations and their real status within the stratified system that stands out as the backdrop for an *exclusively technical debate.*

As several economists have suggested, there is no clear line of demarcation between the "monetarist" and "structuralist" schools, and everything seems to indicate that international grand strategy should consider an intermediate line of action that combines both positions, in accordance with the definition of the situation of each country in this matter. A rational approach to the monetary problem seems to demand, then, a deviation from the "structuralist" school which, if carried to its ultimate consequences, could lead to excessive inflationary pressures with their disintegrating effects on the social system. At the same time it calls for a deviation from the "monetarist" solution, which, by restraining wages excessively, could have disastrous results in the same sense. The study of the Chilean case seems to offer sufficient empirical evidence of the rationality of this statement.

Whatever the level of compromise that is adopted between the "schools" it can only be rationally accomplished after carefully weighing the national and international aspects of grand strategy in its monetary phase. In another part of this study it has been said that a rational attitude before a determined situation should be taken as a function of the particular definition of that situation. If the IMF is effectively trying to apply a "universal solution," a general prescription for all countries as claimed by its critics, such an attitude would imply irrational conduct, because it would disregard the specific definition of each underdeveloped nation.

The case of instability in the market for primary materials provides another illustration of the international implications of development strategy. To avoid repetition of this topic which has already been set forth in Chapter II, we now limit ourselves to the consideration of some aspects that seem relevant to the formulation of grand strategy: (1) international aid for development is inseparable from the problem of instability in the market for primary materials, through the *atimic* effects involved in the latter; (2) a rational solution to the problem can only be achieved by means of an understanding between underdeveloped regions and developed regions, for the reasons given in Chapter II; (3) developed countries insist upon the aspect of international aid which serves to emphasize their position of superiority in relation to the underdeveloped areas, but grand strategy requires that the underdeveloped countries compensate for their subordinate position, stressing the fact that international aid can be completely illusory in some cases, as a consequence of losses suffered through fluctuations in the international prices of primary materials; (4) policy-makers in developed and underdeveloped countries are beginning to realize this problem. As an illustration it is appropriate to recall the declarations of Ambassador Stevenson with respect to the losses suffered by Latin American coffee-exporting countries and the investigations carried on in the United Nations concerning this point. It is also proper to point out that during the discussion of U.S. aid to Latin America in the meeting of the Committee of 21 of the OAS in Bogotá (1960), the Latin American countries emphasized the fact that Latin America was losing one billion dollars annually as a result of the relation of prices and volume in the interchange of primary materials.[38]

Nevertheless, as indicated in Chapter II, the underdeveloped countries have been unable to formulate a coherent, systematic, and continuous strategy in this respect. The problems posed for grand strategy can be enunciated in two questions. (1) Which is the more adequate way to seek a solution to this problem, the regional or the universal? Said in another fashion, and again taking the Inter-American System as an example, should Latin America reach a direct understanding with the United States within the Inter-American System in order to achieve the solution, or should it seek it in universal terms, uniting its efforts with those of underdeveloped countries in other regions that have a similar problem?[39] (2) Should it seek one solution for all basic products or, on the contrary, several solutions, "commodity by commodity"? The generality of the principles established in the Charter of Punta del Este leaves the way open for any of these alternatives, and it is up to the policy-makers who formulate the grand strategy of development to define a systematic group of international actions to find an adequate solution.

B. *The modernization of the style of life in underdeveloped nations and an international grand strategy of development*

It has been stated that a modern society is characterized by the combination of two fundamental elements: (a) the capacity to produce a regular flow of innovations within the social system (a capacity that is directly related to the style of life prevailing in the socio-cultural world of that society); and (b) the existence of an economy of self-sustained growth. We have noted earlier that the transformation of a nation's social and cultural systems, in order to achieve both objectives, constitutes the basic aim of a grand strategy of development.

In the preceding paragraphs we have been concerned with the international implications of the second of these elements which constitute a modern society. We now turn to study the international implications of the modernization of the style of life.

If modern society is that which possesses the two necessary elements, *a contrario sensu* traditional society may be defined as that society which lacks them, and a transitional society as one in which the two constituent elements of a modern society have begun to develop within the social system.   In other words, a transitional society is one in which a process of socio-cultural change has begun, the aim of which is the modernization of society.

The first aspect of our analysis will attempt to establish the relation that exists between the two constituent elements of a modern society.   Marxist theory has given a clear answer in this respect. Engels wrote:

> The materialist conception of history starts from the principle that production, and with production the exchange of its products, is the basis of every social order, that in every society which has appeared in history, the distribution of the product, and with it the division of society into classes or estates, is determined by what is produced and how it is produced, and how the product is exchanged.   According to this conception, the ultimate causes of all social changes and political revolutions are to be sought, *not in the minds of men,* in their increasing insight into eternal truth and justice, *but in change in the mode of production and exchange;* they are to be sought not in the *philosophy* but in the *economics* of the epoch concerned.[40]

Commenting on the relation between this passage from Engels on the materialist conception of history and Marxist theory, Heilbroner has written:

> The reasoning is not difficult to follow.   Every society, says Marx, is built on an economic base, is ultimately grounded in the hard reality of human beings who have organized their activities in order to clothe and feed and house themselves.   That organization can differ vastly from society to society and from era to era.   It can be pastoral or built around hunting or grouped into handicraft units or structured into a complex industrial whole.   But whatever the form in which men organize to solve their basic economic problem, *society will require a whole superstructure of non-economic activity and thought, and it will need to be bound together by laws, supervised by a government, inspired by religion and philosophy.*   But the superstructure of thought cannot be selected at random.   It must mirror the foundation on which it is raised.   No hunting community will evolve or could use the legal framework of an industrial society, and similarly an industrial community obviously requires an entirely different conception of law, order, and government than does a primitive village.   Note that the doctrine of materialism does not toss away the catalytic function and creativity of ideas.   *It only maintains that thoughts and ideas are the product of*

environment, even though they aim to change that environment. Materialism by itself would reduce ideas to mere passive accompaniments of economic activity. That was not Marx's contention. For the new theory was dialectical as well as materialist: it envisaged change, constant and inherent change; and in that never-ending flux the ideas emanating from one period would help to shape another. Men make their own history, wrote Marx, commenting on the *coup d'état* of Louis Napoleon in 1852, but they do not make it just as they please; they do not make it under circumstances chosen by themselves, but under circumstances directly found, given and transmitted from the past. But the dialectical—the changing—aspect of this theory of history did not depend merely on the interplay of ideas and social structures. There was another and far more powerful agent at work. The economic world itself was changing: *the ultimate reality on which the structure of ideas was built was itself constantly in flux.*[41]

Thus, within the Marxist conception, in the process of interaction between the economic subsystem and the "content of men's minds"—the style of life—it is evident that the former is the primordial factor in social change.

We have made this digression about the relation between both elements within Marxist thought because it is surprising to observe how many Western economists and social scientists—who are very far from Marxism—have unconsciously fallen into accepting the Marxist proposition. The fact that it was economists (the cultivators of the most developed social science) who have played a primary role in the formulation of theories of economic development explains this phenomenon in part. The lack of integration of economic theory with sociological theory and with the theories of the other social sciences (social psychology, political science, anthropology, etc.) made it possible for many to implicitly accept the belief that the modification of a nation's economic subsystem would produce an automatic alteration in its social and cultural systems. For this reason, whatever may be the deficiencies of the efforts by Parsons and his associates to produce an integrated social theory around the theory of action, it would be difficult not to recognize their merits. In effect, they have shown that the economy, as well as the polity, are only subsystems within the social system of the nation and that a study of the subsystems implies an analysis of the interactive processes between them and the social system of which they are parts.

The study made by the Center for International Studies of M.I.T., *The Emerging Nations,* implicitly accepts the subordination of the economic subsystem to the social and cultural systems in the process of interaction which leads to the modernization of the underdeveloped nations. It is significant to point out that if one compares this study with Rostow's *Stages of Economic Growth,* there are no substantial differences observed between the two analyses of the constituent elements of a modern society. The fact that Rostow is one of the authors of *The Emerging Nations* permits the thought that we find ourselves facing a current of integration of the theories of the different social sciences and that, if one were able to bring together the efforts of the co-authors of *The Emerging Nations* and Parsons' group, an integrated theory of development might arise from that multidisciplinary effort that could contribute to the elimination of the fallacy of the Marxist proposition. Similar efforts are being made in the Latin American area among social scientists who have centered their attention on the scientific study of development problems.

Upon the basis of the preceding analysis we shall study the process of modernization of the style of life, starting from a hypothesis contrary to Marxist theory. Within the grand strategy of development in the network of interactions that exist between the economic subsystem and the modernization of the style of life, it is this last element that is the fundamental aspect in the interactive process. In other words, "the extent to which economic (or political) development takes place depends very largely upon the elements situated in the non-rational world of values and value orientations, *a world existing in the minds of men*; thereupon depend what men seek and how they seek it. . . . We might then say that economic development tends to proceed most rapidly when, hereditary and physical environment conditions being given, a people's system of values is most favorable to the selection of development-oriented ends, and when its value orientations are most favorable to the selection of means optimally suited to realize those ends."[42] Translating this into simpler language, we may say that the modern development of the social sciences has come to discover what had already been discovered: that to change a society it is necessary to change the content of the minds of men who constitute that society. Professor Spengler, in a brilliant study, has clearly shown the strategic importance of change in the "content of men's minds" in the process of development.[43]

Our analysis may now continue with the formulation of a question: how can a traditional or transitional society achieve modernization of its style of life, in order that there may be produced within it a regular flow of innovations within the social system, leading to the creation of an economy of self-sustained growth? Or what are the social processes through which a traditional society can learn how to modernize its style of life?

In a search for an answer to this question, a proposition of Myrdal's may serve as a point of departure. Myrdal has said that, from a cultural point of view, an underdeveloped country "has reasons for learning from all the world. It is a policy of self-defeatism," he adds, "which a poor country least of all can afford, to build up barriers against the richer world's civilization and values."[44] Since the process of modernization consists of a modification of the style of life, and this has been produced in the developed world, Myrdal's proposition seems completely acceptable. If an underdeveloped country were to limit the sources through which it can *learn* to modernize itself, this would be limiting the universe of its choice and thus curtailing its own possibilities of modernization.

Following Parsons and Shils we shall distinguish "three major classes of culture patterns: (1) Systems of ideas or beliefs. . . (2) Systems of expressive symbols; for instance, art forms and styles. . . (3) Systems of value orientations. Here the primary interest is in the evaluation of alternatives from the viewpoint of their consequences or implications. . . ."[45]

Culture patterns constitute, at bottom, patterns of "learned significance," in accordance with which an individual or group orients its conduct and obtains satisfactions, if its comportment conforms to the systems of ideas or beliefs, expressive symbols, and value orientations of the human group to which it belongs. An American whose ideology accepts the theory of free enterprise and the styles of life deriving from the introduction of technology into everyday life, and who is an enthusiastic partisan of democratic norms, will surely find greater personal satisfactions than an individual who rejects such culture patterns. If such a person were suddenly transplanted to the Soviet society, he would find total opposition between these patterns and those which guide a Soviet citizen.

In developed societies, culture patterns that orient the behavior of the group's members are inculcated through channels which the society has created to produce the socialization of persons, that is, to obtain congruence of personal conduct with group norms. In other words, the process of socialization of a child is brought about in normal fashion through the means of his integration into a determined culture system whose patterns present a *certain grade of stability.*

In underdeveloped nations, on the other hand, the process of learning requires an alteration of the traditional society's culture patterns. The value orientations, systems of ideas and beliefs, and expressive symbols must all experience a *certain grade of change* if it is desired to modernize the style of life.

From the moment that modernization of a society implies this process of change, we must ask ourselves what are the learning mechanisms. Considering the relations between the person or group involved and the "environment" through which the new patterns are obtained, the processes of learning have been classified into three basic types: identification, imitation, and innovation. A person or group "confronts the problem of acquiring these patterns for itself by creating new ones, or by acquiring them from some existing patterns"[46] that serve as models. "In the former case we have innovation. In the latter case we have either imitation or identification."[47] Whatever the type of process employed by an underdeveloped society to incorporate desired modern patterns into its social and cultural systems, another process is implied, namely, a process of communication between the underdeveloped society and the developed societies. As Marx pointed out over a century ago, "the more developed society presents to the less developed society a picture of its own future."[48] To use terms from modern sociology and social psychology, the former societies serve as models, as reference groups, for the latter in the process of modernization.

Since a modern society is defined as one that is capable of insuring a regular flow of innovations within its social system, it is evident that, of the three processes of learning given above, innovation has the dominant role. Modernization requires a psycho-social process through which the underdeveloped society—stimulated from abroad by the vision of its own future—combines already-known patterns and integrates them into new patterns. As Lerner has shown, there is no "transfer of institutions" or patterns from developed societies to underdeveloped societies but rather a *transformation* of them within the developing society.[49] This transformation requires, in greater or lesser degree, the appearance of patterns that are *totally* or *partially* new to the societies in transition. In both cases, the distinctive trait of learning is a new pattern or innovation. This process necessarily involves a break with the past, a discontinuity, a certain disruption in the societies that assimilate the culture patterns of the modern societies. On the other hand, if we consider the postulate of "self-preservation" of the model, a certain level of innovation appears as an essential condition in order that the transitional society may assimilate new patterns and at the same time conserve those aspects of its own social and cultural systems which are compatible with modernization. This synthesis of the old with the new can hardly be achieved without the appearance of these *new patterns,* even though the process of innovation originates in the imitation of the "model" offered by the developed societies.

The examples given in Table III, with respect to the problems on which scientific research and development of modern societies would materially assist underdeveloped countries, provide good material for illustrating the importance of innovation as the basic process of learning in developing societies. The table distinguishes four fundamental stages of scientific and technological development upon which work is presently needed: (1) basic science; (2) invention or improved technology; (3) adaptive invention to fit known technology to other countries and cultures; and (4) the introduction and spread of known technology. There is no doubt that the first three items constitute areas of innovation, and the last, the introduction and expansion of already-known technology, implies changes of greater or lesser scope in the underdeveloped societies which require the appearance of new patterns of behavior. For example, the importation of television sets into an underdeveloped society signifies an impact upon the habits of use of leisure, on the diffusion of propaganda, and on the family budgets of the population segments able to acquire the new technological expression. This impact affects the economic subsystem (through the introduction of new merchandise that requires a network of commercial distribution and connections with importing firms, alteration of consumption habits, etc.), the political subsystem that enjoys a new propaganda instrument, and the social and cultural subsystems of the total society, because this new means of mass communication is a vehicle through which the revolution of rising expectations takes place. The control and management of this series of impacts often calls for a governmental decision; as a typical case, one can cite that of Chile, where the government has prevented the commercial diffusion of this technological instrument and has established that television transmission stations are to be controlled by the universities, in order that they may serve educational and not commercial ends. In this manner the government has prevented an excessive expenditure of foreign exchange that the country was in no condition to finance, and television has been utilized for the ends already indicated.

The foregoing analysis has permitted us to identify the importance of innovation as a fundamental means of learning for underdeveloped societies. It is now fitting to ask ourselves: what is the relationship of innovation to the grand strategy of development? On answering this question we find again that the national and international aspects of grand strategy appear so intimately united that in reality they present themselves to us as different sides of the same coin.

Modern sociology has identified four types of functional problems that every social system must solve to a greater or lesser degree. "They have been given the following names: (1) pattern maintenance and tension management; (2) adaptation; (3) goal attainment; and (4) integration. . . . Broadly speaking, the social structure of every system does to some extent solve these problems; if it did not, the system would cease to exist as an independent or distinctive entity."[50]

In the process of learning based on innovation, the society in transition sees itself confronted with the solution of these four functional problems. The goal attainment within our model is the modernization of the society, whose external repercussion is an elevation of the nation's real status in the stratified international system. To reach this goal the nation must introduce new patterns into its social and cultural systems, adapting those patterns already known in developed societies to meet its own needs. This adaptation should be carried out so that the conflict produced between the old patterns that tend to subsist (pattern maintenance) and the new patterns, derived from innovation, is subjected to adequate control (tension management) in order that the social system in its entirety be *integrated.*

From the international point of view, the objective pursued by the underdeveloped society (goal attainment) may be brought about by different forms, according to the underdeveloped country's *processes of adaptation* to the other nations that serve as models. The grand strategy of development requires rational planning of these processes so that: (a) the underdeveloped nation may maximize the possibilities of learning in its approach to modernization, and (b) the impacts produced in its social and cultural systems do not generate excessive internal tensions or irrational expressions in respect to the nations that serve as models.

Grand strategy requires, with respect to the first point, that the nation adopt a universalist position. To return to Myrdal's proposition, it is necessary that the nation learn from all the world, not only from determined countries, and that it widen as far as possible its frames of reference. For the process of learning, these must be provided by the developed nations of the Western bloc, the developed nations of the Communist bloc, or by underdeveloped nations, whatever their international political position, that are found to be in a more advanced stage. This aspect of grand strategy is directly related to technical assistance and the reform of educational systems in underdeveloped countries.

As for the second point, international grand strategy requires that nationalistic expressions derived from the objective that the society pursues (goal attainment) be held within rational limits.

Let us examine, first of all, the problems that an underdeveloped nation must meet in relation to technical assistance and the reform of its educational system. International grand strategy of development requires that the relationship between technical assistance and educational reform be carefully established so that the first may serve the aims of the second.

The reform of the educational system constitutes a central aspect of the modernization process of an underdeveloped country. In a developed society education serves the aims of the socialization of the child, of the adolescent, and of the adult. Education is a central route through which the social system succeeds in instilling into its new members the culture patterns that support the *integration* of the society as a system. In the underdeveloped countries, education must serve a much more complex aim: in effect, the problem that the society now faces is how to utilize the educational system in order to inculcate through it new culture patterns from which value orientations that favor the modernization process will be derived. In consequence, in underdeveloped societies education must try to socialize the individual, not with respect to old culture patterns, but with respect to new ones whose introduction calls for grand strategy. Such a requirement supposes the establishment of an educational plan in which this aim is considered as an essential part of grand strategy. Within this context it is important that education can enable the individual to meet the new situations that emerge periodically as a result of social change. That is, one of the basic objectives of educational reform in underdeveloped countries should be the creation of *innovating habits* in the child, adolescent, or adult who receives the education.

The Latin American countries again offer a good example of this problem. In these countries knowledge is transmitted principally as if it were *a body of given data,* not subject to major changes; the teaching system rests upon the *memorization of these data by the student,* and mental habits of critical reasoning in response to all kinds of problems reach a stage of only precarious development even in the period of university education. This educational structure not only opposes the formation of innovating habits which are vital to the process of modernization, but it is also

contrary to the general aims of all authentic education. As Whitehead has established in his work *The Aims of Education,*

We have to remember that the valuable intellectual development is self-
development, and that it mostly takes place between the ages of sixteen
and thirty. . . . In training a child to activity of thought above all
things we must beware of what I will call "inert ideas"—that is to say,
ideas that are merely received into the mind without being utilized, or
tested, or thrown into fresh combinations. In the history of education,
the most striking phenomenon is that schools of learning, which at one
epoch are alive with a ferment of genius, in a succeeding generation
exhibit merely pedantry and routine. The reason is that they are
overladen with inert ideas. Education with inert ideas is not only useless; it is, above all things, harmful. *Corruptio optima, pessima.* . . .
Every intellectual revolution which has ever stirred humanity into
greatness has been a passionate protest against inert ideas. Then, alas,
with pathetic ignorance of human psychology, it has proceeded by some
educational scheme to bind humanity afresh with inert ideas of its own
fashioning. Let us now ask how in our system of education we are to
guard against this mental dryrot. We enunciate two educational com-
mandments, "Do not teach too many subjects," and again, "What you
teach, teach thoroughly." The result of teaching small parts of a large
number of subjects is the passive reception of disconnected ideas, not
illuminated with any spark of vitality. Let the main ideas which are
introduced into a child's education be few and important, and let them
be thrown into every combination possible. The child should make
them his own and should understand their application here and now in
the circumstances of his actual life. From the very beginning of his
education the child should experience the joy of discovery. The discovery which he has to make is that general ideas give an understanding
of that stream of events which pours through his life, which is his
life. . . . I would only remark that the understanding which we want
is an understanding of an insistent present. The only use of knowledge
of the past is to equip us for the present. . . . Passing now to the
scientific and logical side of education we remember that here also
ideas which are not utilized are positively harmful. . . . In scientific
training, the first thing to do with an idea is to prove it. But allow
me for one moment to extend the meaning of "prove." I mean, to
prove its worth. Now an idea is not worth much unless the propositions in which it is embodied are true. Accordingly an essential part
of the proof of an idea is the proof, either by experiment or by logic,
of the truth of the proposition. But it is not essential that this proof
of the truth should constitute the first introduction to the idea. After
all, its assertion by the authority of respectable teachers is sufficient
evidence to begin with. In our first contact with a set of propositions,

we commence by appreciating their importance. That is what we all do in after-life. We do not attempt, in the strict sense, to prove or to disprove anything, unless its importance makes it worthy of that honor. These two processes of proof, in the narrow sense, and of appreciation, do not require a rigid separation in time. Both can be proceeded with nearly concurrently. But in so far as either process must have the priority, it should be that of appreciation by use.[51]

If Whitehead's propositions are valid for developed societies, they are even more valid for societies in the process of modernization, inasmuch as the formation of these habits of critical thought is indispensable to enable a person to adapt himself to a social and cultural system whose characteristic is change, provoked by the confrontation of new with old patterns. These habits of critical innovation are adequate channels to provide the solution for problems related to tension management.

For the transformation of the educational system around this basic idea, a planning policy must necessarily take into account: (a) the measure in which pedagogical techniques—and the content of the instruction itself—of educational systems in developed countries can serve to form innovating habits; and (b) the readjustments at which these systems must aim in order to adapt themselves to the necessities of the country on the three levels of education: primary, secondary, and university. Within the universalist position of learning from all the world, and for the formulation of an adequate educational plan, the policy-makers can solicit the assistance of an international educational organization, UNESCO, which has specialized in the technical study of educational problems. Nothing seems more obvious than to utilize this channel of universal co-operation and thus take advantage of the experience that the more developed nations have acquired in this matter. For example, in the field of primary education one can have recourse to the classification that UNESCO has made of the process of alphabetization which distinguishes three levels: elementary, intermediate, and functional. "Elementary alphabetization has been defined as that belonging to every adult or adolescent who has learned at a given moment the rudiments of reading, but who has not developed that ability to the point of being able to read rapidly, easily, and with full comprehension. It has been said that intermediate alphabetization is met when a person can read and comprehend significance, but cannot write a simple, short account of daily life."[52] Finally, "it is considered that a person has reached the functional level of alphabetization when he has acquired, in reading and writing, theoretical and practical knowledge which enables him to participate efficiently in all those activities which normally presuppose an elementary instruction in his cultural group. Functional literacy assumes maturity, independence, and endurance."[53]

For the strategy of development, the utilization of this knowledge appears to be fundamental, since only the so-called functional level of literacy can contribute with complete efficiency to the modernization process of the underdeveloped nation. The other levels could turn out to be disfunctional in the sociological sense.[54] That is, the uncontrolled explosion of aspirations that an inadequate alphabetization may create can reverberate through the social system in the form of excessive tensions that operate against the integration of the system. Educational planning has to contemplate all appropriate measures for reducing these tensions, through the means of functional alphabetization, and, when they are produced, for managing them through the mechanisms for social control of the system.

The objectives of educational reform thus established, the strategy of development requires the estimation of the educational demand that the modernization process implies. In a society that wishes to modernize itself through democratic means, this demand can be appraised in a far different fashion than it would in a society seeking the same end through another type of political system. We shall concern ourselves here only with this demand in the context of a democratic society in transition. Its estimation must be made from two basic elements: (a) the country's demographic growth and its repercussion on the educational system; and (b) the necessities that a developing society will meet within a long-term perspective. The first element takes into account the fact that the underdeveloped nations have very high rates of demographic growth, and, consequently, the number of persons who must be processed by the educational system is constantly increasing. The second element implies a dynamic conception; that is, the planning in this field—achieved on rational bases—must consider not only present educational requirements but also must foresee the society's future needs as they are derived from the process of development.

The dynamism inherent in an educational system of a transitional society in a *democratic process* of development supposes "a general type of education, whose content permits the effective participation of all the individuals in the society"[55] and whose benefits are extended to all the members of the nation.[56]   Two factors condition educational demand in a society in the rapid process of modernization: "(a) the necessity of attending to the integral formation of the personality of individuals, with no limitation other than their own aptitudes, and taking into account the capacities and skills necessary for the progress of the community; and (b) the requirements imposed by a system of social relations in rapid change, determined, in turn, by *a complex of national aspirations and by the influence of extra-national changes which the interdependence of the contemporary world makes more and more effective.*"[57]   From this second factor emerge two imperatives: the first refers directly to the capacity of the educational system to produce innovating habits that permit the adaptation of individuals to the rapidity of social change; the second assumes a certain flexibility in the system, in order that the different educational levels (primary, secondary, and university) may be adapted to qualitative variations (variations of capacities and skills) and quantitative variations (in terms of a maximum of educational opportunity for all the population) in educational demand.   This means that while the aforementioned levels "must be clearly defined, the structure that contains them must be flexible, to respond to a changed demand."[58]

We have said earlier that education should serve as a channel for personal socialization in order to favor the modernization process.   In this sense it is fitting to point out that the creation of an economy of self-sustained growth implies that the population of a country adopt rational habits of consumption, increasing its propensity to save and therefore reducing superfluous expenditures. At the same time, the creation of positive value orientations concerning economic progress is needed: discipline of work, economic value of the use of time, innovating attitudes for channeling savings into reproductive investments, in short, the appearance of a rational attitude from an economic viewpoint. Such an attitude is directly related to the educational system's capacity to socialize persons, in terms of giving them the possibility of adapting themselves to an economy undergoing rapid and profound change. Returning to the conception of the basic objectives of education formulated by Whitehead, the important thing is not so much the transmission of knowledge that corresponds to a *given* state of scientific and technological advance at the moment in which the education is imparted, but the creation in the individual of the bases of critical thinking which permit the permanent evolution of knowledge so characteristic of modern societies.

The estimation of educational demand likewise requires that the human resources mobilized through the educational system find occupational opportunities in agreement with the abilities and skills transmitted by the system. National societies in process of modernization present different levels of social inequality that "facilitate or impede an efficient recruitment of the talent required to fill positions generated by the functioning of social institutions and the production of goods and services. The process of economic growth implies, therefore, a decision (on the part of the policy-makers) about the nature and type of social stratification which the national community is disposed to accept, in the sense of a level and type of social inequality that may be functional to the tasks of social development. The requirements of a dynamic economy assume a social structure capable of adequately selecting the talent needed for its integration, continuity, and maintenance."[59]

In other words, the estimation of educational demand and the reform of the social structure in terms of functional social mobility and the modernization of the style of life are processes that are interwoven in such a manner that the new style of life (characterized by value orientations favorable to the functioning of the economic subsystem) cannot be produced unless the social structure acquires a sufficient level of flexibility to permit benefits to be drawn, with maximum efficiency, from the human product supplied by the educational system. The creation of an "intellectual proletariat" and of qualified labor that does not find occupations compatible with its skills are indexes of a lack of correlation between the modification of the educational system and the modification of the social structure.   Such lack of correlation is disfunctional to the integration of the national social system, and the social tensions thus created can dangerously affect its stability.

Having achieved, in the terms indicated, the evaluation of the educational system required by the modernization process, the next step in the rational sequence of action for policy-makers consists of matching that demand with the capacity of the educational system.   Such a confrontation will permit the discovery of the system's shortcomings, the determination of their causes, and the identification of the structural changes that the system should undergo in order to adapt itself to the quantitative and qualitative requirements of the new demand.

India's three Five-Year Plans and the report on education in Nigeria offer examples of this type of rational evaluation of educational demand in a transitional society.[60]

In this matching it is fundamental to allow for the role played by the three basic levels of education in relation to the modernization process.   In effect, although it is certain that no modern society can perform adequately without a functionally alphabetized population and a high grade of scholarship at the secondary level, it is necessary to point out the fact that the dynamic development of education at the university level occupies a vital position in the grand strategy of development.   By definition a modern society is one that is capable of producing a regular flow of innovations.   From an economic viewpoint this means that modern society, by means of a constant flow of innovations, is capable of systematically, continuously, and regularly applying the potentialities derived from science and technology to the exploitation of its resources.   Of all the sources of innovation, there is only one that is institutionalized: science.   Its aim is to produce change, and beyond its boundaries, change always finds resistance.[61]   Within underdeveloped societies, the universities are the principal vehicles of scientific advance.[62]   Consequently, if the universities, within the reform of the educational system, succeed in creating or modifying their structure in order to be able to better serve scientific advance, their role as permanent centers of innovation may well be a capital one in the modernization process.

This role needs to be carefully evaluated by policy-makers. W. Arthur Lewis has correctly pointed out in his book, *The Theory of Economic Growth,* that, from the economic point of view, a rational measure on the part of a poor country consists of placing equal importance upon the elimination of illiteracy and upon the creation of a university. The universities play a unique role in the modernization of society, and this is not solely because of their functioning as channels for scientific development and, therefore, for vital sources of innovation. If the quality of education that they impart reaches high levels, the universities become productive centers of an elite, with a modern mentality that can supply the social system with human elements of sufficient leadership capacity to direct, on the diverse planes of national activity, the social processes that modernization requires. The role that these men can play, from the viewpoint of the grand strategy of national development, is so decisive, and at the same time so imponderable, that it would be useless and irrational to attempt to measure the university's contribution to the modernization process with a purely economic criterion (in terms of cost per person graduated from the university). Who can doubt, for example, that an appreciable part of India's capacity to realize its modernization through democratic means can be attributed to the fact that it had the good fortune of possessing, at the moment of its independence, a group of men graduated from the best English university—a true modern elite—who could furnish the leadership that the nation needed? Who could dispute the vital role played in Latin America's development by the elite of economists working in ECLA? Not only a nation but an entire region, and the Inter-American System itself, have benefited from the technical studies and the leadership of this modernized elite.[63]

In the preceding paragraphs we have analyzed educational demand, the shortcomings of the educational system, and the readjustments that should be carried out in relation to future demand. Only when this evaluation has been made will the underdeveloped nation be able to establish the nature of the technical assistance it needs for the modernization of its educational system.

It is the task of the grand strategy of development to qualify this assistance, quantitatively and qualitatively, and, guided by a universalist attitude of *learning from all the world,* to localize the most adequate sources for obtaining it and channeling it toward the achievement of goals fixed by the educational plan. In Chapter II we have seen how the countries of the Colombo Plan have faced this problem with a realistic, total criterion that may perhaps serve as an example to other underdeveloped regions, including Latin America. International grand strategy also requires that the underdeveloped countries—on either a regional or a universal scale, in accordance with a specific definition of the international situation in this respect—unite their efforts to: (1) insure that the countries or international organizations furnishing the technical assistance contemplate adequate priorities as a function of available resources; (2) ascertain that those countries or organizations possess administrative units of teams of qualified men who know the culture and necessities of the countries or regions who are to receive the technical assistance, in order that it may be given in accordance with the realities of the underdeveloped nations and under conditions of maximum efficiency; (3) avoid unnecessary duplication; and (4) see that the assistance is given with reasonable speed. With respect to the first point, it is well to point out that a poorly established scale of priorities on the part of the countries or organizations administering the assistance can represent a wastage of human and material resources, which is translated into a source of frustration for them as well as for those who are to receive it. Again taking the Latin American case as an example, it is fitting to ask if the scale of priorities established by AID of the United States corresponds effectively to a rational planning of technical assistance and to the principles of self-help contemplated so much in the legislation that governs that agency, as in the program of the Alliance for Progress. In effect, AID has fixed the following scale of priorities with respect to Latin America: (a) aid to primary education; (b) aid to secondary education; and (c) aid to university education. On formulating this policy, was the affirmation made by ECLA's director at the conference of Bogotá in 1960 taken into account? (He stated that the Latin American countries could eliminate illiteracy through their own devices, without resorting to foreign aid.) Was the experience accumulated by UNESCO in its Principal Project of Primary Education in Latin America utilized? Was sufficient thought given to the strategic role of university education in the process of modernization of the Latin American nations? The reasonable reply to this series of questions constitutes a part of the international strategy of development, and when countries that lend aid and those that receive it do not have a clear understanding of its importance, technical assistance will not be planned on rational bases.[64]

With respect to the second point, it is well to show, again taking the Latin American case for illustration, that the United States government's administration of its programs of technical assistance—in spite of all the efforts made to date by President Kennedy—has not been efficiently organized. It has failed to place qualified personnel, who know the social and cultural reality of Latin America, into its Latin American programs. It still maintains in key agency posts people whose knowledge of the region is precarious and improvised.[65]

In relation to the third point it is apparent that international planning of technical assistance should avoid useless duplications among governments, international organizations, and private institutions. Such duplications can only mean a wastage of human and material resources, producing tensions and creating "nationalistic" feelings among the various agencies providing technical assistance. There are many examples that could be cited in this respect. Any participating observer of the work of the U.N.'s international organizations and of the international organizations of a regional type has had uncounted opportunities to verify it. In no case are these criticisms to be construed as an underestimation of the effective and meritorious efforts that many of these agencies have made. They are rather the posing of a problem that the international strategy of development must face and solve in accordance with a rational criterion of efficiency. Finally, with respect to the fourth point, we say that the international strategy of development requires that the most expeditious formulas be found for the negotiation of requests for technical assistance. These requests are often subject to such annoying formalisms and mechanisms (one might say of a ritual type) that, in some cases, a request for technical assistance needs to wait a year for a positive or negative answer.[66] It is unnecessary to say that such excessive delay not only gives rise to all sorts of frustrations on the part of the policy-makers from the requesting country, but also such slowness in decision-making prevents the underdeveloped country from being able to count on the required aid at the opportune moment.

To terminate our analysis of educational reform in relation to the grand strategy of development, we refer to the international financing of that reform. The report on education in Nigeria contains some suggestions of extraordinary relevance for grand strategy. On appraising the magnitude of the educational problem in that African country, the committee of experts stated:

> Our task is to forecast Nigeria's educational needs up to 1980. We could have approached this task by calculating what the country can afford to spend on education, and by proposing cautious, modest, and reasonable ways in which the educational system might be improved within the limits of the budget. We have unanimously rejected this approach to our task. The upsurge of Africa is so dramatic and so powerful that proposals which today appear to be reasonable and sensible will in a very few years appear to be short-sighted and timid. One has only to read reports on West African education written fifteen years ago to realize how even wise and experienced men under-estimated the pace at which West Africa is growing up. . . . To approach our task, therefore, we have to think of Nigeria in 1980: a nation of some 50 million people, with industries, oil, and well-developed agriculture; intimately associated with other free African countries on either side of its borders; a voice to be listened to in the Christian and the Moslem worlds; with its tradition in art preserved and fostered and with the beginnings of its own literature; a nation which is taking its place in a technological civilization, with its own airways, its organs of mass-communication, its research institutes. Millions of the people who will live in this Nigeria of 1980 are already born. Under the present educational system more than one half of them will never go to school. Like people elsewhere, their talents will vary from dullness to genius. Somehow, before 1980, as many talented children must be discovered and educated if this vision of Nigeria is to be turned into reality. This is a stupendous undertaking. It will cost large sums of money. The Nigerian people will have to forego other things they want so that every available penny is invested in education. Even this will not be enough. Countries outside Nigeria will have to be enlisted to help with men and money. *Nigerian education must for a time become an international*

enterprise. It is on this level of thinking that we have made our recommendations. We have, of course, taken every precaution to save needless expenditure, but our proposals remain massive, expensive and unconventional. To accomplish them all would undoubtedly be beyond the present resources of the Federal and Regional Governments. But a way must be found. To the best of our beliefs nothing less than these proposals will suffice for Nigeria's development. To entertain any more modest programme is to confess defeat. . . . [Our recommendations] will be practicable only if Nigerian Education seeks outside aid and if the Nigerian people themselves are prepared to accord education first priority and to make sacrifices for it. . . . We recommend that the Federal Government explore the possibility of international aid for Nigeria's schools and universities.[67]

The conclusions of these paragraphs, from the viewpoint of international grand strategy of development, are: (1) one must grant first priority to educational reform in the task of modernization; (2) the cost of such reform cannot be constrained by the budgetary limitations of the underdeveloped nation. Although it is clear that the nation should make every effort to devote the highest possible amount of its resources to the financing of the plan, it is necessary to work from the premise that the part that the country cannot pay must be financed through foreign aid; (3) this massive, costly, unconventional approach is the only realistic one if we realize the educational demand of a developing nation, and any modest forecast along traditional lines to solve this type of problem is doomed to failure; and (4) the government must develop an active international strategy to find foreign resources.

If the primordial role of the educational system as a factor of change and modernization in an underdeveloped society is recognized, the recommendations of the report cited seem to be the only realistic, rational ones to adopt. It is up to the policy-makers of the underdeveloped countries to be aware of the problem as it has been outlined and to carry out the international strategy that makes it possible to obtain the necessary foreign aid. The international strategy of education for development, based on a dynamic conception of educational demand, must replace the opportunistic and improvised approach *guided by a psychology that says it is rational to accept any kind of technical assistance that is offered,* which many underdeveloped nations have followed up until now. The task will become easier if the countries or agencies giving the technical assistance comprehend the urgency of long-term planning for the realization of educational reforms. But if such comprehension does not occur, it is up to the underdeveloped nations to employ grand strategy to obtain this inescapable objective of the process of modernization.

Reform of educational systems touches, nevertheless, but one aspect of the modernization process. In effect, this reform, within the grand strategy, serves as an instrument for socializing *the generations that are being incorporated into the social life* in accordance with the new culture patterns from which value orientations favorable to development are derived. The process of modernization also requires that those *generations already formed* under the old system and socialized in conformance with traditional patterns acquire the new ones. Put in other terms, the modernization process also implies socialization of adults, and this cannot be carried out through the formal channels of the educational system. It requires other types of more complex mechanisms. A developing nation must be morally and psychologically mobilized to produce, in the adult population, the internalization of patterns necessary to the modernization process. A question then arises for the grand strategy: how to attain this objective without giving rise to irrational expressions?

The reply may be found in the international expressions of grand strategy. In the conclusions of Chapter I, we showed that Rostow had indicated that a reactive nationalism was, historically, the most powerful motive for the transformation of transitional societies into modern societies. And we point out, on our part, that the nationalism of the underdeveloped countries is equally a reactive nationalism, reacting against *atimia* or its consequences and trying to enhance the status of the nation in a stratified world dominated by the values of wealth, power, and prestige. It is this awareness of the loss of prestige and of the nation's status which policy-makers must awaken in the national public opinion in order to obtain an internalization of the new values characteristic of a modern society. From this sentiment of privation arises the psychological springs capable of building the solidarity of the national group, and it is this solidarity that makes possible the realization of development tasks. The problem then consists of making this nationalistic explosion rational and orienting it positively, suppressing or reducing the irrational and negative expressions of the affirmation of in-group values before the rest of the world.

For the creation of a rational nationalism, the first task of grand strategy is to define the national interest in terms of development. That is to say, to define the complex of national tasks constituted by the diverse aspects of the development plan in its national and international projections. The second task is to confront those objectives with the current state of social order, to provoke in the national group the idea of privation, of dissatisfaction, from which a crisis psychology may emerge. The third task is the diffusion of an awareness of this *atimic* state. The fourth task consists of the propagation of the ideology of development, as the only way that the national group has to improve its prestige and status. The fifth task is that of emphasizing the relations among the national and international aspects of development, in the sense that in this way the national group, while elevating its status in the stratified international system, may also furnish its members with higher standards of living and a reduction in social inequalities.

In summary, a rational nationalism can emerge if the members of the national group succeed in identifying themselves with the goals pursued by the nation. In the creation of this group consciousness it is necessary that the idea of the loss of "national prestige" be channeled toward tasks implanted by development and not toward expressions of conflict with other national groups. It is also essential that the grand strategy succeed in creating an atmosphere of crisis in national values and in associating development tasks with an increase in the status of the nation, as well as with increases in equality, justice, and living standards. In this fashion there will appear those psychological mechanisms that permit the integration of adults into the modernization process.

The creation of this crisis psychology appears as the axis of the entire process, and the underdeveloped countries offer it fertile soil. In effect, the sentiment of privation of material and cultural goods—provoked by comparison with the developed world; the state of dissatisfaction, insecurity, and tensions arising from the revolution of rising expectations; and the sensation of threat to the very survival of the national group in conditions of dignity and respect before the rest of the world—constitutes an adequate climate for the production of group solidarity, wherein old habits, rooted in traditional patterns, can give way to value-orientations favorable to the development process. This psychology, similar to that of a state of war against an external enemy, can bring about the change of culture patterns while maintaining the integration of the social system.

The idea that national independence and prestige will be seriously impaired, until a state of modernization in the society is attained, is the *leitmotiv* that should guide the grand strategy of development. The creation of a psychology of war against obstacles opposing the process of modernization must impregnate the action of the policy-makers and resound over all the nation through mass communication media.[68]

2. *Relationship between the basic structure of the model and international actions in the patterns of power and prestige*

Having established those elements which comprise the basic structure of the model, it is now proper to analyze the type of relationship existing between international actions derived from that structure and international actions of the underdeveloped nations in the patterns of power and prestige.

The study of the basic structure of the model revealed to us that international actions are organized around two fundamental objectives: (a) international actions designed to promote the creation of an economy of self-sustained growth; and (b) international actions designed to bring about the modernization of the style of life.

In the construction of the basic model we pointed out the Marxist fallacy and held that within the grand strategy of development the modernization of the style of life is the fundamental factor in the interactive process. It is evident that policy-makers should adopt international actions under both headings (a) and (b), but in so doing they should not lose sight of the necessity for giving to the transformation of the style of life all the importance it derives from its primordial role in the achievement of the grand strategy's ultimate goal.

We may now study the manner in which the system of action of the basic structure of the model is merged with international actions in the patterns of power and prestige. The conception of development planning as grand strategy permits us to find the key to this integration. The objectives of grand strategy are defined by the model's basic structure, and since they show the orientation of the system of action, international actions in the patterns of power and prestige merely fall in the category of specific strategies, subordinated to the grand strategy.

We may now ask what should be the goals of these specific strategies in the power and prestige patterns, in order to serve the ends of the grand strategy. The grand strategy calls for the adoption of certain international actions, and the obtaining of the aims of such actions depends on the degree to which the nation is capable of influencing other countries—developed or undeveloped —or international organizations to achieve the modification of their actions in accordance with its own. For example, if within the grand strategy, the change of the IMF's monetary policy, the attainment of an agreement for regulating price fluctuations of primary products, or the modification of priorities of technical assistance from the countries or agencies furnishing it appears as a necessity, these aims may be more easily achieved when the influence that the interested nation has over those countries or organizations is greater. This influence depends in large measure on the position that the nation occupies in the patterns of power and prestige within the stratified international system. Consequently, the specific strategies in these patterns should have as a basic goal an elevation of the nation's real status. Nevertheless, as these strategies are subordinated to the grand strategy, the nation's international actions in such patterns may only be developed within limits that do not perturb the actions of grand strategy.

If we compare this requirement of specific strategies with the typologies established in Chapters III and IV, we can construct a table in which we may observe the compatibility or incompatibility of international actions, in the power and prestige patterns

TABLE XXI

GRADE OF COMPATIBILITY OF INTERNATIONAL ACTIONS IN THE
PATTERNS OF POWER AND PRESTIGE, DERIVED FROM THE
TYPOLOGIES OF CHAPTERS III AND IV, WITH THE OBJECTIVES
OF THE GRAND STRATEGY OF DEVELOPMENT WITHIN THE MODEL

International Actions Derived from the Typologies		Actions in the prestige pattern	Grades of Compatibility with the Objectives of the Grand Strategy Established in the Basic Structure of the Model		
Actions in the power pattern		Actions in the prestige pattern	Compatible	Compatible in the grade in-dicated	Incompatible
In its coercive dimen-sion (military power)	In its influential dimension				
Power policy on a local scale					X
Military power limited to national security				X	
Renunciation of power policy on local scale			X		
	Power policy in its influential dimen-sion (all types)		X		
		Leadership in accord-ance with the real status of the nation in the economic pattern	X		
		Leadership in dis-agreement with the real status of the nation in the eco-nomic pattern			X
		Leadership on the educational plane	X		
Power policy on world scale before nation has elevated its economic status					X
Power policy on world scale as a subordinate aspiration to elevation of economic status				X	

derived from these typologies, with the orientation of the grand strategy. (See Table XXI.)

This classification permits us to observe the three principal relationships that follow. (1) International actions in the power pattern in its coercive dimension are compatible with the grand strategy of development only from a negative point of view. That is, when the nation renounces this type of action (countries that do not practice power policies on a local scale) or when it is subordinated to the elevation of economic status. Put another way, a policy of military power cannot achieve an elevation of the nation's real status in the power pattern that serves the attainment of the ends of grand strategy. If a nation renounces a policy of power in its coercive dimension and thus conforms to the objectives of grand strategy, logically it cannot elevate its status in the power pattern. If, on the contrary, it decides on a power policy, its actions will be in contradiction with the goals of the grand strategy. (2) Only international actions in the pattern of power in its influential dimension are always in conformity with grand strategy and permit an increase in the nation's real status in this pattern. (3) International actions in the prestige pattern are adapted to the goals of the grand strategy if the form of leadership selected is in agreement with the nation's economic status. Only in this case will such actions comply with the double objective of elevating the nation's prestige status and serving the ends of the grand strategy.

Let us now consider in what manner the ends of specific strategies may be achieved by underdeveloped nations. It is necessary to draw a distinction in this respect between those nations which have adopted a neutralist position and those which adhere to the Western bloc. It is not to be doubted that the latter have a more limited universe of international selections than do the former. As pointed out by the Center for International Affairs of Harvard University,

The "nonalinement" position in international politics has the very practical effect of maximizing the power of neutralist nations in world diplomacy and is thus a response to their weakness. Possessing neither military nor economic strength, the neutralists have developed the tactics of negotiation into an effective instrument of policy. The growth of world public opinion has had the effect of democratizing diplomacy. Neutralist nations have both contributed to and exploited this development. By playing such roles as arbiter, conciliator, and negotiator in a context of world opinion which is moving from a norm of partisan bipolarity toward a more fluid tripolarity, they succeeded in maximizing the source of influence available to them in world politics. It is not mere coincidence that India places great stress on the United Nations as the arena for the conduct of world politics, for it is in the United Nations that world public opinion is given formal recognition and some authority. The discrepancy between equality of voting strength within the United National General Assembly and the actual power positions of various nations no doubt creates serious problems by throwing the relationship between authority, power, and responsibility out of joint. On the other hand, there is also no doubt that such a situation maximizes the influence of the ex-colonial nations. At the same time, given the growing Soviet and American preoccupation with the post-colonial, neutral nations, their position of neutrality can be materially advantageous.[69]

Recently Talcott Parsons, in his first attempt to apply his theory to the field of international relations, has presented an original point of view with respect to the bipolar character of the world system. We shall utilize it to illustrate our analysis of specific strategies in the patterns of power and prestige. Parsons has said that the division of the world into two rival blocs and the fact that the whole world has come to be a single political system have produced a political structure with some similarities to a biparty system. In this perspective the fighting of the rival parties—the Communist and Western blocs—within the cold war may be compared to a great campaign for the conquest of an "electorate" made up of world public opinion. In this campaign both "parties" try to present to the electorate the advantages to be derived from the adoption of their political solutions and from the acceptance of their ideologies, insisting upon the differences that separate them rather than showing points of agreement between them. Thus they utilize, to a certain extent, the same techniques used on the national plane to conquer the electorate.

Following Parsons' comparison, we may say that within this world "electorate" the neutralist underdeveloped nations find themselves in a privileged position. In effect, they constitute the "uncommitted electorate," and through the very dynamics of a biparty political structure the two "parties" are obliged to give special concern to this sector's opinion. Each makes an effort to obtain the support of these nations in its electoral campaign or, if that is not possible, tries to insure that they maintain their "uncommitted" position as a means of preventing their aiding the rival "party." Many examples might be cited in this respect, but we shall mention only one. For the first time in the history of the cold war, the rival "parties" have permitted eight neutral nations to participate in the Geneva Conference on Disarmament. Within the "biparty" structure, it is logical that no member of the underdeveloped "electorate" already allied with one of the two "parties" has been invited. What reason would there be for it, since these nations are already supporting one of the "parties" and are consequently "represented" at the Conference? The eight neutral nations, conscious of their roles as "arbiters," "conciliators," and "negotiators," have not lost this opportunity to maximize their influence. According to information furnished by the *New York Times*, "the eight neutral states suggested a compromise between the Western and Soviet positions. The neutrals proposed that when 'suspicious events' occur in any country (and are registered on seismographs in the outside world), that country voluntarily invites an international inspection. If it refuses to issue such an invitation, the other powers could abrogate the treaty. Both Arthur Dean of the U.S. and Russia's Valerian Zorin responded cautiously that the neutral proposal offered some ground for further negotiations."[70]

From the viewpoint of our analysis it is significant to show that some of the eight neutral nations—India, for example—are nations that act as leaders within the uncommitted "electorate." This explains why they were chosen by the rival "parties" to take part in the Conference. If one of these "uncommitted" leaders supports the propositions of one of the "parties," the repercussion on the rest of the "electorate" will be magnified by the fact that it is a leader and not merely a member of the electorate.

It is clear, then, that the neutralist nations have discovered an adequate way to develop specific strategies which permits them to increase their international status in the patterns of power and prestige.

Let us study next how the underdeveloped nations of the Western bloc can develop specific strategies in this field. The Parsonian comparison demonstrates that it would be an oversimplification to consider these specific strategies as attempts at "blackmail." The fact that each nation tries to increase, where possible, its prestige and influence in an effort to achieve the goals of grand strategy, is derived from the very structure of the "biparty" system. If the leaders of the rival parties and the leaders of the uncommitted electorate are trying to maximize their own prestige and influence within the stratified international system, the underdeveloped members may, with equal reason, assert their rights within each "party" in the dynamics of the electoral campaign. The existence within each party of pressure groups with different interests is a characteristic of biparty systems on the national plane, and their transposition to the international political system does not substantially alter the nature of the phenomenon.

In Chapter III we pointed out the neutralist tendencies that have begun to arise in the Latin American nations and the manner in which Brazil was assuming the leader's role in these tendencies. Within the context of this chapter we shall see how the necessity of accepting the dynamics of these tendencies, as an almost inevitable consequence of the cold war, has been recognized in several different studies prepared under the direction of the Foreign Relations Committee of the United States Senate.[71] The following paragraphs from these studies are significant for our analysis:

(1) One political conviction, shared by most articulate opinion in the new nations, has been a source of considerable dismay in the United States. This is the profound desire for withdrawal from the power conflict between the West and the Soviet bloc. The label attached to this sentiment is "neutrality," or "nonalinement." The United States has never really decided how it should regard a nation that has announced its neutrality in the conflict between democratic and communist countries. At times, U.S. statesmen have announced that they regard this neutrality as immoral and irresponsible. At other times, spokesmen for the American Government have accepted neutrality grudgingly, with expressions of regret and real sorrow at the neutral nation's inability to distinguish between right and wrong. The records of congressional hearings leave no doubt that questions about neutrality of specific nations enter into decisions about the size and direction of U.S. foreign aid. . . .

(2) To insist, either through such psychological warfare as stigmatizing neutrality as immoral or employing more overt tactics as withholding or skimping on economic aid, can at best win us reluctant

alliances with governments that can readily be overthrown on the very issue of too close an association with a military power. In many parts of the free world, evidence of U.S. rigidity or intolerance on this issue can antagonize those liberal elements who are our natural political allies on the issues of the day and of tomorrow. Liberal and moderate left parties throughout the Western community are strong, and quick to belabor any indications of rigidity in the U.S. position. . . .

(3) A people [the United States] with a long tradition of isolation, particularly during major periods of the nation's growth and development, ought to be superbly tolerant of countries which are currently experiencing a not dissimilar evolution and demonstrating the same symptoms on the international scene. *It sometimes seems to our friends abroad that our national preoccupation with the danger of international communism so dominates our thoughts that we cannot concede legitimacy to a position of neutrality that we ourselves held for most of our early history. . . .*

(4) *We should . . . be relaxed about the new nation's natural urge for nonalinement with any big power in the cold war. Rather than trying to get them excited about our rivalry with the Russians, we should interest ourselves in the emergent nation's aspirations for modernization.* [This statement is proposed as a recommendation for the formulation of future U.S. foreign policy.][72]

Although the preceding considerations are made with special relation to the already neutral group of nations, they may be equally applied to the underdeveloped nations allied with the Western bloc. They express a tendency on the part of significant groups within the United States to favor a tolerant attitude toward neutralism.

Over such a base the underdeveloped nations of the Western bloc can construct their specific strategies for maximizing their international influence. These strategies may be developed on different levels: (1) within the Western bloc itself; (2) within world international organizations; (3) in relations of underdeveloped countries of the Western bloc with the neutral nations; and (4) in relations with the Soviet bloc. To illustrate the development of the strategy on these different levels, we again take the Latin American nations as a case study. These constitute over two-thirds of the underdeveloped nations allied with the United States (see map, page 112).

Within the Western bloc the Latin American nations can develop these strategies through one or several of the following measures. (a) Within the Western Hemisphere, they can reinforce their relations with Canada, whose nationalism grows day by day, as a reaction against an increasing dependence on the United States. (b) Within the Organization of American States, they can attempt to strengthen the powers of the Secretary General, as a means of fortifying the Organization itself, giving it a more equalitarian base in accordance with the principles contained in its Charter. If the Secretary General of the OAS had powers similar to those of the Secretary General of the United Nations, he could act with greater independence from the nationalistic urgings of the member states, which are often in conflict among themselves. A transformation of the OAS into a true international organization of sovereign states, taking the United Nations as a model, might induce Canada to join in. The structure of the Inter-American Development Bank, which is also characterized by the existence of a secretariat with wide powers, could itself serve as a model, *mutatis mutandis,* for the achievement of this end. Finally, the British Commonwealth, which has evolved from a structure of power toward one of free states, might also serve as an example.

The Latin American nations, acting within the OAS as a pressure group, might bring it about that the United States would *practically* recognize the equalitarian ideology of the Charter and stop considering this organization as a power structure for the service of its foreign policy.[73] If our hypothesis is valid that one of the sources of international prestige is the congruence of international policy and value orientations, a new American attitude in the sense indicated above would strengthen its position before the "rival party" and before world opinion. In effect, there would then exist complete agreement between the ideology and value orientations of the United States, both in their national and international aspects, and the assumed attitude. The United States would increase its prestige within the hemisphere; it would demonstrate a profound historical comprehension of the dynamics of the "bi-party" system; it would greatly weaken a permanent source of Cuban attacks; and it would suppress existing tensions within the Inter-American System stemming from the continual contradiction in the comparison between the member nations' formal status and their real status.

With respect to the Alliance for Progress, it would be demonstrated that the emphasis of American policy in relation to Latin America rests more on Progress than on Alliance. The Latin American countries should undertake a massive information campaign within the United States to create an atmosphere favorable to such a policy. Important groups of American university specialists in Latin American affairs, of businessmen, of policy-makers, and of the press might well favor the development of this strategy, if it were implanted as a means of fortifying the Inter-American System.

Finally, (c) in the development of this strategy within the Western bloc, the Latin American countries should reinforce their political, economic, and cultural relations with the countries of Western Europe, especially with those that have been historically connected to Latin America.

Within the international organizations of a world character, such as the United Nations and its specialized agencies, the development of the strategy should be based on a rational policy of promoting the modernization of the underdeveloped world. The Latin American countries should systematically co-ordinate their policies with the neutral nations in terms of maximizing their influence, which permits them to achieve the objectives of the grand strategy. Such co-ordination would not have an exclusive character but rather one of co-operation with the developed nations of the Western bloc.

In their relations with the neutralist underdeveloped world, the strategy of the Latin American countries—the group of underdeveloped nations with the longest history of independence—should take on universal dimensions with the object of increasing contacts of all kinds with the Asiatic and African nations. Experiences of fruitful innovation in the international field, such as the work of ECLA, the creation of the Inter-American Development Bank, the Latin American Free-Trade Association, and the Central American Common Market should be placed at the service of the underdeveloped countries of those two continents as models of inspiration. At the same time the negative experiences of Latin America might well serve to show those countries certain errors that the Latin Americans have committed in their process of modernization. Finally, as for their relations with the Soviet bloc, the Latin American strategy should further the establishment of economic and diplomatic relations with that bloc, in the same manner and for the same reasons as given by the developed nations of the Western bloc.

3. *Relations between national and international aspects of grand strategy*

In the preceding paragraphs we have analyzed the basic structure of the model and its relationship to specific strategies in the patterns of power and prestige. We have thus described the model of the grand strategy of development by analyzing its international aspects. It is now fitting to establish the relations between the national and international aspects of the grand strategy which can only be separated for analytical reasons. In effect, grand strategy is a complex of actions, integrated into systems and subsystems that are developed as much on the national level as on the international level. As we have stated in another part of this chapter—following Professor Dawson—"the mutual interaction of foreign policy and national politics [is of such a nature] that these two elements in the totality of the political process form a continuum and . . . neither can be adequately understood in isolation."[74]

An exhaustive and adequate analysis of these relations would demand for itself alone a separate study and a considerable theoretical and empirical effort, which has not yet been done. The present analysis will attempt only to show some aspects that seem to be significant. Consequently, our analysis should be regarded as both tentative and disputable. The analysis has been made with a profound awareness of the gross character of the judgments made.

In Table XXII we have attempted to point out the place occupied by the grand and specific strategies of development in the complex of systems and subsystems of the underdeveloped nation and to establish some of their basic relationships with the international system. In the construction of the table we have utilized principally several aspects of the theoretical schema of Parsons

THE PLACE OF GRAND STRATEGY OF DEVELOPMENT IN THE COMPLEX OF NATIONAL AND INTERNATIONAL SYSTEMS

Developed countries
"The more developed society presents to the less developed society a picture of its own future."[1]

International System
Nation-states are the main units of the International System. The International System has many subsystems: the two rival blocs, the regional and world international organizations, etc.

Reference Group behavior.[2]

Revolution of rising expectations

Underdeveloped countries
They have a low real status within the International System.

National Society
It is a complex social system composed of many subsystems, its *social structure* is characterized by a certain type and degree of social stratification. In underdeveloped countries the type and degree of social stratification is characterized by a low degree of social mobility.

POLITY The polity is a subsystem parallel to the economy in which "the generation and allocation of power occurs through a set of structures and processes."[3] The political subsystem "is a system of interactions to be found in all independent societies which performs the functions of integration and adaptation, (both *internally and vis-à-vis other national societies*) by means of the employment or threat of employment of more or less physical compulsion. Is the *legitimate order-maintaining or transforming system of the society.*"[4] It is composed of *political and governmental* structures.[5] Within it the policy-makers make the decisions connected with the formulation and implementation of grand and specific strategies of development *in its national and international aspects.* The political subsystems of underdeveloped countries can be classified according to their degree of competitiveness and political modernity (see Table XXIII).

ECONOMY The economy is a subsystem parallel to the polity. In an underdeveloped society this subsystem is characterized for its incapacity for self-sustained growth.

CULTURAL SYSTEM "The cultural-system focus is . . . on 'patterns' of meaning, e.g., of values, of norms, of organized knowledge and beliefs, of expressive form."[6] This with the social system of the national society forms a socio-cultural sphere. "This sphere [has] the properties of *creating and maintaining* a patterned cultural tradition." At the same time, it involved organized systems of structured or "institutionalized interaction between large numbers of individuals."[7] In underdeveloped societies, the style of life characteristic of the socio-cultural sphere is incapable of producing a regular flow of innovations and an economy of self-sustained growth.

→Grand and specific strategies of development are subsystems of the polity. Specific strategies of development are subsystems of grand strategy.

Development (or modernization) *is the collective goal of the national society*, both internally and vis-à-vis other national societies. This collective goal is motivated and driven by a reactive nationalism—reacting against *atimia*—attempting to enhance the real status of the nation.

International strategies of development are aimed: (a) to obtain within the International System the means necessary to implement the ends of modernization; (b) to raise the real status of the nation.

National strategies of development are aimed to produce changes in the socio-cultural sphere of the society and in the economy in order to meet the two requirements of a modern society: (a) a capacity to produce a regular flow of innovations, and (b) a capacity for self-sustained economic growth.

———This line shows the relationship between the real status of the underdeveloped country in the International System and the choice of development as the collective goal of the national society. — —This line shows that the formulation and implementation of grand and specific strategies of development are dependent on the decisions made in the political subsystem.

1. Karl Marx, *Capital.*
2. The fact that developed societies are models for underdeveloped societies originates patterns of reference group behavior.
3. Talcott Parsons, "Power, Party and System," in S. Sidney Ulmer (ed.), *Introductory Readings in Political Behavior* (Chicago: Rand McNally and Company, 1961) p. 128.
4. Gabriel A. Almond and James S. Coleman (eds.), *The Politics of the Developing Areas* (Princeton, N.J.: Princeton University Press, 1960) p. 7. Italics supplied by author.
5. *Ibid.*, p. 532. Italics supplied by author.
6. Talcott Parsons, "An Outline of the Social System," in Talcott Parsons, Edward Shils, Kaspar D. Naegle, and Jesse R. Pitts, *Theories of Society* (Glencoe, Ill.: The Free Press, 1961) I, 34.
7. *Ibid.*, p. 33.

and of the study of Almond and Coleman on the political systems of seventy-five underdeveloped nations.

For the interpretation of the table it is necessary to consider the nature of the process of interaction that is developed in the complex network of systems and subsystems shown. In the first place, as far as the national aspects of grand strategy and of specific strategies are concerned, national development presents itself as a total phenomenon that involves a coherent complex of processes among social, economic, and political factors of the national society, "in which the whole cannot be expected automatically to prosper as the result of the stimulation of one or more of the parts."[75]

Secondly, in this process of interaction that takes place within the national society, international aspects of the grand and specific strategies constantly intervene, integrating themselves and forming part of it in a decisive manner. For example, let us suppose that the policy-makers within a democracy have developed specific strategies to reform the educational system and to industrialize the economic subsystem, counting on international technical assistance and economic aid. Let us also assume that such aid is not opportunely supplied, and the execution of the plans is prevented. This may create tensions of a diverse nature within the political system; if they take on large dimensions and are skillfully exploited by parties or by pressure groups opposed to the democratic regime, a replacement of the democratic system by an authoritarian system may also be forthcoming. If such tensions are of lesser degree, the failure of the policy-makers in the realization of international strategies and the consequent loss of prestige within the political system may provoke their replacement by other policy-makers who will eventually begin to re-define the national and international aspects of grand strategy in order to acquire prestige and to maintain themselves in power. In this manner the formulation and implementation of grand strategy will be seriously affected. If the policy-makers excluded from power have succeeded in channeling the reactive nationalism within the criteria of rationality, the new policy-makers may be inclined toward new forms of nationalism, in which the countries or international organizations furnishing technical and financial aid will play the role of a "scapegoat." This scapegoat mechanism can lead the nation toward irrational expressions of nationalism within the international system.

The example mentioned, while showing the nature of the process of interaction between the national and international aspects of the grand strategy, also permits us to explain the placement of the grand and specific strategies in Table XXII. This table shows that their formulation and implementation depends primarily upon the political subsystem of the national society. It is within this subsystem that the policy-makers adopt the corresponding decisions, and it is principally through the government structures of this subsystem that the specific strategies are implemented and carried out. Within these structures the role of public administration is fundamental. As pointed out, "Development administration is the process of formulating policies necessary to achieve development goals and the mobilizing, organizing, and managing of all necessary and available resources to implement policies. Policy and administration are indistinguishable aspects of a continuum. Both are development administration."[76]

In order that the international aspects of the grand and specific strategies may be carried out, it is necessary that the political subsystem of the nation comply with certain requirements. In Table XXIII, Almond and Coleman have classified the political systems of underdeveloped nations. The classificatory criteria were: (a) the degree of competitiveness; and (b) the degree of political modernity. Given the array of disparate systems shown in the table, it was only at the highest level of generalization that the authors were able to make statements concerning their common properties. These fundamental features are pointed out in the footnotes of the table, and the reader is referred to them for the proper interpretation of the analysis. One of them—the lack of integration of underdeveloped societies—is particularly significant for our analysis and for the interpretation of the table. Following Levy, we can say, "Membership in a society is . . . a matter of degree. An individual is a more or less well integrated member of a society to the extent that he accepts and orients his action *without conflict* to the structures [of the society] in general, but particularly to the strategic and crucial institutions of that society."[77] Be-

TABLE XXIII
CLASSIFICATION OF POLITICAL SYSTEMS IN UNDERDEVELOPED AREAS

Classificatory Criteria		Countries by Areas						
Degree of Competitiveness	Degree of Political Modernity	Southeast Asia	South Asia	Near East	Africa		Latin America	
Competitive	Modern			Israel			Chile	Uruguay
	Mixed	Malaya	Ceylon	Lebanon			Argentina	Costa Rica
		Philippines	India	Turkey			Brazil	
Semi-competitive	Mixed	Burma		Algeria	Cameroons	No. Rhodesia	Colombia	Panama
		Indonesia		Iran	Central African	Nyasaland	Ecuador	Peru
		Thailand		Jordan	Republic	Rep. of Congo	Mexico	
				Morocco	Chad	Sierra Leone		
				Tunisia	Dahomey	Somalia		
					Gabon	So. Rhodesia		
					Ghana	Tanganyika		
					Guinea	Togoland		
					Ivory Coast	Uganda		
					Mali Federation	Upper Volta		
					Mauritania	Union of So.		
					Niger	Africa		
					Nigeria			
Authoritarian	Mixed	Cambodia	Pakistan	Iraq	Angola		Bolivia	Haiti
		Laos		Libya	Belgian Congo		Cuba	Honduras
				Sudan	Liberia		Dominican	Nicaragua
				U.A.R.	Mozambique		Republic	Paraguay
					Ruanda-Urundi		El Salvador	Venezuela
							Guatemala	
	Traditional			Afghanistan	Ethiopia			
				Saudi-Arabia				
				Yemen				

NOTE: Almond and Coleman analyze the above table on pages 533-36 as follows:

"The political systems covered in this survey are listed in Table XXIII according to the degree of competitiveness (competitive, semi-competitive, and authoritarian) and degree of political modernity (modern, mixed, and traditional). These classifications have been made with a profound awareness of the gross character of the judgments they represent, as well as of the fact that most of the systems concerned are in transition. The present classification is regarded as both tentative and disputable. Its only purpose is to bring all of the systems together in one framework for the analysis that follows.

"Given the array of disparate systems shown in Table XXIII, it is only at the highest level of generalization that one can make statements about their common properties. At that level, at least three features stand out. One is the "mixed" character of their social, economic, and political processes. Most of the countries are still overwhelmingly rural; the majority of the populations are illiterate. Per capita income in these countries remains very low. Social and geographical mobility is relatively high in the modern sector but very low in the rest of the society. The subsistence element persists as an important factor in most of the societies, and industrialization is either just getting underway or remains only an aspiration. The central structures of government are in most instances modern in form, but the authoritative as well as the political functions tend to be performed through a variety of "mixed" structures embodying both modern and traditional elements. These admixtures of modernity and traditionality are in some instances fusional, in others, isolative in character.

"A second common feature of these societies is their lack of integration. This is due in part to the ethnic, religious, racial, and cultural pluralism characteristic of the societies, in part to the limited and uneven operation of the processes of modernity. The critical fact, however, is not that these societies are pluralistic—pluralism is one of the key attributes of most modern societies—but that interests still tend to be defined predominantly in terms of tribe, race, religion, or communal reference group. The persistence and the predominance of such groups retards assimilation into the new national societies. Moreover, so long as interests are primarily rooted in and find expression through communal groups, they are far less amenable to aggregation in a competitive and bargaining process. Only in the modern sector of these mixed societies does one find the emergence of non-communal functionally specific interest groups.

"A third modal characteristic is the wide gap which exists between the traditional mass and the essentially modern subsociety of the Westernized elite. The latter controls the central structures of government and essays to speak and act for the society as a whole. This elite subsociety is the main locus of political activity and of change in the society at large. The character of the principal actors and participants in the elite subsociety is variable: in the new states and colonies of Africa, and in the new states of Asia, they constitute the urbanized, Western-educated minority; in the white oligarchic states of Africa and Latin America they constitute to varying degrees a culturally defined elite. The principal differences among the societies sharing this characteristic are the degree of access to the elite subsociety, and the extent to which there is communication between the two sectors in the form of such mediators as provincial elites, or an intermediate class in transition between the traditional and modern sectors. The gap between the two sectors illuminates the mixed character of the social and political processes in these countries as well as the degree of malintegration on the vertical plane.

"In addition to these general characteristics common to most of the seventy-five countries covered in this study, there are others which can be more appropriately summarized under the headings of the common outline the area authors have employed, namely, the processes of change and their political implications, and the functions of the political system."

SOURCE: Gabriel A. Almond and James S. Coleman (eds.), *The Politics of the Developing Areas* (Princeton, N.J.: Princeton University Press, 1960), pp. 533-36.

cause the process of modernization has been diffused in a fragmentary and uneven fashion among the underdeveloped nations, there exists a great mass of population that is not integrated within the society or is only partially integrated. If we take the Latin American nations as an example, we may say that the large indigenous groups of countries such as Peru, Bolivia, and Ecuador are on the limit of a total lack of integration. If we look at the Chilean case, where the indigenous proportion is insignificant, we find, on the other hand, that the *campesinos* are typical examples of poorly integrated individuals in relation to the large sectors of the urban middle and upper classes. If we now examine the level of modernization of the elite of these classes, we again find a difference in the degree of integration, with respect to the same classes, inasmuch as this elite could withstand a favorable comparison with the elites of any developed nation.

These uneven levels of integration of individuals within national societies directly affect the functioning of the political system, since its efficacy largely depends on a certain cohesion of the national group around certain fundamental value orientations. The possibilities of conflict between the large, backward masses and the modernized elites derive from the fact that the latter constitute subcultures, subsocieties, and minorities with respect to the former; a lack of consensus with respect to the basic objectives of the national society as a total human group is a consequence of the inadequate integration of the nation. This fact, in turn, reverberates in direct fashion on the possibilities of supranational integration. We pointed out earlier that the Latin American countries and the members of the Arab League seemed better prepared for supranational economic integration than the other underdeveloped nations because they have a longer record of independence. We indicated that this fact gives a certain plausibility to the Myrdal hypothesis that movements toward supranational integration require previous national integration. If we now make the parallel between the level of supranational economic integration of the Latin American nations and that achieved by the countries of Western Europe, we find a new illustration of Myrdal's hypothesis. Finally, if we observe the political difficulties that the British government has had to face because of its decision to join the European

Common Market, we can state that only in a nation with such a high level of internal cohesion could a government have survived the political tensions provoked by such initiative. It is not hazardous to advance the hypothesis that, if this high grade of national integration did not exist, nationalistic sentiments would have sufficed to displace the power of the policy-makers who are attempting the supranational integration. Again, looking at the national aspects of integration, we can show that a society in the process of modernization—the United States in the nineteenth century—*needed a civil war to integrate the subsociety of the southern states into the national society.*

The foregoing considerations permit us to formulate some conclusions about the conditions—the prerequisites—that a national society must comply with if it wishes to be able to carry out the objectives of the grand and specific strategies.

The basic prerequisite refers to the national society in its entirety and requires that the society must have a *minimum grade* of integration, which permits a certain amount of cohesion in the national group for the realization of collective aspirations both internally and with respect to other national societies. The present level of scientific knowledge does not allow us to determine just what these *minimum grades* of integration and cohesion are that make an acceptable functioning of the political system possible.

Working from the base established by Almond and Coleman (see Table XXIII), that there exists a modernized elite within the underdeveloped nations that "controls the central structures of government and essays to speak and act for the society as a whole," we may analyze and determine what are the prerequisites for an "acceptable functioning" of the political subsystem. The first prerequisite is that the stability of the system and of political processes permits that the policy-makers of the modernized elite maintain themselves in power, or at least that they be normally replaced (without violence) by other members of the same elite to allow the implementation of the grand strategy of development; and, secondly, that the political structures of the system possess the flexibility and efficiency necessary to permit these policy-makers to exercise the leadership required by the rapidity of social change and to thereby operate simultaneously in the diverse fields of the

specific strategies in order to avoid tensions and disequilibria produced within the social system by the speed of change.[78] An example will clarify this concept. If the reform of the educational
system is not accompanied by changes in the system of social
stratification, the new, modernized people created by the reform
will not find employment opportunities compatible with their
talents and skills, and they will constitute, in greater or lesser degree, a technical and intellectual proletariat that is dissatisfied and
frustrated. Far from favoring the modernization process, this can
operate as a disintegrating element in the social system. The third
prerequisite is that the government structures of the political subsystem insure a minimum level of efficiency in the functioning of
the organs of public administration charged with the execution of
specific strategies.

Having summarily determined the prerequisites of the grand
strategy of development, we shall now illustrate its relations by
means of a "case study" based on an examination of the Chilean
and Mexican experiences. The analysis will be centered fundamentally upon the comparison of the democratic systems of both
countries in relation to Table XXIII.

Let us consider, first of all, Chile and Mexico from the viewpoint of the level of national integration. The fact that Mexico
has a large mass of indigenous population not completely integrated
into the national life, a greater proportion of illiterates, and a lesser
proportion of persons possessing secondary and university education might make one think that Chile, as a national society, enjoys
a greater level of integration.[79] If this hypothesis were valid, one
might suppose that Chile has more completely achieved the minimum grade of national cohesion that is a prerequisite of grand
strategy. The observation of Table XXIII permits us to appreciate
that, in accordance with the two classificatory criteria of political
systems used therein, the Chilean system is competitive and politically modern, while that of Mexico is semicompetitive and mixed
(politically semimodern). The greater modernization of the
Chilean political system is in agreement with the hypothesis relative to Chile's greater integration as a national society. In both
countries there likewise exists a modernized, high-quality elite, and
as for qualified technical personnel, each possesses a group of

economists who have distinguished themselves in the works of the Economic Commission for Latin America. One might also believe that the efficiency of the bureaucracies in the two countries and the democratic stability enjoyed by them over many years are comparable. Given this, one might think that the Chilean political system possesses conditions superior to those of the Mexican system for the realization of the grand strategy of development and of specific strategies. Nevertheless, a study of the rates of economic growth experienced by the two countries demonstrates exactly the contrary thesis to be true. Although Mexico's rate of growth is the highest in Latin America, that of Chile falls in seventh place.[80]

The differences in population and resources, which give Mexico a very favorable position relative to Chile, do not wholly explain this fact, since countries with populations and resources inferior to those of Chile—such as Ecuador—also have higher rates of growth. Even allowing for the fact that Mexico had a social revolution and an agrarian reform, which Chile did not, does not explain this phenomenon. The key to the differentiation might lie, in our judgment, in the distinct characteristics of the political systems in the two countries. The Mexican political system—classified as less "modern" and less "competitive" in accordance with Table XXIII—is structured in such a manner that the policy-makers can exercise a more effective leadership, a leadership more in consonance with the rapidity of social change required by the grand strategy of development. On the other hand, the Chilean political system is distinguished by a multiplicity of parties. While in the Mexican system there exists a dominant, but nondictatorial, party—the Partido Revolucionario Institucional, or PRI—that controls the functioning of political structures, Chile's multiparty system is so competitive that political processes are developed with unusual slowness.

In the Mexican system the executive power—dependent upon the dominant party—relegates a passive, secondary role to the Congress. In Chile, in spite of the existence of a presidential system that gives great power to the executive, the Congress—divided into numerous factions as a consequence of the multi-party system —has a role of extraordinary importance and can limit, reduce, or curtail the leadership capacity of the executive power. In this fashion, the greater competition found in the system and its higher level of "political modernization" operate as factors contrary to the realization of a grand strategy of development. Within this context, the fact that the Chilean economic development process received an impulse of considerable magnitude when a party—the Radical—exercised a certain predominance in the system for some fourteen years gives some plausibility to our hypothesis. This hypothesis is that a democracy with a dominant party of the Mexican type offers better conditions for implementing a grand strategy of development, even though its grade of "competition" and "political modernization"—measured in accordance with the Anglo-Saxon model—may be inferior. Qualified observers of the Chilean system—nationals as well as foreigners—are in agreement that if Chile wants to carry out a grand strategy of development, she needs to modify her political system in order to insure an effective leadership by the executive power.

The consequence of this analysis for the grand strategy of development might permit the enunciation of a general hypothesis: that underdeveloped countries should introduce innovations of greater or lesser scope into their political structures in order to be able to comply with one of the key prerequisites of the grand strategy of development. The Anglo-Saxon model of democracy should be a point of departure for the construction of new democratic models, adapted to the requirements of the rapidity of social change which the underdeveloped nations are experiencing. We are far from insinuating with this observation that the Latin American countries should "imitate" the Mexican model. On the contrary, underdeveloped countries, *learning from all the world,* seeking outside their borders for valuable experiences of other nations, should choose those elements that can be useful for their own needs and by innovation combine them into new patterns. Thus a democratic political structure might be assembled that would favor, not obstruct, the realization of the grand strategy of development.

4. *The model of the grand strategy before reality: an outline for comparison*

The aim of this section is to present a schema that may serve for the comparison of the model of grand strategy with reality.

Any attempt at an exhaustive comparison of the model with reality would overlook the present state of scientific knowledge in this field. In effect, there do not exist any empirical investigations that have studied the international actions of an underdeveloped country, considering them as an internally organized and congruent system of action for achieving the ends proposed by the grand strategy of development. The typologies identified in Chapters II, III, and IV only offer us examples of the international behavior of an underdeveloped nation in each of the three variables—economic, power, and prestige—of the stratified international system. But we do not know how such international actions are organized in their reciprocal relations. That is, we do not know how they are structured within the system of international action of the underdeveloped nation. Do actions in the economic pattern have primacy over those in the power and prestige patterns, as the model establishes? Or does the lack of rationality in the nation's system of international action give primacy to actions in the power or prestige patterns, thus deviating from the model? For this reason, any attempt to compare the model—which is a system of action—with empirically studied international systems of action would lack a scientific base.

These considerations explain why we limit ourselves to only identifying the level of abstraction of the model and to pointing out some tendencies of concrete systems of action that seem to be derived from the typologies.

Every model is an abstraction with respect to the reality that it attempts to analyze, since from the universe of relevant variables the model only selects those that offer the greatest significance for a given analysis. On making explicit the areas in which the abstraction of the model rests, we intend to identify some of the sources from which the deviant comportment of the system of international action may spring.

The model's level of abstraction with respect to reality derives from (a) the postulates of the model, and (b) the prerequisites that we pointed out in examining the relationships between the national and international aspects of grand strategy.

With respect to the postulates of the model, in order to avoid useless repetition, we refer the reader to the section of Chapter V entitled: "The Rational Orientation of the System of Action and Its Postulates." Each one of these postulates represents a basic supposition of the model that, if not met in reality, may represent a deviation from the fundamental orientation of the grand strategy. The sole discussion of the examples given in that section would permit the establishment of isolated hypotheses of systems of hypotheses identifying variables that might show how, in reality, the nation's international behavior can move away from the abstract world implicit in those postulates. For reasons of space and time we shall limit ourselves to the analysis of the relationships between two of the postulates of the model and one of the prerequisites. We refer especially to the abstract world implicit in the first and fourth postulates. On page 202, summarizing the content of the first postulate, we said that our model assumes that whatever may be the advantages of short-term rationality in international actions, long-term rationality always prevails. Such advantages cannot supersede the benefits on the international scene that the underdeveloped countries may derive, either from gratifications or from value orientations flowing from self-sustained economic growth and technological maturity. On page 207, surveying the fourth postulate, we said that our postulate establishes: (1) that some patterns of rationality are predictable in the international stratified system; (2) that rational policy-makers must be able to predict roughly the behavior of other nations pursuing their own goals, of other policy-makers acting on behalf of their own nations, and of relevant groups within the nations pursuing certain goals of their own; and (3) that some ambiguity in the predictions is inevitable but, nevertheless, that rational behavior is still possible.

Let us relate these two postulates to the prerequisite that assumes a certain grade of stability in the political subsystem of the underdeveloped nation which permits the policy-makers of the modernized elite to maintain themselves in power and to be normally replaced (without violence) by other members of the same elite for the implementation of grand strategy.

Analysis of these relationships permits us to identify one possible source of deviation from the model. Let us again take the Latin American case to illustrate these relationships. In general terms, it may be said that one of the characteristics of the political systems of these countries is their instability. This generates frequent changes of policy-makers, and it often happens that the new policy-makers have different conceptions of development policy, both in its national and international aspects. On the other hand, the struggle for power within these political systems sometimes takes on such sharp features that the policy-makers who are governing must show concrete results to the public as a means of staying in power. It would be difficult to conceive of a more inappropriate framework of action in order that the long-term criterion of rationality of the model's first postulate could prosper or for the continual rational evaluation of the international situation required by the fourth postulate. Within this context one can formulate the hypothesis that the impact of the instability of the political system on the strategy of development will translate itself into a predominance of short-term criteria of rationality over the long-term criteria assumed by the model.

As Homans has shown, "When the future is uncertain and science weak, the pursuit of immediate reward is by no means irrational even by the austere standards of the Theory of Games; 'a bird in the hand is worth two in the bush' is by no means an unintelligent policy. And so far as the pursuit of rationality entails study, forethought, and calculation, and such things hurt, as they often do, the pursuit of rationality is itself irrational unless their costs are reckoned in the balance. The costs of rationality may make rationality irrational."[81] Following Homans' reasoning, even for those policy-makers who altruistically pursue a development policy based on national interests, the cost of long-term rationality may appear too high in political terms for replacing short-term criteria of rationality. If such a type of process is produced within the political system as a result of the instability of the system, the essential postulate supporting the model of the system of action would be destroyed.

The analysis of typologies permits the identification of some tendencies which are also opposed to the realization of a grand strategy of development. We shall limit ourselves to showing two of them that are related to international actions in the economic and power patterns. Notwithstanding the necessity for a supranational economic integration of the underdeveloped countries, only a small minority of them have conformed their international actions to this basic requirement of the grand strategy of development. If the hypothesis that the lack of national integration is the chief obstacle to supranational integration is valid, there is little possibility that in the more or less immediate future rational tendencies will emerge in this sense.

In the pattern of power, Chapter III showed us that, almost without exception, the underdeveloped countries are practicing a power policy on the local scale, obliging them to spend an appreciable portion of their total budgets on armament, thus reducing resources indispensable to development and giving rise to international rivalries that seriously affect the rationality of their international system of action. Even in the case of India, which seems pledged to a rational development policy, the proportion of these expenses is alarming, and for this reason the thesis that its system of international action is rationally oriented could be questioned. Recent reports, published in the *Manchester Guardian Weekly,* reveal that the defense expenditures of that country will climb to 255 million pounds sterling in 1963, exceeding those of 1962 by some 29 millions. Such figures are even more disquieting if one considers that the Ministry of Finance showed that for the same year, 1962, the country would have a budgetary deficit of 90 million pounds which will grow to 110 million in the next fiscal year.[82]

The reason that has been given to justify such expenditures is that they are necessary to safeguard the territorial integrity and security of the nation.[83] If such reasons are effective, the Indian grand strategy of development will continue to adjust itself to patterns of rational conduct, since as long as the system of nation-states subsists, the goal of national self-preservation provides a logical basis for such decisions. If the increase in India's military budget arises from her conflict with Communist China and her dangerous location between the two leaders of the Soviet bloc, the Western bloc could question only with difficulty the rationality of these decisions. These events would have demonstrated once again that the postulates of the model's abstract world do not always present themselves in reality. In this case, the second postulate would not have been met, and the deviant behavior would be attributed to it.

It would be difficult not to detect a note of pessimism in the preceding considerations, with respect to the possibilities for a grand strategy of development in the real world of the stratified international system. Men who struggle and who are guided by such value orientations as the dignity of the human being and his inalienable rights, justice, and truth might feel discouraged over the verification that a quick comparison between the abstract world of the model and reality has been sufficient to reveal such significant sources of deviation.

To such pessimistic expressions one would have to reply that progress, modernization, and development are not the consequences of any inevitable historical law. Developed nations that have contributed to the enrichment of Western culture, such as Germany, have demonstrated various grades of abysmal irrationality during the Hitler period. And the two rival blocs, guided by the two super-powers that serve as reference groups for the rest of the world, are on the verge of provoking a nuclear catastrophe that will destroy the fruits of development so arduously acquired. Is this a correlation among development, modernization, and rationality?

To the scholars who recognize value orientations peculiar to Western culture falls a task from the daily conquest of progress, that of contributing to the scientific study of the international system. This will be done by means of a reciprocal fertilization between theory and empirical investigation. They must also gradually discover, in the slow and difficult advance of science, the sources from which the irrationality of the present world spring. On doing this, as Myrdal has suggested, it would be well that they explicitly formulate their value judgments. The concepts of "modern society" and "development" are loaded with value implications. The scholar, as a scientist and as a citizen, can make them his own, as goals to be achieved by means of grand strategy. It is this task that we have attempted to perform. In so doing, we have tried to avoid the presentation of values as facts, and facts as values, and we have attempted to maintain our objectivity in the analysis of both. We have shared neither the illusion nor the philosophy that there is an upward evolution toward modernization, development, and rationality in the historical process, nor have we tried to present an artificial correlation between development and rationality. Development, progress, and the perfection of man constitute a struggle that must be decided daily, and only through it will there surge a greater rationality in the relations between men and nations. A rational nationalism can only emerge when it is understood that the goal of the nation is the perfection of man and that only in the measure to which the nation fulfills this end is its existence as a unit in the international system justified. If rationality were couched in terms of placing men as the end and nations as means, the rival nationalisms of the developed and underdeveloped worlds would perhaps not accuse each other of irrationality. This level of analysis of rationality has not been used in this book.

NOTES

1. Government of India Planning Commission, *Second Five-Year Plan*, 1956, p. 1.
2. Max F. Millikan and Donald L. M. Blackmer (eds.), *The Emerging Nations* (Boston-Toronto: Little, Brown and Co., 1961), p. 12.
3. *Ibid.*, p. 19.
4. For a study of the relationships between economy and society see Talcott Parsons and Neil J. Smelser, *Economy and Society: A Study in the Integration of Economic and Social Theory* (Glencoe, Ill.: The Free Press, 1956).
5. *Ibid.*, pp. 246-94.
6. India, *Second Five-Year Plan*, p. 1.
7. Corporación de Fomento de la Producción, *Plan Nacional de Desarrollo Económico, 1961-1970* (Santiago de Chile, n.d.), pp. 7-18.
8. Pan American Union, *Alliance for Progress*. Official documents emanating from the Special Meeting of the Inter-American Economic and Social Council at the Ministerial Level (Washington, D.C.: Pan American Union, 1961), p. 47.
9. Many writers have pointed to this fact. We shall limit ourselves only to the recent work of Millikan and Blackmer, *The Emerging Nations*.
10. Albert O. Hirschman, *The Strategy of Economic Development* (New Haven, Conn.: Yale University Press, 1960), p. 209.
11. See Millikan and Blackmer, *The Emerging Nations*, p. 12.
12. Gunnar Myrdal, *Teoría Económica y Regiones Subdesarrolladas* (Mexico, D.F.: Fondo de Cultura Economica), p. 18.
13. C. N. Vakil, "The Unity of the Social Sciences," in *Round Table Conference on the Teaching of the Social Sciences in South Asia* (UNESCO, New Delhi, 1954).
14. These studies have been published by the Latin American Faculty of the Social Sciences: *Aspectos Sociales del Desarrollo Económico* (Santiago de Chile:

Editorial Andres Bello, 1959. A later study on the same theme was made under the auspices of ECLA, UNESCO, and the UN, at a meeting held in Mexico between December 12 and 21, 1960: *Informe del Grupo de Trabajo sobre los Aspectos Sociales del Desarrollo Económico en America Latina.* Economists, sociologists, and specialists in political science participated in this study.

15. Latin American Faculty of Social Sciences, *Reports on the Project to Create the Latin American Schools of Economic and Public Administration* (Santiago de Chile: Editorial Universitaria, 1962), p. 193.

16. José Vera, *Planificación, Concepto y Evolución* (mimeographed). Project of definition for the *Dictionary of Social Sciences* in the Spanish language, prepared by the Latin American Faculty of Social Sciences under the auspices of UNESCO.

17. Millikan and Blackmer, *The Emerging Nations,* p. 12.

18. B. H. Liddell Hart, *Strategy* (New York: Frederick A. Praeger, 1961), pp. 335-36.

19. In the description of "grand strategy" and "specific strategies," I have used the description of "Elements of National Development Programs" contained in one of the appendices of the *Alliance for Progress.* I have also utilized some of the general concepts of national development contained in *An Act for International Development, Fiscal Year 1962,* Department of State Publication 7205 (Washington, D.C.: G.P.O., 1962).

20. *Alliance for Progress,* p. 11.

21. *Ibid.,* p. 4.

22. Statement by Felipe Herrera, President of the Inter-American Development Bank, at the inaugural session of the Third Meeting of the Board of Governors of IDB, on April 23, 1962.

23. P. N. Rosenstein-Rodan, "International Aid for Underdeveloped Countries," in *The Review of Economics and Statistics,* Vol. 43, No. 2 (May, 1961), 109-10. Technical assistance, although considered by Rosenstein-Rodan as part of aid, is not included in his study as "capital inflow" because of its particular nature.

24. *Ibid.,* p. 110.

25. As an example of this type of declaration one can cite the declaration of Cuba's Minister of Finance, Regino Botti, at the meeting of the Committee of 21 of the OAS in the Conference of Bogotá in 1960: "In the first place, Cuba emphatically proclaims, in this tribunal, before the peoples of Latin America and the world, that the economic development of the underdeveloped nations must be before everything else the result of the effort and sacrifice of its own peoples. The participation of foreign investments in the financing, of development should, consequently, play a secondary role. Cuba does not deny, nevertheless, the advantages that may be derived from relations between countries able to export capital and underdeveloped countries, provided that such relations are made on a plane of equality and respect for the sovereignty of the weak peoples and that they serve to elevate the levels of life of the large masses of population of the less developed countries.

"These principles accepted, the Cuban delegation wishes to make it equally clear that it does not accept as a form of development financing direct foreign investments of any kind. Neither does Cuba accept mixed private investments, with the participation of foreign monopolies, even when they are a minority. With respect to indirect investments, Cuba is disposed to receive them when they are necessary and convenient for the development of its economy, as long as they comply with a series of conditions. In the first place, these investments must not be linked to requirements of a political character, whether from international alliances or from determined forms of internal economic organization. In the second place, they must be designed only for ends that the country itself deems necessary, and they are to be distributed in the order of priorities that the country itself assigns. In the third place, they must be effected at relatively low rates of interest (for example, 3% per annum), and the terms of amortization must be more than 10 years in duration. The Cuban delegation feels that indirect investments in underdeveloped countries should preferably be made through an international organization, in which no country or bloc of countries has a majority participation nor attempts to impose any investment criterion contrary to the national sovereignty of the recipient countries, nor tries to favor, directly or indirectly, the interests of the great, imperialistic monopolies." From *Panorama Económico,* 216 (October, 1960), 291. ECLA and the OAS jointly appointed a consultant group in December, 1959, to look into the question of foreign private investment in the Latin America Free-Trade Area. "More specifically, it was to examine the practicability of establishing common aspects of policy with respect to private foreign capital, to investigate the value of incentives in stimulating the flow of such capital and to suggest practical means of financing the expansion and modernization of existing domestic industries, as well as means of dealing with the adjustments required in response to greater competition in the Free-Trade Area." This report analyzes the current attitudes towards foreign investment. See United Nations, *Foreign Private Investment in the Latin American Free-Trade Area: Report of the Consultant Group Jointly Appointed by the Economic Commission for Latin America and the Organization of American States* (New York, 1961).

26. For an excellent exposition of this theme, see Celso Furtado, *Desenvolvimento e Subdesenvolvimento* (Rio de Janeiro: Editora Fondo de Cultura, 1961); and Albert O. Hirschman (ed.), *Latin American Issues: Essays and Comments* (New York: The Twentieth Century Fund, 1961), p. 108.

27. Hirschman, *Latin American Issues,* p. 95.

28. David Felix, "An Alternative View of the Monetarist-Structuralist Controversy," in *Latin American Issues,* pp. 82-84.

29. Investigation by the Latin American Faculty of Social Sciences into psychological insecurity and the search for authoritarian solutions among wage-earners in Santiago, Chile.

30. For a criticism of the monetary policy of the Chilean government in recent years, made by a leader of the opposition in the Senate, see Eduardo Frei, *Chile Tiene un Destino: Pasado y Presente de una Crisis* (Santiago de Chile: Imprenta Raposo, 1962).

31. Joseph Grunwald, "The Structuralist School on Price Stability and Development in Latin America," in *Latin American Issues,* note, pp. 108-9.

32. *Ibid.,* p. 109.

33. *Ibid.*

34. Felix, "An Alternative View," in *Latin American Issues,* p. 83.

35. As examples one can cite the following issues of *Panorama Económico:* "La Dictadura del Fondo Monetario" (No. 220, March, 1959); "El Fondo Calla, Pero Manda" (No. 201, April, 1959); "Alternativa Frente al Fondo: Los Hechos Nos Dan la Razon" (No. 203, June, 1959). Professor Anibal Pinto has also published a book containing his opinions of the IMF's monetary policy: *Ni Estabilidad Ni Desarrollo: La Politica del Fondo Monetario Internacional* (Santiago de Chile: Editorial Universitaria, 1960).

36. *Hispanic American Report,* Vol. 12, No. 6 (August, 1959), 352-53. For the study of the negotiations between Brazil and the IMF see the following issues: Vol. 12, No. 3 (May, 1959), 176 ff.; Vol. 12, No. 4 (June, 1959), 236 ff.; and Vol. 12, No. 5 (July, 1959), 296 ff.

37. *Panorama Económico,* 203 (June, 1959), 187.

38. *Ibid.,* 216 (October, 1960), 286.

39. The Charter of Punta del Este specifically considered the problem. See in this respect Number 12 of the objectives of the Alliance for Progress, Title IV of the Charter, and the resolutions included in Appendix C that refer specifically to the problem of the basic export commodities. Pp. 11, 20-22, 39-45 of *Alliance for Progress.*

40. Quoted by Robert L. Heilbroner, *The Worldly Philosophers* (rev. ed.; New York: Simon and Schuster, 1961), pp. 119-20.

41. *Ibid.,* pp. 120-21. Italics supplied by author.

42. Ralph Braibanti and J. J. Spengler (eds.), *Tradition, Values and Socio-Economic Development* (Durham: Duke University Press, 1961), pp. 30-31.

43. *Ibid.,* cf. pp. 3-56.

44. Gunnar Myrdal, *Rich Lands and Poor* (New York: Harper & Brothers, 1957), p. 68.

45. Talcott Parsons and Edward A. Shils (eds.), *Toward a General Theory of Action* (Cambridge, Mass.: Harvard University Press, 1959), p. 8.

46. *Ibid.,* p. 128.

47. *Ibid.,* pp. 128-29. We have preferred the expression "innovation" to the Parsonian term "invention" because we consider the word innovation to be more comprehensive. We share completely in this respect the opinion of H. G. Barnett, who says: "To a limited extent 'invention' is also used as a synonym for 'innovation.' There would be no objection to a consistent equation of these two terms were it not that popular usage puts a more restricted meaning upon invention than is intended for the word innovation. For most people an invention is a thing, and the label seems inappropriate when applied to novel behavior patterns, theories, and social relations. While maintaining that there is no psychological distinction between the conception of a new object and a new act or theory, the present study retains the conventional implications of the term 'invention.' When it is used it means simply a technological innovation, a new thing. Custom has also governed the use of the term 'discovery.' It is fruitless to try to establish a rigorous and meaningful distinction between 'discovery' and 'invention,' and nothing is to be gained by re-defining the two words. On the contrary, communication is facilitated by conforming to ordinary usage. Beyond this purpose no significance should be attached to differential employment of 'invention' and 'discovery.' Both are names for 'innovation.'" From H. G. Barnett, *Innovation: The Basis of Cultural Change* (New York: McGraw-Hill Book Company, 1953), p. 8.

48. Quoted by Daniel Lerner, *The Transfer of Institutions* (mimeographed), p. 8.

49. *Ibid.*

50. Harry M. Johnson, *Sociology: A Systematic Introduction* (New York: Harcourt, Brace and Co., 1960), pp. 52-53.

51. Alfred North Whitehead, *The Aims of Education* (New York: Mentor Books, 1961), pp. 13-15.

52. Karel Neijs, *Las Cartillas de Alfabetización: Evaluación y Empleo* (Paris: UNESCO, 1961), p. 12.

53. *Ibid.*

54. For an analysis of the cases in which alphabetization can be disfunctional, see Lerner, *The Transfer of Institutions.*

55. *Bases Generales para el Planeamiento de la Educación Chilena* (Santiago de Chile: Ministerio de Educación Publica, 1961), p. 19. A commission named by the Ministry of Education of Chile, composed of experts in planning and education, principally from the University of Chile, UNESCO, and the United Nations, wrote this report. In our analysis of educational demand we shall follow this report closely, as well as a report on the reform of education in

Nigeria, written by British experts, Americans, and Africans at the request of the Ministry of Education of Nigeria: *Investment in Education: The Report of the Commission on Post School Certificate and Higher Education in Nigeria* (Nigeria: Federal Ministry of Education, 1960).

We have also considered the estimation of educational necessities in relation to the national development plan made by the Indian government: *Third Five-Year Plan: A Draft Outline* (Government of India Planning Commission, 1960). The comparison of these three studies has permitted some generalizations concerning the calculation of educational demand in three underdeveloped nations belonging to three different regions: Latin America, Africa, and Asia.

56. *Bases Generales,* p. 19.

57. *Ibid.,* p. 20. Italics supplied by author.

58. *Ibid.*

59. *Ibid.,* p. 24.

60. See note 55.

61. For the analysis of the relationship between innovation and science, see Talcott Parsons, *The Social System* (Glencoe, Ill.: The Free Press, 1951), especially Chapters VIII, X, and XI.

62. This affirmation does not have the same level of validity in some developed societies. For example, in the United States, while the universities contribute powerfully to scientific advance, certain fields of scientific and technological advance are channeled outside the university system. This takes place especially in relation to the technology of warfare, which is channeled partly through private industries that have teams of scientists and technicians.

63. It is known that ECLA supplied the basic data for an economic translation of the Alliance for Progress. The Director of ECLA, Raúl Prebisch, turned over to Ambassador Stevenson in Santiago de Chile a memorandum entitled: "Some Reflections on the Need for an Economic Development Policy in Latin America," March, 1960, in which the basic objectives of a program of economic co-operation on a continental scale are clearly formulated. In this memorandum there appeared the figure of 20 billion dollars as an estimate of the foreign aid that Latin America would need to finance its development plans. The author is grateful to the President of the Inter-American Development Bank, Felipe Herrera, for providing him with a copy of this document.

64. A similar problem may be posed with respect to the policy of the Special Fund of the United Nations. In effect, since its creation the Special Fund of the United Nations has shown itself to be reluctant to carry out programs of technical assistance in the university field—a reluctance resulting from the belief that its aid should be translated into a rapid increase in the per capita income of the underdeveloped countries. Within this criterion, programs of technical assistance in the university field were rejected. Later, the Special Fund modified its policy and began to carry out programs in the university field, but the old exclusively economic criterion persisted as a backdrop which does not recognize the strategic role of university education in the process of modernization of underdeveloped societies. The author had the opportunity to expound these views at the first session of the Administrative Council of the Special Fund held in New York in 1959, which he attended as a delegate of the Chilean government. Later he has had the satisfaction of verifying that his appraisal, initially rejected, has been accepted, although in a limited form, by this international organization.

65. The author has received this information from Americans in diverse universities in the United States who specialize in Latin American affairs. Without a doubt, the efficiency of the American administration in this aspect is still very far from the spirit of the "New Frontier" proclaimed by President Kennedy. It is significant to point out in this respect that qualified American scholars have demonstrated to the author that studies of the relations between innovation and

public administration are still in an incipient stage. One of the few American authors who has called attention to this problem is Professor Rostow, in his work, *The United States in the World Arena: An Essay in Recent History* (New York: Harper & Brothers, 1960). See especially the chapter entitled "Bureaucracy, Innovation, and the Individual," pp. 493-502.

66. This is the period required for the transmission of a request presented in Santiago de Chile to the administration of the Point Four (now AID) program. Functionaries of this organization expressed their hopes to the author that this situation will be modified as a consequence of the new structure of this agency.

67. Nigeria, *Investment in Education,* pp. 3, 41, 47.   Italics supplied by author.

68. For the study of the relationship between the psychology of crises and war and innovation, see H. G. Barnett, *Innovation,* especially pp. 80-89.

69. *Ideology and Foreign Affairs: The Principal Ideological Conflicts, Variations Thereon, Their Manifestations, and Their Present and Potential Impact on the Foreign Policy of the United States.* Study prepared at the request of the Committee on Foreign Relations, United States Senate, by the Center for International Studies, Harvard University (Washington, D.C.: G.P.O., 1960), pp. 60-61.

70. *New York Times,* April 22, 1962.

71. *United States Foreign Policy.* A compilation of studies prepared under the direction of the Committee on Foreign Relations, United States Senate, 87th Congress, 1st Session; Senate Document No. 24 (Washington, D.C.: G.P.O., 1961).

72. *Ibid.,* Study Number 6, *The Operational Aspects of United States Foreign Policy,* by Maxwell Graduate School of Citizenship and Public Affairs, Syracuse University, pp. 574 ff. Italics supplied by author. Similar considerations and recommendations are contained in Study Number 10, *Ideology and Foreign Affairs,* by the Center for International Affairs, Harvard University.

73. The statement that the OAS is a power structure dependent upon United States foreign policy is derived from the very history of the organization. It would suffice to cite that only in 1923 did the post of director of the Pan American Union (former name of the organization) become available to a Latin American. Before that time the director was named directly by the Department of State. The dependence of the OAS on the United States is openly discussed in Latin American circles in Washington as something evident and unquestionable.

74. Raymond H. Dawson, *The Decision to Aid Russia, 1941: Foreign Policy and Domestic Politics* (Chapel Hill, N.C.: The University of North Carolina Press, 1959), p. xi.

75. K. H. Silvert and Frank Bonilla, *Education and the Social Meaning of Development* (mimeographed), a preliminary statement with the professional collaboration of Thomas Ktsanes, Virginia Ktsanes, and Frieda M. Silvert (New York: American Universities Field Staff, Inc.), p. 1.

76. Richard W. Gable, *Plan for Research and Publications in Public Administration,* prepared for the Agency for International Development (Washington, D.C., 1961), p. 23. On the role of public administration in development, see also United Nations, Seventh Period of Sessions of ECLA, *Public Administration in Development Policy: Preliminary Examination of the Latin American Experience* (La Paz, Bolivia, 1957), and *Reports on the Project to Create the Latin American Schools of Economics and Public Administration,* published by the Latin American Faculty of Social Sciences, with the financial co-operation of the Inter-American Development Bank (Santiago de Chile: Editorial Universitaria, 1962). In this latter study it is stated that a proper study of the process of public administration in Latin America should be made taking into account the fact that public administration is a part of the political system of Latin American countries.

These political systems are the product of a given historical and socio-cultural setting.

77. Marion J. Levy, *The Structure of Society* (Princeton, N.J.: Princeton University Press, 1952), pp. 123, 547. Italics supplied by author.

78. We employ the expression "political structures" of the system in the sense defined by Almond and Coleman.

79. *Cooperation for Progress in Latin America,* a statement on national policy prepared by the Research and Policy Committee of the Committee for Economic Development (New York: 1961), p. 25.

80. We have based this observation on the often-cited study of P. N. Rosenstein-Rodan.

81. George Gaspar Homans, *Social Behavior: Its Elementary Forms* (New York: Harcourt, Brace and World, Inc., 1961), p. 82.

82. *Manchester Guardian Weekly,* March 22, 1962, p. 5.

83. *Ibid.*

INDEX

Agency for International Development (AID), and educational reform, 254-55; mentioned, 37, 76

Act of Bogotá, and social development, 82; mentioned, 71, 72, 77, 83, 85

Africa, and power politics, 99, 108; and neutralism, 111; and prestige status, 135; mentioned, 29, 50, 55, 67, 69, 114, 147, 148, 256

Alaska, 143

Algerian War, 21

Alliance for Progress, and Western Hemisphere idea, 83; and population growth, 83; and Marshall Plan, 83-84; goals of, 83-90; ten-year plan of, 84, 86; institutional framework of, 84-90; and *atimia*, 84, 90; and national development plans, 84-90, 215; and problem of basic commodities, 85; and self-sufficiency of Inter-American System, 85-90; and supranational integration, 85; and foreign aid, 86, 87, 88; and technical assistance, 87; Committee of Nine and, 87; *ad hoc* committees, 87, 88, 89; ECOSOC and, 87; and per capita rate of growth, 88; and U.S. leadership, 89-90; and social revolution, 90, 120; implementation of, 89-90; origin of term, 94; and Cuba, 120-21, 226; and Western Europe, 224; mentioned, 29, 38, 71, 77, 86, 196, 222, 223, 232, 254, 269

Almond, Gabriel A., 192, 272, 273, 276

Alvear, Marcelo T., 150

Anticolonialism, and power politics, 106

Arab Common Market, 57

Arab League, and supranational integration, 275; mentioned, 57, 60, 61, 67, 69

Argentina, and power politics, 103-5; and prestige status, 149-60; and leadership, 149-60; army of, 153; economic independence of, 156-57; technological advance of, 157; military power of, 157; third international position of, 157-60, 162; foreign reserves of, 159-60; mentioned, 28, 116, 180, 194, 204

Asia, and power politics, 99; neutralism of, 111; prestige status of, 135; mentioned, 29, 44, 50, 55, 71, 73, 74, 147, 148

Atimia, and ideology of equalitarianism, 22-30; concept of, 24; and technological maturity, 24-25; social development and, 25; technological leadership and, 25; definition of international situation and, 25-30; and governing elite, 26; and common man, 26; and nationalism, 30; and systems of international action, 30; and national economic status, 37-38; and primary commodity market, 61-66; and gratification, 190; and deprivation, 190; and rational action, 198; and modernization, 258-60; mentioned, 103, 138, 183, 193, 236

Australia, 48, 63, 73, 146

Austria, 63, 111

Avellaneda, Nicolás, 160

Baghdad Pact (METO), 67

Balaguer, Joaquín, 206

Bandung Conference, 110-111

Barnett, H. G., concept of innovation, 288

Betancourt, Rómulo, 189
"Blue Streak," production of, 15
Bogotá Conference, change of U.S. foreign policy at, 82; mentioned, 254. *See also* Act of Bogotá
Bolivia, economy of, 121-24; National Revolutionary Movement in, 121; and International Tin Council Agreement, 122; and power politics, 121-24; and foreign aid, 225; and national integration, 275; mentioned, 153, 178, 194, 226
Botti, Regino, 286-87
Bowles, Chester, and Alliance for Progress, 94
Brazil, navy of, 24, 103; agricultural development of, 46; nationalism and, 115; neutralism and, 115; as key country, 116-17; and power politics, 124-26; take-off, 126; and prestige status, 143-46; and leadership, 143-46, 266; and Operation Pan-America, 145; neutralism and, 145-46; and monetary policy, 233-35; mentioned, 28, 55, 139, 146, 149, 152, 153, 158, 159, 187, 188
Brazilian-Argentine relations, 103, 104-5
British Commonwealth, and power structure, 268; mentioned, 63, 71, 97, 201, 226
Burma, 62

Cameroons, 108
Canada, technical maturity of, 11; and economic status, 16; spontaneous development of, 53; national image of, 130-31; and Western Hemisphere, 268; mentioned, 63, 126, 143, 146, 225
Capital inflow, estimation of, 41-44; and technical assistance, 286
Castro, Fidel, 119, 169
Castro, Raúl, 121
Center for International Studies of M.I.T., and integrated social theory, 240
Central American Common Market, Costa Rica's recent entry to, 92; mentioned, 269
Central American Free-Trade Area, 60
Ceylon, 62, 73, 74
Charter of Punta del Este, 38, 71, 72, 77, 85, 86, 89, 224, 237
Chile, navy of, 10, 104; and power

politics, 103, 104; and higher education, 141-42; and prestige status, 141-42; and monetary policy, 231, 232; and national integration, 275, 277-79; political system of, 277-79; and grand strategy of development, 277-79; mentioned, 28, 152, 153, 158, 176, 178, 194, 204, 214-15, 222, 235, 244
Chilean-Peruvian relations, 103
Churchill, Winston, and value-orientations, 201-2
Coleman, James S., 192, 272, 273, 276
Colombia, and Latin American Free-Trade Area, 92
Colombo Conference, 44
Colombo Plan, compared with Inter-American System, 70-73; White Paper on, 71, 72, 74; principal features of, 73-77; and Marshall Plan, 73; duration of, 76-77; administrative machinery of, 75; and national development plans, 215; mentioned, 29, 69, 70, 174, 222, 225, 254
Colonialism, and propaganda, 137; and anticolonialism, 148
Committee of Twenty-one, OAS, 28
Communist China, and economic status, 17; and power politics, 124-26; and technological maturity, 126; traditional image of, 134-35, 136; compared with India, 134; conflict with India, 283-84; mentioned, 48, 55, 113, 116, 119, 143, 146, 174
Communist world, 43
Conference of Independent African States (ACCRA), 67
Content analysis, of Peron's speeches, 153-56
Costa Rica, prestige of, 21; and Central American Common Market, 92; and power politics, 108-9; and university education, 108, 141-42; and prestige status, 141-42; mentioned, 189
Cuba, OAS membership, 118; and power politics, 118-21; and Western Hemisphere idea, 118; revolution, 118; and neutral nations, 118; sources of international influence, 119-21; and Alliance for Progress, 226; and foreign aid, 286-87; and private investment, 286-87; mentioned, 113, 152, 178, 196, 268
Cuban revolution, and U.S. prestige, 120

and economic status, 16, 17; mentioned, 63, 111

Switzerland, and international politics, 95; mentioned, 48, 111

System of action, concept of, 181-82; and Parsons' theory, 182

Taiwan, 113

Take-off, Rostow's, 11; preconditions of, 12; and India, 17; concept applied to supranational integration, 60; Deutsch's concept of, 93; mentioned, 139

Technical assistance, concept of, 45; and regional organizations, 66-90; channels of, 76; and Alliance for Progress, 87; to neutral nations, 114; and formulation of development plans, 222; and educational reform, 246-58; and grand strategy of development, 246-58; and U.S., 255; and duplication of effort, 255; and "capital inflow," 286; mentioned, 6, 38, 44

Technological leadership, and *atimia,* 25

Technological maturity, and welfare state, 12; and economic maturity, 12, 14; and leadership, 13; and economic status, 16; and *atimia,* 24-25; and power status, 98; and world power politics, 125; and Communist China, 126; mentioned, 11, 24, 45

Terms of trade, UN study of, 39, 40

Thailand, 113

Theory of games, 282

Trade, distinguished from foreign aid, 226-27

Traditional society, Rostow's, 11; mentioned, 12

Triffin, R., 23

Trujillo Molina, Rafael, 189, 205

Turkey, 113

Ulate, Otilio, 109

Underdeveloped countries, origin of term, 27-30, 195

United Arab Republic, 111

United Nations (UN), power of, 97, 268; mentioned, 27, 29, 39, 40, 41, 49, 51, 61, 62, 66, 67, 69, 74, 135, 185, 195, 199, 222, 236, 255, 264

United Nations Educational, Scientific and Cultural Organization (UNESCO), and primary education, 255; mentioned, 176, 185, 217, 248

United Nations Special Fund, 108

United States, technological maturity of, 11; and economic status, 17, 19; navy of, 24; spontaneous development of, 51, 53; and international politics, 95; and national prestige, 128-130; traditional image of, 129-30, 133-34, 136; and propaganda, 137; and Peronist Argentina, 157-60; universalism and foreign policy, 193-97; and monetary policy, 229-36; and technical assistance, 255; and neutral nations, 265; mentioned, 13, 22, 43, 71, 79, 86, 89, 97, 103, 108, 111, 113, 117, 120, 122, 143, 146, 153, 169, 171, 174, 175, 176, 178, 183, 184, 187, 195, 215, 224, 225, 226, 237, 264, 266-67

United States Senate, Foreign Relations Committee of, 266

United States State Department, and neutralism, 114

Universalism, as value-orientation, 193-97; and U.S. foreign policy, 193-97; and Russian foreign policy, 193; and Latin America, 193-97; and Inter-American System, 193-97; and neutralism, 196; and rational action, 199

Urquidi, Victor, 58-59

Uruguay, prestige of, 21; and power politics, 104; mentioned, 28, 153

Vakil, C. N., 217

Venezuela, and international politics, 95; mentioned, 178, 189

Vietnam, 113

Warner, W. Lloyd, 20

War of the Pacific, 103, 194

Weber, Max, 96, 166-68, 169

Western Europe, spontaneous development of, 51, 53; and Alliance for Progress, 224-25; mentioned, 71, 215, 225, 226

Western Hemisphere, idea, 77, 79, 81, 118, 120; and North Atlantic Community, 79; and Marshall Plan, 80; balance of power in, 119; and particularism, 194; and Canada, 268; mentioned, 20, 24, 151

www.ingramcontent.com/pod-product-compliance
Lightning Source LLC
Chambersburg PA
CBHW020337270326
41926CB00007B/213